T0386240

THE LANDSCAPE OF SILENCE

AMALENDU MISRA

The Landscape of Silence

Sexual Violence Against Men in War

HURST & COMPANY, LONDON

First published in the United Kingdom in 2015 by
C. Hurst & Co. (Publishers) Ltd.,
41 Great Russell Street, London, WC1B 3PL
© Amalendu Misra, 2015
All rights reserved.
Printed in India

Distributed in the United States, Canada and Latin America by
Oxford University Press, 198 Madison Avenue, New York, NY 10016,
United States of America

The right of Amalendu Misra to be identified as the author
of this publication is asserted by him in accordance with the
Copyright, Designs and Patents Act, 1988.

A Cataloguing-in-Publication data record for this book is
available from the British Library.

ISBN: 9781849042826 *hardback*

This book is printed using paper from registered sustainable
and managed sources.

www.hurstpublishers.com

… for Francisco Berlin Valenzuela

Of all the secrets of war, there is one that is so well kept that it exists mostly as a rumour.

Will Storr, The Rape of Men, 2011.

CONTENTS

PREFACE

This book is about sexual violence. It is about sexual violence of a particular kind. It is about sexual violence in its myriad form against boys and men in armed conflicts and war.

So far as I am aware, this inquiry is the first systematic attempt to develop a general theory of sexual violence against the male sex in the above conflict settings. I have endeavoured to explore a terrain that still remains obscure and ambiguous. While on the surface it appears as a political question once you peel away one layer you find a whole mélange of issues buried deep within, one after another.

While I write as a political scientist/conflict theorist I use various social sciences' methods to reflect and meditate on such questions as the place of the physical body, hatred, power, violence, humiliation, trauma, jurisprudence and the art of, or the lack of, reconciliation in such a context.

Any critical inquiry on such a complex and taboo topic requires sustained and extensive interaction with the victims. For, it is the victims who are the key protagonists in such an undertaking. Effective firsthand information on sexual violence experienced by boys and men in armed conflicts and war, however, is notoriously hard to come by. This is owing to two interrelated factors. First, the perpetrators or aggressors generally hide from accountability. Second, given the nature of the abuse, the victim often hides from the secondary harm of social humiliation.

Fortunately, for me and for this study, several victims willingly came forward to describe their experiences. I also had a glimpse into the minds of the violators who at one time or other had been part of a vile enterprise—part of a mob that carried out 'a job' in varied conflict settings—from Northern Ireland to India. Their contribution led me to explore the issue in several new directions. They alerted me to details which otherwise would have escaped my scrutiny. Needless to say this study is richer, thanks to their decision to open up and speak out.

The terrain this book explores is both difficult as well as disturbing. The language that is used to describe this particular form of violence is often direct. Some of the narratives can be deeply offensive and distressing. Since the central objective of this undertaking is to introduce the readers to the exactness of such crimes, I have neither tried to airbrush the rawness of the theme nor attempted to tip-toe away from engaging with difficult questions.

This will not be a lengthy overture, for I have said what I want to say in the main body of the book. Steeped in the dark tragedy of many broken and conflict-ridden societies, this study turns to the nature of man's inhumanity to man. The work may be summed up as an attempt to *see* and to *show* what happens to man and what conclusions are forced upon him, when he is placed within a certain framework of interaction.

AM   *Los Isotes*, Veracruz, January 2015.

ACKNOWLEDGEMENTS

I would like to thank all those quoted in this book, and also the many others who gave generously of their time and knowledge, in particular, Bhikhu Parekh and Noël O'Sullivan. At Lancaster, Christine Sylvester, David Denver, Michael Dillon, Patrick Bishop and Mark Lacy have been endless sources of inspiration. I thank them for their generosity.

Preparing a nuanced portrait that contains much of the details of such atrocities is fiendishly soul-destroying work. Luckily, for me, I have had the good fortune to have a select group of friends who perpetually kept me entertained when I thought of abandoning it all.

For their unconditional friendship and unstinting encouragement—sometimes spanning over the past two decades—I thank R. Narayanan, Maggie O'Sullivan, Pramila Parekh, Alba Teresa Bellido Diaz, Clare Coxhill, Ambrogia Cereda, Angel Rivero, Luisa Fernanda Hernandez Mora, Trilok Nath Mishra, Rakesh Agrawal, S. G. Pandian, Peter and Daphne Glazer, Zafar Jaspal, Jose Jorge Eufracio, Bill Wynn, Emma Norman, David Mena Aleman, Gurharpal Singh, Karin Fierke, Rafiq Ali Master, Adrian Guelke, Steve and Denver Lalonde, and Issahaq Mohammed Nurudeen.

In recent years, Maricruz Montana Fernández, Omar Torres, Sara Dawn Moore, Ignacio Hernández García, Jitendra Nath Misra, Yinka Olomojobi, Manuel Amante Martínez, Luz del Carmen Serrano Hernandez, and Pablo Morales Domínguez have contributed to my many non-academic interests in various ways. I thank them all profusely.

I thank the anonymous referees who read the manuscript and alerted me to issues, which I would otherwise have missed. I owe a great deal to Olga Alekseeva-Carnevali, who read parts of the manuscript with painstaking care and diligently provided many critical suggestions

ACKNOWLEDGEMENTS

for its improvement. The book is much richer for her efforts. I thank Simon Harris for his astute copy-editing and Jon de Peyer and Daisy Leitch for editorial assistance.

Thanks also to María Rebeca Fernández Granja who has been a source of intermittent distraction for the past six years.

Michael Dwyer has been exemplary in his patience with my relentless request for extensions and inquiries. I could not have expected a better editor.

A special debt of gratitude goes to Jueves Peluso, a Siamese-Angora kitten that arrived unannounced one July afternoon, kept me alert and grew up with this book.

Finally, I dedicate this book to jurist and a constant friend Francisco Berlin Valenzuela.

INTRODUCTION

The more obscene the crime, the less visible it is.

Michael A. Sells, *The Bridge Betrayed*, 1996: 11.

Your initial response is correct: in an unregulated armed conflict or war women experience sexual violence at the hands of the enemy. But it is not the complete answer. Let us rephrase the question. Do you think women are the 'only' victims of such violence in these conflicts? If you still said, 'Yes', you are conforming to a widely held perception, but there exists a gap in your knowledge.

The perceived knowledge you are in possession of informs you that in such settings, 'specific forms of violence happen to differently gendered bodies' (Shepherd, 2010: 75), that is, unlike its female equivalent the male body does not have a sexual representation or value in war: bodies of the male enemy are marked out for killing, while those of women are set aside for sexual violation. This misconception is 'rooted in traditional assumptions about male wartime roles' (Carpenter, 2006: 89). Throughout human history male members of the enemy have often been subjected to sexual violence. Yet it is rarely mentioned. If anything, there resides an overwhelming silence over it. The topic is conspicuous by its very absence from any such discussion—scholarly or otherwise.

The limited statistics that exist on sexual violence against boys and men in armed conflicts and wars almost certainly vastly under-represent the number of such victims (Russell, 2007: 22). The breadth of sexual violence suffered by boys and men in armed conflicts can be frighteningly unlimited (Lewis, 2009: 10). Male rape is, in fact, endemic in many of the world's conflicts (Storr, 2011: 7). In the past decade alone, 'sexualized violence against boys and men—including rape sexual humilia-

1

tion, sexual torture, mutilation of the genitals, sexual enslavement, rape, forced incest and forced rape—has been reported in 25 armed conflicts across the world' (Russell, 2007: 22).

Contemporary sexual violence against these two constituencies is not limited to a few deviations. Sexualised violence against boys and men can emerge from a diverse breadth of conflicts—from localised riots and pogroms to civil wars and full-blown inter-state wars (Wood, 2006: 308).

Its scope is far wider than one could ever imagine. Sexual violence against boys and men varies in prevalence and form and is not confined to state forces, armed opposition groups and private contractors. The 'range of sexual violence committed against men in armed conflict crosses the full gamut of possibilities; all permutations and combinations are present' (Sivakumaran, 2007: 257–8).

Explored within the wider context of armed conflict, this particular violence is that complex whole which may include rape, sodomy, physical mutilation, public humiliation, and any other capabilities and perversions employed by the perpetrator. Such variations in violence are often the direct result of the overall condition of the conflict, the culture of the violator, and the nature and character of the victim's ethno-political and religio-nationalist identity.

It is more likely to occur when the victim is perceived as ethnically distinct from the perpetrator. As a community becomes more factionalised along ethnic and religious lines there is a greater likelihood of sexual violence (Butler, Gluch & Mitchell, 2007: 675). If a particular ethnic or religious group is known for or is trying to establish its own pure, distinct and autonomous identity, then that 'purity' is deliberately assaulted in the form of sexual violence in order to defile it.

As we have noticed in recent years (in the wake of some high-profile cases such as Abu Ghraib) these constituencies of boys and adult males can experience forms of sexual torture and sexual assault while in detention for their alleged opposition to an occupational force.[1]

Albeit late, recently stories of sexual violence against men in various theatres of conflict have slowly begun to infiltrate the mainstream. The civil wars in the Balkans and Rwanda in the late twentieth and early twenty-first centuries were watershed events that forced a section of the international community to take notice. Having said that, such forms of violence against enemy civilians and enemy combatants were fairly widespread in the 1970s and 1980s.

Various authoritarian regimes from Chile, Argentina, Guatemala and El Salvador in Latin America to Sri Lanka and India in Asia, and the Democratic Republic of Congo and Sierra Leone in Africa, regularly subjected boys and men to frequent sexual assaults in a multitude of forms including custodial rape. Staying in Latin America we find that there were several instances of state-sponsored sexual violence against male dissidents of Chilean dictator Augusto Pinochet during his two-decade-long rule. The explicit aim here was to crush the opposition and send a message of terror to anyone who opposed Pinochet's regime (Cienfuegos & Monelli, 1983). We also have fragmentary episodes of wartime sexual violence against men during the Greek civil war (Gaugaard et al., 1983). In those theatres of conflict where sexual violence against the male sex has been properly investigated such violence has been recognised as regular and unexceptional (Sivakumaran, 2007: 259).[2]

It is now conclusively established that several male prisoners belonging to the partisan side in El Salvador's civil war did undergo forms of sexual violence by their right-wing captors (Agger, 1989; Wood 2006). In fact an overwhelming 76 per cent of male political prisoners surveyed in El Salvador's civil war in the 1980s reported at least one instance of sexual torture or abuse (Stemple, 2009: 613).

While there has not been any scholarly study of sexual violence during the Vietnam War (owing to plenty of documents still being classified) reports of such undertakings have nonetheless surfaced from time to time. According to one such source, the Tiger Force of the 101st Airborne carried out acts of sexual violence against male civilians over a seven month period in 1967 (quoted in Wood, 2006: 316). In all these conflict situations sexual violence against the captive was quite severe in cases and contexts where the detainee was alleged to have political sympathies that ran contrary to the concerned regimes.

Considering male victims—a brief history

The very act of sexual violence against the enemy during armed conflict and war has a long established tradition. As a form of warfare it has been well documented since Biblical times.[3] In many ancient societies where male-male sex was not condemned or considered deviant the practice of sexually violating defeated male captives and prisoners-of-war was an accepted norm. For the Ancient Egyptians this was a divinely ordained practice. Their gods Horus and Set, who practised male-male sex, provided the Egyptians with the required legitimacy to engage in such practices in real life (Walker, 1952: 129). Evidence suggests that Egyptian soldiers freely sexually preyed upon their male captives following an armed victory. Elsewhere, other communities made such practices part of their official policy.

Darius the Great, the third king of the Persian-Achaemenid Empire, required subjected territories to provide castrated young men from their communities as war-tributes. Hence we have a royal dictat demanding Babylon and the rest of Assyria to send him 1,000 talents of silver and 500 castrated boys as tribute (Tannahill, 1980: 247). Such demands, it would appear, helped institutionalise the use of able-bodied males as sacrificial victims.

If one were to focus on Classical Greece and the conduct of war among various city-states it becomes amply evident that male enemy captives were treated very much as 'spoils of war', and freely used as sexual slaves by the victorious party (Neill, 2009). This may be due to the fact that bisexuality was an accepted practice among the ancient Greeks.[4] Thus whenever a city state went about raising an armed campaign against its enemy the captured male population was 'ravished', to quote the phrase from Isaiah's description of the fate of the Babylonians.

As is evident from the accounts of the historian Arrian, when he went about his conquest Alexander the Great was always eager to inherit the male sexual slaves of the fallen opponent ruler. He also keenly pursued good-looking men among the captive enemy for his and his troops' sexual consumption (Arrian, 2004). If prisoners refused to sexually submit then they were sexually tortured and violated before being put to death.

The Romans were also very active in trafficking 'handsome' boys and men for sexual consumption among themselves and for trade with Eastern civilisations. This slave trade in 'desirable' males or, to put it in the contemporary parlance, 'male human trafficking' was so conspicuous that it even reached the highest courts in some empires. The greatest historian of the period, Herodotus, mentions one such incidence.

A slave trader from Chios named Panionion, specialised in handsome young boys whom he castrated and then sold, through the markets at Ephesus and Sardis, to the Persian court and other eastern customers. One of his victims became the favourite eunuch of King Xerxes (quoted in Finley, 1977: 164).

At one point in Roman civilisation it became almost customary for the rich, noble and powerful to openly engage in the procurement of captured young male subjects from conquered territories, castrate them and later use them as slaves or sexual partners in domestic settings. Existing historical records inform us that, not to be outdone by his peers, one Roman nobleman, Plantianus Praetorian Prefect, had one hundred boys emasculated, and then gave them away to his daughter as a wedding present (Durant, 1944: 666).

Several other ancient civilisations (Amerindian, Islamic, Japanese— where homosexuality in warfare was largely prevalent) not only actively sought male-male sexual predation in the event of a military success but also were severe when the subjugated failed to fulfill the desires of the victorious. In the event of the captive male refusing to undergo the sexual demands of his captor the outcome was most commonly sodomy, rape, mutilation of the reproductive organ of the dissenter and eventual beheading or spearing to death.[5]

'The Persians who succeeded to the Assyrian empire appear to have been the first to castrate prisoners in cold rather than hot blood' (Tannahill, 1980: 247); a form of deliberate and calculated enterprise one might say. Sexual violence against enemy males was very much a part of conventional warfare in ancient Persia. Intimate mutilation—of at least some male enemy captives—was a recurring phenomenon. Some of the murals from Persepolis depict victors of many battles parading with large plates stacked high with their enemy's penises (Del Zotto & Jones, 2002).[6]

However, credit must go to the Romans for inventing and eventually mastering the art of sexual warfare against the male enemy combatants. Emperor Caligula, famous for his inventive sadistic exploits against his enemies, considered this undertaking 'truly Roman' (Kiefer, 1976: 413). During his brief reign he revelled in an extraordinary passion for cruelty, and unconcealed sexual sadism against his male enemies. Unsurprisingly taking direction from his conduct the 'conspirators who killed him drove their swords through his sexual organs' (Kiefer, 1976: 314).

Turning to another Roman Emperor, Nero, we find an occasional passion for sexual violence against male challengers to his throne/rule. According to the historian Tacitus, shortly after coming to power Nero personally sexually violated and raped his half stepbrother Britannicus before poisoning him to death.[7]

The power dimension

Throughout this long period of over two millennia, sexual violence against male enemy combatants and civilians was very much anchored in the context of the 'spoils of war'. In the pre-modern era many civilisations practised forms of male-male sexual subjugation within the context of warfare. In mediaeval Japan 'love between enemy warriors' was not only an accepted custom in ancient warfare it also permitted the victor to use the captive enemy male as his sexual trophy (Neill, 2009).

According to some scholars, forms of male-male predatory sexual relationship existed between the European colonial masters and their subjects in the far-flung parts of their Empires. The capacity of the white colonial body to appropriate and sexually violate non-white colonised bodies had an established pattern. According to Richard Aldrich, for white Europeans the colonies offered a more liberal environment. European men 'saw sexual opportunities as one of the benefits of empire' (Aldrich, 2003: 57). Reflecting on this in the context of a dominant-dominated relationship, some critics have even gone a step further by suggesting that sex in one form or another was a 'driving force' for many of the European colonial powers including the British Empire (Hyam, 2003; Woollacott, 2006). As a result there were a significant number of colonial officials engaging in sex with native boys and men who were often powerless to protest (Hyam, 1990). Although not strictly wartime sexual violence, these undertakings were unilateral hegemonic power relationships establishing a pattern of conquest and subjugation.

Systematic mass wartime sexual violence (especially rape) did not end with the advent of modernity. It simply assumed a new explanatory framework. That sexual violence could be used as a highly effective method in conventional warfare was keenly explored by various armies and political leaders throughout the twentieth century. Such undertaking assumed a strategic character, which until that time was missing from this discourse.

In the last century, many conflicts involved systematic sexual violation. Nazi soldiers, for instance, raped non-German women in conquered territories and when Allied troops and Stalin's Red Army entered Germany they openly carried out mass sexual violation of German women.

This mode of violence had tacit institutional approval. It was tolerated and even encouraged by the Soviet command structure, starting from field officers all the way up to the supreme leader Stalin. It is suggested that when formal complaints were made by the Germans against the excesses of sexual violence in East Prussia, Stalin responded with the comment that 'we lecture our soldiers too much. Let them have some initiative' (quoted in Naimark, 1995: 72).[8]

According to some critics, this endemic pattern of sexual violence in European history would appear to suggest a form of institutionalised punishment against the resistant population no matter which ethnic, racial, religious or national background they came from (Wood, 2006: 309).

Similarly, a little known aspect of the Japanese atrocity in Manchuria during their military campaign in the East is the horrendous sexual violence inflicted upon men. Sexual violence by the Japanese in the East (apart from using Korean and Chinese women as sexual slaves in the form of comfort women) included various forms of sexual abuse of men, including rape, the forcing of men to have intercourse with family members or the dead, and the forcing of celibate men (monks) to have intercourse (Wood, 2006: 311; Chang, 1997: 88–9, 95). The objective here was not only to use men and women as spoils of war but also to send the message that the Japanese had complete supremacy over the masses in the conquered territory. Hence when they invaded the British-occupied Andaman Islands in 1944 they went about raping many of the Indian male inhabitants in charge of the island in order to humiliate them and make the colonial administration realise the impotency of its authority.

While the Japanese were busy violating their victims in the East, around the same time their Nazi allies were devising methods to render their male enemies sexually impotent on an industrial scale.[9] Towards the latter part of the war an unknown German engineer infamously developed what came to be known as a 'castration mine'. This particular weapon was 'a type of land mine with a dual explosive charge. When an unfortunate infantryman stepped on it, the first charge exploded and hurled the mine to just below waist level. Then the second charge blew up and so did the testicles' (Reuben, 1969: 14). We do not have documentary evidence that could allow us to discern the exact reason why the Nazis were using this device. However, with the benefit of hindsight one could safely argue the primary purpose behind the 'castration mine' was to make the enemy sterile and make Allied infantrymen very afraid of treading in German-held territories.

Fortunately, the use of the 'castration mine' was limited to the wars on the Western Front. Plenty of Allied combatants who were maimed by these mines but were lucky enough to live, returned home only to experience a slow and painful withering away of their manliness. According to some critics 'the weapon was a limited success; the enemy combatants were understandably reluctant to march through a field sown with these weapons' (Reuben, 1969: 14).

One would have assumed that with the end of the general anarchy that was synonymous with the Second World War period, humanity and nations would finally move away from such abominable practices. Ironically, in spite of the emergence of global norms such as the *Universal Declaration of Human Rights* in 1948 and subsequent rulings banning such violence against civilians and enemy captives these practices were pursued in earnest. If anything many advancing armies once in the enemy territory employed the full gamut of sexual violence in order to achieve the twin objectives that Nazi Germany had originally espoused.

Such practice was undertaken in earnest when West Pakistani troops went about raping East Pakistani (Bangladeshi) men and women in a very well organised and coordinated manner with almost military precision (Brownmiller, 1975; Agger, 1989). In the 1990s this practice was revived when Yugoslavia fell into a civil war. Serb militias and military made it a part of their offensive against Bosnian Muslims and Croats. In Rwanda the ancient Tutsi practice of adorning the royal drum *Karinga* with male enemies' severed genitals (Taylor, 2002: 166) eventually gained a mass currency albeit differently during the genocidal war in 1992 when extremist Hutus liberally used that past narrative in order to subject their enemy Tutsi counterparts to similar violence before putting them to death. In the current century Janjaweed militias in the western Sudanese region of Darfur have been engaged in similar acts for over a decade with almost impunity (Handrahan, 2004; Toften & Markuen, 2006).

In the Sierra Leonean civil war in the 1990s the conflict became synonymous with excesses of sexual violence. The period was not only marked by 'indiscriminate' rape and torture of civilians but was particularly notorious for it condemned the victims to undergo forms of torture that broke all the sacred social taboos. Following the end of the civil war it appeared that rebels frequently forced male Sierra Leoneans to rape their male as well as female family members, or watch them dance naked or be raped by the rebels (TRC Sierra Leone/Final Report: 292–6; also see Human Rights Watch, *We'll Kill You if You Cry*, 35–42).

Then there is the predatory sexual violence against civilians during a community's transition from war to peace. In contemporary international society such predatory behaviour can be traced to many theatres of conflict. Particular societies in the midst of post-conflict recovery such as Afghanistan, Congo and Haiti, have become havens for such predatory behaviour. Boys and vulnerable adult males have become subjects of violation not only by the locals, but also by outside peacekeepers whose job it was to protect the people (Higate, 2007; Bastick, Grimm, & Kunz, 2007). In 2011 it was found that several Haitian boys and men were individually or collectively raped by Uruguayan and Pakistani peacekeepers.[10] In many instances UN peacekeepers are found to commit such violence and abuse with impunity (Bastick, Grimm, & Kunz, 2007: 173).

A weapon of war

Male-to-male rape and other forms of sexual violence against boys and men have been used during conflicts since ancient times to feminise enemy combatants and soldiers, (Linos, 2009: 1549) to break down their morale and enforce complete subjugation upon the defeated enemy. It often had a political motive behind it. In the view of some critics, 'in ancient conflicts between various societies and regimes male rape in times of war was considered as an absolute right of the victorious soldiers to declare the totality of enemy's defeat and to express their total and absolute power and control' (Zawati, 2007: 33). The rationale in this context was a fairly simple one—'a man who had been shorn of some or all of his manliness was equally shorn of his capacity to take revenge on his enemies'.

Moreover, following his sexual humiliation and abuse the enemy male (as is the case with female) is no longer the same individual. A part of his identity is lost forever. Or, as Brownmiller puts it, rape is a castrating experience that brings about an everlasting curse of impotence (Brownmiller, 1975: 38).

Consequently one can identify three key patterns of sexual violence against men in the twentieth century: sexual assault and rape as part of the general interrogation process; sexual violence as an intimidation and humiliation strategy in order to breakdown the enemy's political conviction/identity; and rape of prisoners by soldiers or forced rape between the captives as a form of vengeance (Peel, 2004). In all these instances the violator operates from a self-defined social order where the violated is placed in a hierarchy where he is considered as an inferior and thus a legitimate object of humiliation, violence and terror.

Sexual violence against boys and men during an armed conflict is an act of domination grounded in a complex web of cultural preconceptions (Bastick, Grimm, & Kunz, 2007: 9). Many primitive, ancient and even some modern societies and cultures maintained that in the context of military engagement 'when a victorious soldier emasculated a vanquished enemy and sexually penetrated him, the victim would lose his manhood, and could not be a warrior or a ruler anymore' (Zawati, 2007: 33). As a result very often it was the officers and nobles of the enemy group that were handpicked to undergo this violence and indignation. The Ottoman Turks, for example, often had personnel who specialised in these forms of torture and violence.

Interestingly, for the Ottomans there was nothing homosexual about such practices. Sexual violation was simply a form of warfare that aimed at complete subjugation of the enemy; to break his morale and force upon him a form of indignity from which he could never escape. Additionally, such indignation meted out to a member of the officer class or military personnel in command robbed that particular individual of any military or moral authority over the soldiers under his command. Put simply, then, as now, it was very much a tactical, strategic endeavour aimed at defeating the enemy.

This age-old practice was once again evident in some recent theatres of conflict such as Iraq. In this instance the sexual torture and violation of Iraqi men was conducted in a systematic manner in order to crush the spirit of the political detainees who opposed and resisted the Allied invasion of their country (Taguba Report, 2004; Zawati, 2007).

An overview of contemporary conflict locations also introduces us to the fact that men and women are both perpetrators of such violence. As some studies have suggested, 'women can be as susceptible as men to the process of "soldierisation", which imbues in them values and roles of warrior masculinity, processes most likely more pronounced among women who are in or close to combat roles' (Barkawi, *et. al*, 1999: 185). Growing participation of women in contemporary armed conflicts and wars has meant this constituency's familiarity with male 'warrior masculinity'.

This, in turn, has led some of them to embrace the same violent practices as their male counterparts. As a result we have instances of female militia and soldiers conducting sexual violence against boys and men in many recent theatres of conflict (as I will highlight subsequently in the context of Abu Ghraib, Iraq, Rwanda and the DRC).[11] The existence of male victims of female agents of sexual violence is a growing phenomenon (Alison, 2007: 89): the female participation in this undertaking is only a matter of difference of numbers.[12] Or as one critic put it, "the female perpetration of wartime sexual violence has remained somewhat hidden maybe due, at least in part, to the fact that researchers have simply not asked about the sex of perpetrators with rare exceptions (Cohen, 2013: 386)." It needs to be acknowledged, therefore, that although primarily an intra-gender undertaking, in some conflicts and situations, this may turn very much into an inter-gender as well as intra-gender affair.

Interpreting it—the thick …. and the thin view

There exists both a narrow and a wide interpretation of sexual violence in armed conflicts and war. According to the British medical journal *The Lancet* 'sexual violence in armed conflicts comprises assaults to the genitals, non-consensual sexual acts, and objects pushed through the anus'. Similarly it classed rape as non-consensual anal penetration with a penis (*The Lancet*, 2000).

While the narrow view, as the term suggests, focuses only on the physical harm brought upon by the victim owing to the perpetrators' action the wider definition tries to be much more inclusive. The United Nations, for example, has a much wider interpretation of sexual violence in armed conflicts and war. According to the scope of this interpretation:

'Sexual violence was determined as any physical or psychological violence carried out through sexual means or by targeting sexuality and included rape and attempted rape, molestation, sexual slavery, being forced to undress or being stripped of clothing, forced marriage, and insertion of foreign objects into the genital opening or anus, forcing individuals to perform sexual acts on one another or harm one another in a sexual manner, or mutilating a person's genitals.' (quoted in Johnson et. al. 2010: 555; also see UN E/CN.4/Sub. 2/1998/13, 1998: 7–8).

So a broader view of sexual violence in armed conflict may include acts or actions which may lead to both physical as well as psychological harm. The International Criminal Court (ICC) in its *Elements of Crimes* framework, for instance, defines sexual violence as crimes against humanity if they fulfill the following three cumulative criteria: first, the perpetrator or aggressor must inflict severe pain or mental suffering upon one or more persons; second, the tortured person or victim must have been in the custody or under the control of the perpetrator; and third, the pain that the victim suffered or was suffering did not arise only from, and was not inherent in or incidental to, lawful sanctions (*Elements of Crimes*, International Criminal Court (ICC) Doc. ICC-ASP/1/3 (part II-B), arts. 6 (a)–6(e); 9 September 2002).

According to the International Criminal Tribunal for the Former Yugoslavia (ICTY), sexual violence leading to rape during an armed conflict or war may refer to:

The sexual penetration, however slight (a) of the vagina or anus of the victim by penis of the perpetrator or any other object used by the perpetrator; or (b) of the mouth of the victim by the penis of the perpetrator; where such sexual penetration occurs with the consent of the victim (quoted in Lewis, 2009: 34–5).

Eventually, according to the statue of the International Criminal Court, someone might be guilty of sexual violence if they:

… committed an act of a sexual nature against one or more persons or caused such person or persons to engage in an act of a sexual nature by force, or by threat of force or coercion, such as that caused by fear of violence, duress, detention, psychological oppression or abuse of power, against such person or persons or another persons, or by taking advantage of a coercive environment or such person's or persons' incapacity to give genuine consent (ICC, *Elements of Crimes*, Art. 7 (1) (g)-6).

Finding a vocabulary

While it is easy to establish (at this stage) the rationale for studying sexual violence against boys and men there is another line of inquiry which refuses to go away. This particular query can be framed along the following trajectory: what is the intellectual justification behind studying sexual abuse and violence against boys and men in armed conflicts and war as a separate category? Why not study it alongside the everyday occurrence of such violence in a domestic framework? It is well known that boys and men regularly experience such violence when they are in incarceration. Similarly, stories of their sexual abuse in an everyday societal context abound. Surely the victim experience of the violation either in the context of war or in peacetime could be similar. Or, is it?

It is not the intention of this study to quantify, measure or evaluate the 'male experience' of such abuse in a domestic context. It does not intend to engage in a debate to establish whether those violated in arenas of armed conflict are worse off compared to those who have experienced such violation during peacetime. While it does recognise the fact that 'rape or sexual abuse is intended to canalize aggression of the perpetrator and demoralize the victim' (Loncar et al., 2010: 199) in either of these contexts highlighted above, it nonetheless seeks to establish the fact that there is a whole untold story with intricate behavioural patterns that puts wartime sexual violence and male experience in a completely different autonomous category.

As the reader will encounter it throughout this study the wartime sexual abuse against the male gender operates along a very complex set of explanations. It has elements of ethnic cleansing; it may be conducted within the framework of an atavistic nationalism; it may be used to delegitimise the autonomous group identity; it could be a simple issue of exacting revenge against the enemy; or as with the case during peacetime domestic context such acts could be simply opportunistic in nature undertaken to satisfy the perpetrators' or violators' own specific sexual needs.

'Violence against the helpless does turn out to have a specific vocabulary of its own' (Cavarero, 2010: 1). While the terminology of sexual violence is inclusive and captures the essence of this particular undertaking it is by no means exhaustive. Instead what we have are narratives of experience, which although can be put in the general category of sexual violence, are nonetheless unique in their own context because of the overall political nature of the conflict that determined that particularised form of violence. Examined individually the above-mentioned cases would form a part of the narrative that ranges from cruelty, castration, humiliation, sodomy, rape and finally death.

On the whole the narrative that emerges while assessing this gender-specific violence in the context of armed conflict and war is that such undertakings as a rule of thumb are clearly organised, premeditated prior to their implementation, strategically defined and conducted within a clearly held political belief or imagination. In fact it is these very character attributes that put it under an altogether separate category for intellectual and academic exploration.

Balancing the bias

Most of the contemporary scholarship on sexual violence in armed conflicts is not only biased towards the female gender but is heavily influenced by feminist monopolisation of that space that has sought to describe such violence as binary in nature: it is only perpetrated against the female gender by male members of the society. Note for instance this standard definition by a highly influential critic who describes sexual violence as 'a collective noun to encompass all forms of male violence against girls and women' (Kelly, 2000: 45). Thanks to this biased interpretation where the feminist concern is primarily to highlight the victimisation of women by men (Graham, 2006), male sufferers have simply become 'absent victims' in such gender analyses of conflict dynamics (Jones, 1994). Therefore it would not be incorrect to suggest that there is a conceptual and definitional confusion over gender-based violence (Carpenter, 2006).[13]

If one were to take a random sample of some of the contemporary conflicts it becomes abundantly evident that men are sometimes sexually violated as frequently as women. In the former Yugoslavia, for instance, of the 6,000 Serb-held concentration camp interns in the Sarajevo Canton, 5,000 were men and 80 per cent of them had been raped either by their captors or were forced to rape each other (Mudrovcic, 2001: 64; Sivakumaran, 2010: 263). Similarly, in Liberia, in a survey of 1,666 adult combatants some 32.6 per cent had experienced forms of sexual violence while another 16.5 per cent were forced to be sexual servants by their own military leadership or the enemies (Johnson, 2008; Sivakumaran, 2010: 263). In Eastern Congo, a byword for sexual violence against women for the last decade, some 22 per cent of men surveyed have reported conflict-related sexual violence (Storr, 2011: 7). According to the American Bar Association that ran a sexual violence legal clinic in the city of Goma, more than 10 per cent of its cases in June 2009 were men (Gettleman, 2009: 2).

However, in spite of this overwhelming sexual violence against the male gender, if we focus on just one of the conflicts, former Yugoslavia, we are faced with the fact there was hardly any mention of it in the international press. For one critic:

The international media, so fervent in reporting rapes of women, shied away from the topic of sexually assaulted men. Pictures of the starved bodies of Muslim men from the camps run by Bosnian Serb force were on the front pages of international magazines, as were photos of tearful, raped women. But nobody published a photo of a raped man. The national press within former Yugoslavia offered a similar picture. Rapes of women were newsworthy; rapes of men were not (Zarkov, 2001: 72).

Similarly, while plenty of newsreels were spent documenting the sexual atrocities against women victims in Liberia's civil war there was hardly any mention of the condition of men who were simultaneously undergoing a parallel experience.

Moreover, even when there is evidence present on the ground that suggests that the male members of the society have gone through various degrees of sexual violation like their female counterparts those researchers documenting it might simply decide to overlook it. A 2002 survey on sexual violence in Sierra Leone by *Physicians for Human Rights*, for instance, made an exhaustive study of female sexual victimisation, but completely ignored the condition of male victims. It is not clear why the authors of this otherwise excellent study did not touch upon the male victimisation process while there was plenty of evidence confirming this all around. Similarly a report by the Benetech Human Rights Data Analysis Group and the American Bar Association titled *Truth and Myth in Sierra Leone: An Empirical Analysis of the Conflict, 1991–2000* that provides a sustained interrogation of sexual violence during the conflict "the issue of male rape victims was seldom broached (Cohen, 2013: 384)."

Michele Leiby in her study on the Peruvian civil war found that the Peruvian Truth and Reconciliation Commission set up to document the horrors in the post-conflict phase often coded men's experiences of sexual violation in the hands of the enemy as simple 'torture'. But when it assessed the condition of women who had gone through similar experiences it put them down as victims of 'sexual violence' (Leiby, 2009). Why such errors and irregularities?[14]

Such irregularities have led some critics to argue that male 'sexual violence research is beset by selection bias' (Cohen, Green & Wood, 2013: 10). In addition if one were to broaden the area of criticism then one could argue there are a whole host of actors both undermining and inhibiting our comprehensive understanding behind it. While governments, aid agencies and human rights defenders are aware of it they barely acknowledge its possibility (Storr, 2011: 7).

True the primary reason why there exists an absence of required knowledge about this form of violence has to do with a lack of societal concern regarding sexual violence against men and the hesitancy of the victims (owing to multiple factors) to report their violation. There is not only individual and communal hesitancy to recognise this atrocity but there is also a culture of non-recognition pervading the NGOs and

INGOs who often posses intimate knowledge of such conflict dynamics (Stemple, 2009: 612).[15]

This being the context, it is not just the fault of researchers not reporting such crimes, the media shying away from it, NGOs in the field ignoring it or feminist critiques pursuing a gender-bias agenda. There is a culture of silence surrounding this violence. It is a silence that is orchestrated by a number of actors. Hence to clear the analytical haze that dominates this field we have to take a holistic approach to this very issue.

Methods

The core underlying concern in any case or event-based research is not only to throw light on an issue but also to bridge an existing knowledge gap. It is, as some critics have argued, about unearthing and describing a chunk of 'reality' (Daymon & Holloway, 2002: 106).

Looking back I realise the seeds for this study were sown way back in the late 1990s, when I was a graduate student in a small city in north-east England. My time in that city coincided with the arrival of groups of refugees (mostly male) from the war-torn Balkans. The halls of residence where I lived had falling student numbers. To see through the challenging times the management had decided to take on board some of these male refugees. Thus began my first encounter with the topic and the beginning of the learning process surrounding it. What started as post-dinner table discussion with one of these residents turned into revelations about deep personal traumas and private tragedies. Soon I realised that each one of those refugee residents had been affected by this specific violence in the war and now harboured a deep physical and emotional injury.

Later I would come across similar experiences among Sri Lankan Tamil refugees living in the British Isles and Western Europe. My fieldwork in Central America and South Asia introduced me to facets of this horror played out often times openly during communal clashes and civil wars.

This study is informed by both first-hand qualitative data gathering, as well as evaluation of these events from secondary sources (available in the public domain in the form of newspaper stories, journal articles, field reports of human rights bodies, NGO studies, international legal rulings, TV documentaries, and excerpts present in the visual media such as *Youtube*). As the discerning reader will realise I have interwoven these two sets of sources in this study.

As far as the primary data gathering is concerned, although not bracketed by boundaries of time, most of the interviewed participants' victimisation took place in various conflict locations and wars between 1980–2010. Altogether I undertook thirty-two open format semi-structured interviews conducted in informal public spaces: over post-dinner conversation, in cafes, while observing life from park benches, during long walks on the seafront and so on conducted intermittently between 1998–2000, 2003–2005, and 2008–2010.

Individual interviews were conducted over sustained periods of time comprising of several meetings. All ethical issues concerning anonymity and confidentiality were fully observed during the course of such interviews. The information was gained through voluntary informed consent. All of the victims' identities will remain anonymous: the narration is often in third person singular mode and actual names are replaced by fake ones.

A study such as this, with explanations framed in various theoretical contexts, necessitates a process of purposeful sampling of cases. I have, on occasion, used a single event in various contexts to bring forth several layers of meanings and ways of evaluating that event.

So far as intellectual justification for studying sexual violence against men in war is concerned one could highlight a number of reasons. Most importantly, it is understudied and under-reported. By and large male victims of sexual violence in armed conflicts and war continue to be an unrecognised constituency. Recognition and identification of this conceptual gap throws light on a problem with grave implications. A part of the objective of this study is to draw attention to the problematic discourse in conflict literature that treats sexual abuse and violence experienced by the male individual during armed encounter and war solely as 'torture survivors'. It is the absence of the sexual component of their suffering in such discourse and policy undertaking that this work tries to highlight.

With respect to sexual violence against the male gender this study encompasses both boys and adult men. While stories about sexual violence against the male gender in domestic settings, prisons and in peacetime abound, this book does not purport to reflect on, analyse or interrogate such incidences of violence. The primary and abiding concern throughout this study is to examine, explore and interpret sexual violence against male gender in conflicts. Sexual violence against boys and men in conflicts is unique, in the sense that the aggressor, owing to a very complex set of reasonsing and cognitions, entertains this undertaking.

The framework of analyses, therefore, is entirely different from the domestic contexts.

Returning to the theme specified, overall, it would appear, such experience has been excluded both from the history of warfare and from the readers' understanding of the nature of armed conflict and war.

Engaging in a 'structural' explanation in the study of specificities of violence it also highlights why there exists a disparate engagement with this topic as an academic subject of inquiry (that is women's experience gaining a voice and male experience being largely silent or missing).

Ontological security, which focuses on the security of oneself, and one's identity in the context of sexual violation in war, is rather inadequate in its current form. Our comprehension of violence in war is guided by specific' inherited understandings: while sexual violence against women falls into the category of orthodox, their male counterparts' experience is considered unorthodox and thus its occurrence impossible—male combatants in an armed conflict and war may boast and confess to the fact that they have raped women but they would not admit to raping men (perpetrators of such violence are never in a hurry to discuss why they did it nor are they keen to confess it). Consequently the experience of female victims of sexual violence finds a natural voice in mainstream international relations, feminist studies, political theory and war studies but male victims, because of their unorthodox experience, are left out.

Furthermore, the lack of knowledge on the wider impact of war, ignorance surrounding this specific occurrence, and failure to confront it head on may have something to do with our own incomprehension of war as a subject, seen through the particular optics of ontology of violence. As Barkawi posits, 'the social political and cultural processes of the war itself remain a black box' (Barkawi, 2011: 708). Simply put, despite its constitutive function for politics and society, war in general and some aspects of war in particular, have never been made the object of an academic discipline (Barkawi & Brighton: 2011: 126–143).

'War' and the attendant violence it spawns, 'consumes and reworks social and political orders' (Barkawi, 2011: 705). Seen from that perspective this particularised experience requires sustained interrogation in the context of 'order' and 'disorder'. What one needs to do in such scenarios is to weave this specific experience back into the overall narrative of war.

Therefore, this study is as much an inquiry into the ontology of violence as it is a phenomenological study of war. It goes behind war as an experience and tackles questions such as—how do victims as well as perpetrators (violators) reflect on sexual violence and how does it affect their consciousness? Hence inter alia the rationale for the pragmatic application-related value of this study.

My attempt here is not to highlight 'male experience of sexual violence' as an independent discipline. My way of posing the question is primarily ontological. Such an ontology of war centres upon the examination of 'what war *is*, and about the challenges of knowing about it' (Barkawi & Brighton, 2011: 134).

This method in social science not only helps us identify, categorize and describe the fundamental structure of what exists, but also provides us the foundational assumptions from which a line of inquiry can proceed (Barkawi & Brighton, 2011: 134). What I have tried to do is to engage in discursive analyses and compliment the dominant narrative on violence in war. I aim to highlight *prima facie* how 'human activity' could 'produce a world of things' (Foucault, 1972). And, critically, how discourse produces facets of knowledge.

In addition, I try to broaden the debate about the nature of contemporary warfare by examining sexual violence against male victims as constituted through behavioural responses. Such an approach, I believe, can alone offer our first complete view of the nature of conflict in warfare.

Conclusion

War occurs in the realm of experience rather than via (de)personalised strategies. Broadly this study proposes a new methodological take on war as a 'lived' experience. The intention behind this undertaking is to treat the experiences of victims of these atrocities as a resource with which to develop a new analytical framework. Hence methods and approaches to deal with this subject matter are at once interdisciplinary and direct.

A careful reading of such forms of violence from an interdisciplinary perspective offers the prospect of a valuable holistic understanding. As such, it tries to locate the normative explanations behind this particular undertaking and the resulting outcome from a varied perspective—ranging from anthropology to political theory, moral philosophy to sociobiology, and law to psychology.

On the whole it is an exercise in 'unmasking' events and studying them up close. If this book is to be properly understood, it must be read not as a work on politics, still less a sort of policy study, but purely and simply as a treatise on conflict behaviour. The title indicates that. This book deals with the condition of a particular kind of victim; but it also deals with the whole condition of our being a part of that experience.

1

THE BODY

It [*the body*] is outside itself, in the world of others.

Judith Butler, *Frames of War*, 2009: 52.

From antiquity to the modern age, human sexuality has been a fundamental agent of progress, order and happiness. Hence some individuals, communities and societies, in order to gain an upper-hand in conflicts or wars, have tried to enforce a particularised version of sexuality upon their opponent.

Any discussion surrounding sexuality invariably leads us in the direction of the place of the body in that discourse. The analysis that follows is primarily an exercise in articulating and conceptualising the event of sexual violence on the male body in the context of armed conflict. Given this specific undertaking there are multiple interrelated lines of inquiry associated with the body, which dominates the debate in the subsequent pages.

In the main I focus on the following questions: Why does an enemy male's body have sexual significance? What are the metaphors, symbolism and representations associated with it? Why is it that some bodies are selected or elected for sexual violation over others? Or, what is the attractiveness of violation in relation to a specific body? Similarly, what are the key motivational aspects behind such undertakings? Why, for example, do specific conflicts spawn particularised forms of sexual violence against the male body and others do not?

Within this broad framework of analysis I seek to answer the sexual subjectivity of a given opponent's body and the value that a violator

21

attaches to it. In this context I ask why the violator prefers sexual violation of the victim's body over its complete physical elimination—as is the
case in most armed conflicts and wars. While engaged in this evaluation,
I also shed light on the intricate relationship between body and soul and
seek to problematise the meaning and significance of the body prior to
and after its violation. In doing so, I seek to offer a theorisation of the
male body in the context of sexual violation in armed conflicts and war.

In the libertarian discourse it is generally understood that a living body
is the possession of the individual personality of which it is a part. It is
based on the simple proprietary premise that as embodied persons we
possess ourselves (Cohen, 2008: 103). To the owner of this body it is a
kind of property that one invests in, it gives us back to ourselves. Also, it
is through the body that the very personhood is conceived and maintained. Ontologically it signifies an inalienable sovereignty of that individual over his body. It is ours to control (Cohen, 2008: 104); we can do
what we want to do with it (Gill, Henwood & McLean, 2005: 48). Yet,
there is a caveat. All those mechanisms and understanding that gives the
individual supreme authority over his physical being is very fragile indeed.

In spite of the general normative understanding behind the body and
the specific rights of its owner over it, even in peacetime or in a non-war/
non-conflict context, one's body may not be completely one's own. If the
'body is the vessel which holds the true self locked within it' (Elias, 1969),
it is easily exposed to another's desires and designs.

The body's relevance and consequently the treatment that accrues to
it are made possible in contexts and situations 'where we encounter a
range of perspectives that may or may not be our own. How I am encountered, and how I am sustained, depends fundamentally on the social and
political networks in which this body lives' (Butler, 2009: 53).

The political implications arising out of specific physical bodies closely
affect conflict dynamics. The body's sexual embodiment is a cause for
concern. In some theatres of political conflict it becomes the most cov-
eted object of confrontation and control. Trespassing 'the boundary' of
this body assumes paramount importance to the violator. If that is so, to
borrow Butler's analogy again, in the context of conflict and war, 'certain
kinds of bodies will appear more precariously than others, depending on
which versions of the body, or of morphology in general, support or
underwrite the idea of human life that is worth protecting, sheltering,
living, mourning' (Butler, 2009: 53).

Within the context of armed conflict and war one can ask three questions in relation to the 'body'. First, what is a body? Second, what can a body do? Third, what can you do to a body? I will return to the second and third questions in chapter two (on biopower). But let's concentrate here on the first question that is intended as an exploration within a broadly interactionist analysis.

In the discourse and activism surrounding conflict and war a given physical human body can have two sets of meanings. Let me adapt Giorgio Agamben to the present discussion. Using Agamben's trajectory in *Homo Sacer—Sovereign Power and Bare Life*, one could situate it in the following manner. A body can be classified as *Zoé* (bare life) or *βios* (qualified political life) (Agamben, 1998). From the perspective of the opponent in a confrontation with a bare life the latter can be easily violated, ruptured and dispensed with. Not of high value a *Zoé* at times could provide momentary satisfaction to the veritable desires of the aggressor. By contrast *βios*, while it has all the physical attributes of *Zoé*, has an additional value as a medium on which a given subversive (ethno-religious or political) message can be etched. In this trajectory the living body and its possessor are primarily essentialised.

While the assignation of the body is crucial in understanding the subsequent treatment it receives, there is another crucial factor that also contributes to determining the course of events and experiences that this given body would experience. In this particular context, we can also think about demarcating the human body through identifying its boundaries (Butler, 2009: 52). This boundary condition underlines all acts of appropriation (Cohen, 2008: 107). The body, then, is circumscribed within a well-defined perimeter. The value classification and the boundaries a given body possesses determine the process of violation as well as non-violation it may encounter.

The 'human body is soft and susceptible, and it is very vulnerable in its nakedness. Anything can penetrate it. Every injury makes it harder for the body to resist' (Canetti, 1979: 17). Yet, for the violator the modes of materialisation of the violation of the victim are also dependent on the temporal, spatial and physical conditions of that body itself. In the morphology of the body, a body can be strong or weak, young or old, virile or effeminate, submissive or resistant, disabled or able bodied and so on. It is the particular physical condition of that body (and several other attendant factors) which ultimately determines the nature of exertion of his violence.

Therefore, while the human body as a general principle is vulnerable to external manipulation by the manipulator, its attractiveness to perform such undertakings are governed by the very physical manifestation/ state of that body.

Consequently, sexual violation of a disabled or old body is not only aesthetically unpleasant but that endeavour has very little prospect of establishing the virility of the violator. Thus while an old, weak or disabled body is ignored or consigned to a quick process of physical elimination a young, virile and strong body is put into sexual violation. The key underlying objective of the violator is to defile the body that is at its prime. While engaging in this selection process our violator is not only practising what one might call aesthetics of violence but is also gauging that body's ability to work as a sounding board for its long-term message.[1] Violation of an able, young body contains the possibility of a lasting outcome. Therefore this undertaking is about complete submission of a body that is both strong and healthy. Violation of this body either directly or indirectly establishes our perpetrator's complete and long-serving sovereignty over that sound physical body with an equally undamaged psyche. Since the violator's aim is to exert maximum long-term damage s/he seeks out and targets these specific bodies.

This being the narrative, one critic has rightly asked if there exists a pattern of hierarchy among enemy bodies, which disposes them to receiving such violence (Stemple, 2009: 630). In the view of some scholars there exists a clear pattern of 'hierarchy of harm' in relation to the specific bodies (Graham, 2006). The would-be victim finds himself in an extremely volatile situation if he possesses a very healthy and attractive body and his ethnicity, religion or nationalism is directly in opposition to his enemy. Consequently the targets are not simple victims to be picked up at random but are carefully screened and occupy a clearly defined hierarchy of classification.

Conversely, when the body is not aesthetically pleasant or the violator has a superior sense of his own racial identity, the latter may force the captive victims to engage in sodomy, mutual masturbation and rape. While forcing this violation from a distance the violator is proclaiming a binary divide between the untainted image of himself and his community, and the shattered image of the fallen, less than human identity of the victim and the community, culture and religion that he belongs to.

Violation, denigration and subjugation of the body create a heightened level of bodily self-consciousness in the owner. He is suspended in a manufactured precariousness. He has no rational explanation behind the given treatment of his body by his violator(s). He is left to carry the burden of an inferior self-consciousness following this experience. This bodily experience and the inescapable awareness of it is often the dominant factor in the victim's rejection of the world around him. The most dominant marker of this experience is signs of the natural inferiority of the possessor vis a vis others in the community. But by and large the victim carries the shame and burden of guilt and with that banishes all forms of autonomy from his self. I explore in greater detail the effects on the physical and mental state following such violation in chapter six.

Sexual bodies

The subtle and not so subtle correlation between the body, sovereignty and sexuality comes alive in the works of Georges Bataille. According to Bataille human sexuality is inextricably linked to violence and the dissolution of the boundaries of the body and self by way of irregular and uncommon impulses. Therefore, by and large, sexuality concerns two key forms of polarised human impulses—excretion and appropriation—as well as the regime of the taboos surrounding them (Bataille, 1985: 94–5). Following Bataille, it is the classification of the body of the opponent into *Zoé* and *ßios*, which ultimately determines the nature and character of the violator's infliction.

Thanks to a steep rise in irregular warfare, the body of the male civilian and soldier has been pushed into a world of sexual insecurity (Misra, 2008). In some conflict locations this prevailing insecurity may enforce a new context for such violation. Here the original political project surrounding violation may have little or no meaning. The bodies here take the form of *Zoé* or bare life in contrast to *ßios* or a high-value body capable of carrying a political message. The dominant thinking here is to use the body of the other (the easily available *Zoé*) to give expression to one's own feelings of desire, frustration or needs.

Such being the narrative there may be occasions when the body of a victim may be used by people belonging to his own side, violating it in order to escape their own frustration and abject condition. If the conflict condition were the metaphorical and literal representation of extremity then those who inhabit it may at times engage in practices that previously were the purview of the enemy violator.

Note, for instance, the widely reported cases of rape of Iranian prisoners of war (PoW) by their fellow Iranian prisoners while held in Iraq following their capture in the Iraq-Iran war (1980–1988). Captured Iranian soldiers in Iraqi-held camps often raped their fellow Iranians in the darkness of the night. The explanation behind such undertaking was that 'that particular violator' was revolting against the abject condition in which he found himself and the fellow Iranian prisoner's body became his momentary passage.[2]

Faced with extraordinary situations those inhabiting this space will stoop below their own humanity if the occasion permits a temporary escape from the surroundings. It is the abject desperation to escape from this condition—albeit temporarily—that might explain cases of victim on victim sexual violence in the camp.

Irrespective of whether the violator was the enemy or belonged to the victim's own community there is no escaping the fact such violation involves two autonomous bodies. It is a double act. Therefore it is imperative that one also seeks to extrapolate the meaning and significance of this act on the violator's personality.

If one were to open up this debate there could be these sets of questions: What about the body of the perpetrator? What role does it play in this interaction? Is the perpetrator always involved in a psychological relationship with his victim? Is his or her body completely insulated from that of the victim? Or are there occasions when both their bodies (that of the perpetrator and that of the victim) come into some sort of interplay?

It is now common knowledge that there exists a particular variety of individuals who are drawn to members of the same sex. What happens when these individuals find themselves in situations when they are presented with bodies that can act as vehicles of their suppressed desire? What if the perpetrator's congenital constitution made his homosexual drive much stronger in the face of easily available bodies? It would be inaccurate and unhelpful to presume that the perpetrator does not use the occasion to enact his own private pleasures on such the body of his opponent caught up in the maelstrom of conflict.

What if a specific body is strung out across difference? How does one articulate this desire? Let's use Frantz Fanon's analogy to elicit some explanation. In *Black Skin White Mask* Fanon wonders, albeit in a different context, 'just as there are faces that ask to be slapped, can one not speak of person or persons who ask to be raped?' (Fanon, 1967: 177). Certainly there is an erotic charge in this interpretation. Perhaps Fanon is deploying his own prejudices in this statement. Yet, there is no escaping the fact that, at times in psychosexual organization of bodies a given physical disposition may amount to the exertion of a specific form of violence: a form of affectation leading to a certain outcome.

Commodification

The parameters that define the body as an object of violation do not automatically emerge from the body itself; rather they enter the decision making process of violation through the violators' own preference. Thus while some conflicts become synonymous with the gross sexual infringement of the male body (such as the Bosnian and Guatemalan civil war) others are mercifully free from it (Israeli-Palestinian conflict, for instance). This context-dependent transitivity of the body may yet face an entirely different process in some other conflicts.

Earlier, I argued that there is an intricate relationship between the body and individual ownership over it. In the context of armed insurgency and war, however, some specific bodies become 'objects of desire' where the person being a part of that body is forced to give up his physical self to the ownership of another person. This 'specific body' is appropriated and kept very much as a valued property and for personal use and disposition. The 'body-as-property' formula is exploited to the full in some conflict locations where there is internecine war and a prevalent culture that encourages such external ownership.

External ownership, of course, involves trade in these objects of desire or commodities. It is dictated by what experimental psychologist Steven Pinker calls 'sexual economics' of the body (Pinker, 1998: 474). As posited earlier, the desire to possess and violate an individual body, therefore, is value- and condition-specific. According to 'the German', a self-styled Afghan pimp making the most of the chaotic Afghan post-war hiatus, the buying and selling of young and adolescent boys to a network of clients is an accepted undertaking like any other business. But more importantly, this undertaking is governed by a careful exploratory exercise guided by the very physical conditionality of those specific bodies. To quote 'the German':

I go to every province to have happiness and pleasure with boys, some boys are not good for dancing, and they will be used for other purposes… I mean for sodomy and other sexual activities (see Quraishi, 2010).

Our itinerant businessman 'the German' is part of a larger cultural practice known as *bacha bazi* (Bacheh-baaazi) and *chai*boys whose inherent objective is sexual commodification of specific bodies.[3] What we have here is an active and conscious process of 'survey' and 'consumption' of specific bodies. War spurs hitherto dormant desires. It throws open immense possibilities for an immoral minority to trade in on 'fashionable permissiveness'.[4] It provides the perfect cover and context to procure and violate specific bodies. The likes of 'the German' are its schemers and plotters.[5] That given sets of bodies are to be procured, traded in and exploited is not limited to war-torn Afghanistan alone. In south Sudan (prior to its independence in 2011) this was a commonly known practice.[6]

In both these contexts such predatory masculinity against the other's body is not only tolerated but often times culturally sanctioned. In the view of Enayatullah, a 42-year-old in Baghlan province, in war-torn Afghanistan 'having a boy has become a custom for us, … whoever wants to show off should have a boy' (Brinkley, 2010).

Apart from the immediate concerns surrounding legality and ethicality of the whole enterprise, there are some other larger questions to answer. For instance, 'showing off' involves procurement, or at least possession, of a given body. If a live body can be procured and possessed it raises several complex questions associated with ownership.

Procurement of such a body raises questions about its management. Following the procurement of the young boy a discursive exercise about the place of his body in the public domain begins—between the individual who is physically a part of it, the warlord who now controls/owns it and the onlookers who are part of this new knowledge. Needless to add this is very much an undertaking to reorient all the three parties to the place of this given body in the grammar of ownership. The physical body at the centre of this debate and site of sexual violation is now separated from the individual self. Upon procurement the new owner of this body establishes what one might call fresh proprietary sovereignty. In the new body-as-property arrangement the person who is physically a part of it is now the secondary owner of that body; while primary ownership is held by the rebel leader, tribal elder or warlord who has now acquired it.

If a given body is indeed a property it throws up all manners of challenges and problems associated with tangible matters. As Cohen argues, 'in order for something—or some thing—to be someone's—or some one's—property, the boundary that has been drawn around it must be defensible (Cohen, 2008: 107). Thus those engaged in such practices go to lengths to protect their 'property'. That being the context, feuds and killings between various strongmen following robbery or attempted robbery of their *chai*boys in Afghanistan or 'boy slaves' in Sudan are not uncommon.

Furthermore, if the body of the other is, indeed, the property of someone else, in such circumstances, 'property ownership constitutes a form of dominion, and dominion manifests a force or power that resists and repels all opposing forces or power within its domain' (Cohen, 2008: 107). While normally it may refer to warding off competing individuals and groups from taking over ownership, very often this power projection may be against the secondary owner of the body (the actual person who is physically part of himself or the slave).

For Majok, a twelve-year old boy caught up in the civil war in Sudan, life consisted of attending to his master's cattle all through the day, and later at nightfall he was regularly raped by his primary owner. The master in question had a whole group of young boys: 'he often went to collect other boys at nightfall took them to a special place and raped them' (Silwa, 2004: 1). While many of these victims put up with this daily torture, some did try to escape. Their master either killed those who did try to escape, or on occasion had one of their limbs hacked off for insubordination. Once again applying the proprietary principle, we are confronted with the fact that the inability of the person inhabiting the body to protect itself from usurpation leads not only to servitude but on occasion death:

I watched my master and four Murahaleen [soldiers] violently gang-rape a young Dinka slave boy. The boy was screaming and crying a lot. He was bleeding heavily, as he was raped repeatedly. I watched his stomach expand with air with each violent penetration. The boy kept screaming. I was very frightened, and knew I was likely next. Suddenly the boy's screams stopped as he went completely unconscious. My master took him to the hospital. I never saw him again. (Silwa, 2004: 3)

Why put the body through so much pain? This, of course, arises due to questions surrounding acquisition and the subsequent management of an external body. To quote Cohen, 'if a boundary does not contain the domain within which this force or power—this agency or subjectivity— can freely act, then the distinctiveness of the property is lost' (Cohen, 2008: 107). Hence procurement of the body implies procurement of undisputed control over it. If at any point there is an attempt to circum-scribe the authority over this property the primary owner of this given body (who resides outside it) can go to extreme measures to demonstrate his ownership over it.

Governability

Our common understanding of the body as 'both formally discrete and politically, socially, and/or psychologically fundamental to its owner' (Cohen, 2008: 106), faces unique problems during times of socio-polit-ical disruptions such as armed conflicts and war. In such situations, the actual ownership over the body and the ability to do things to it becomes context-dependent. In other words, the hitherto exclusive control of the individual over his own body becomes contested. Instead of the actual person (whose body it is) deciding his body's functionality it becomes subject to the other's system of organisation and disposition.

In Foucault the study of the body is organised around the notions of discipline and regulatory controls of 'governability' (Foucault, 1991: 143). Hence, from the perspective of the violator, the body of the victim is both a 'functional site' as well as a 'disciplinary space'. The body of the living victim is all that the perpetrator needs in order to impose his/her vision of what that individual's life from now on is going to be like. It serves as a canvas on which the perpetrator can etch his/her particularised notions of disciplinary measure, punishment or retribution. For all intents and purposes it is the functional site for such enactments. Similarly it comes to serve as a disciplinary site in the sense that others belonging to his community can take lessons from the bodily experiences of the victim.

Governability in this sense imposes a condition of existence—what it means to have a violated body. It dictates how the prisoner of this body shall feel about himself from here after. Governability may also imply imposing a permanent enslaved condition on the violated. It determines the space in which it (the violated body) is going to operate. Ironically while the space might be vibrant, the body (or the person living in this body) may be dead to this vibrancy. External governability over the body, in such contexts, creates a new regime of control, which can be framed along these lines: You (the victim) can have the body, but I (the aggres-sor), shall have an indeclinable control over its future. Mildly put it is a despotic act that establishes a life-changing experience for the violated.

From Iran to Zimbabwe and Peru to Kashmir many regimes trying to control their dissident opponents' 'soul power' do employ such violation in order to permanently impose a structure of governance that keeps the violated in a constant state of fear, submission and isolation.

In Indian-held Kashmir, for instance, the quarter-of-a-century long separatist war over competing nationalisms created a discourse and policy framework whereby the restive population came to encounter a blanket violation of their physicality and absence of any recourse to address it. To counter the separatist insurgency the Indian Army often used sexual violence against both women and men in order to inflict 'collective dishonour' on the Kashmiri body politic.

Coupled by the stigma of violation of bodily integrity and unable to face up to the new reality many militants, insurgents and would be separatists went back into self-isolation. The challenge for these violated men to publicise the atrocity of the security forces and military was compounded by an almost macabre Catch 22 situation: 'these violated individuals had to report to the very authorities who violated them'; and there was explicit 'pressure exerted by military authorities on the local police not to file a First Information Report on behalf of sexually violated and rape victims' (Kazi, 2009).

Turning to another conflict location, Zimbabwe, to highlight the manner of this bodily governance against perceived opponents of the government, let the victim speak of his bodily experience:

They removed all my clothing, then one of the militia put on a condom and raped me. ... I was crying and there was a lot of blood. Then the second militia did the same thing ... When it was over, they put me in handcuffs and chains and left me without my clothes (Hill, 2003).

Our Zimbabwean victim like countless other such victims in other conflict settings such as Kashmir, was subsequently freed. What is interesting here is: Why was the regime putting them through this torture releasing them back into the public space? Once again this could be answered within the process of bodily governance.

In normal conditions of penalty the prisoner would have been housed in some kind of formal penal architecture in the form of concentration or PoW camp, jailhouse, penitentiary, correction home and so on. But by sexually violating the body of the prisoner and leaving the victim to live with his body and that experience, the perpetrator is doing away with the need for any such formal architecture to house the prisoner.

On these occasions the experience that the violator forces upon the victim is transmuted to an external/public disciplinary space. Following this specific undertaking the prisoner remains safely imprisoned in the experience within him. It is this particular knowledge about the correlation between bodily experience and the subsequent burden of psychological imprisonment, which lies at the heart of such undertaking on the part of the perpetrator. Violation and subsequent release of the victim into the public domain commits him to a perpetual enslavement. Furthermore his bodily experience is transmitted to the collective and the latter assumes a similar servitude by association (as I discuss in detail in chapter six).

Feminising Masculinity

There are two ways of violating the male body. It can be direct or indirect. As we have seen sexual violation of the male body can be undertaken by an enemy aggressor or the latter may force his or her captives to perform forms of sexual acts against each other while in custody. For instance, the Serb militias apart from castrating their Bosnian Muslim prisoners also forced them to rape each other. Contrast that with reports of Afghan warlords raping their victims or openly engaging in the practice of acquiring 'toy boys' for their sexual entertainment and gratification. While violation of the body was the outcome in all these instances the manner in which it was conducted was significantly different from one another. What made the Serb militias enforce rape between their Bosnian Muslim captives? And why did the Afghan warlord prefer to rape his enemy captive?

Forms of wartime sexual violation could be argued to be culturally specific. According to some observers such asymmetric reactions have a lot to do with cultural norms 'in which one participant (the receptive partner) in (both consensual and coerced) male-male insertive anal sex is viewed as feminine and/or homosexual while the other participant (the insertive partner) is viewed not as feminine or homosexual, but as masculine' (Lewis, 2009: 7). Similarly some other cultures might come to associate any form of male-male sex as homosexual.

Therefore the reason why the Serb militias did not rape their victims was for the simple reason that that very act could have tainted them with homosexuality. For the Afghan warlord, however, there were no such cultural a priori prohibitions or socially-constructed threats. Throughout this study we will encounter such contrasting behaviour. That there could be social as well as political dimensions to such culturally conditioned deviant behaviour and ways of perceiving masculinity and femininity in conflict settings was first detected by Brad Epps. While studying the tumult of the Cuban revolution Epps found that:

Designating less a libidinal relationship between individuals of the same gender than a particular role, position, or style of behaviour, homosexuality, male homosexuality that is, primarily designates those men who exhibit 'feminine' traits or otherwise show that they assume so-called passive or receptive positions in sexual intercourse. The *maricon*, very much more than the 'active', 'insertive', 'masculine-acting' *bugarron* is here the subject in questions. The latter indeed is a figure who, is not necessarily, 'labeled' or 'stigmatized' as homosexual and who may even find his masculinity reinforced by penetrating other men (Epps, 1995: 232–33).

If the above construct is any help the Afghan warlord or strongman who engages in the practice of *bachhabazi* (rape of boys and keeping them in a state of sexual slavery as discussed earlier) earns a certain amount of respect among his fellow fighters for having the supreme masculinity of penetrating other men. Some cultures, in fact, may permit and encourage such practices of direct violation of other men or enemy soldiers. The rape of British-Arab war hero T. E. Lawrence by the Ottoman Turks, which I will touch upon later, can be seen in this context.

Armed conflicts and wars spawn what one might call militarised bodies. These bodies are 'almost archetypical masculine ones: bodies built to fight, defend, and protect as much like machines as possible' (Pile, 2011). How do you demobilise such a military machine? The violation of the male enemy's body through sexual penetration or rape, in some instances is aimed at 'reducing' this very militarised bodily representation to a lower rank and ascribing him the status of a 'feminised male'. In fact a whole gamut of symbolic and metaphorical meanings go into the construction of such images.

This is the story of Dhia al-Shweiri, one of the Iraqi inmates of Abu Ghraib prison. Let al-Shweiri speak of his transformative experience.

"We are men. Beatings don't hurt us; it just a blow. But no one would want their manhood to be shattered. [Our captors] wanted us to feel as though we were women, the way women feel…"

[During Saddam Hussein's regime I was] "electrocuted, beaten and hung from the ceiling with hands tied behind back. But that's better than the humiliation of being stripped naked."

"Shoot me here," he added, pointing between his eyes, "but don't do this to us." (al-Shweiri, China Daily, 2005; also quoted in Franks, 2014: 569).

According to one critic, 'when an individual is forced into a passive position, that individual is feminised, and the feminisation of passivity reinforced' (Shepherd, 2010: 77). For Gear, the very act of sexual penetration of a male victim by his enemy captors at once strips him of his innate masculinity. In his view, in a psychoanalytical framework penetration is something reserved for, or associated with, the female sex (Gear, 2007: 214). As anthropologist Pierre Bordieu explains:

Penetration, especially when performed on a man, is one of the affirmations of the *libido dominandi* that is never entirely absent from the masculine libido... [I]n a number of societies homosexual possession is conceived as a manifestation of 'power'. An act of domination (performed as such... in order to assert superiority by 'feminising' the other and that, understood in this way, ... it condemned the victim to dishonour and the loss of the status of a complete man and a citizen ... (Bourdieu, 2001: 21).

If our male victim found himself in a situation where he was sexually penetrated, that sent out a message both for his aggressor and the victim that the person receiving this treatment is incapable of preventing this abominable act from happening in the first place. Therefore he forfeits the right to consider himself a 'real man'.

His primary identity has thus been reversed, as becomes all the more evident if we evaluate the above sets of arguments against some concrete evidence. According to one of the survivors of such violence from the DRC, while they were raping him his violators kept saying, 'you're no longer a man, you are going to become one of our woman' (Amnesty International, 2004: 19; also quoted in Sivakumaran, 2007: 271). This is not a unique comment. Many Iraqi prisoners who were sexually violated by the American soldiers while in detention in one form or another have gone on record to express similar sentiments. For these survivors, their captors, while violating them were guided by many different objectives. However the prominent and overwhelming objective was to imprison these victims into a construct that denied them their full masculinity (MacKinnon, 2006b: 25).

Using individually centred violence to undermine the position of an enemy's ethnic or religious group has a long history. The enemy violator is often privy to this knowledge. He is aware of the fact that these violations, even when they are localised and subtle, have a knock on effect rendering this individual event into a communal one. In these contexts it is considered by the enemy aggressor that by harming one of the opponent's members or leaders it can inflict injury upon that entire community. This symbolic logic of transposing one single instance of violence upon one entire group finds a perfect host in sexual violence against men. Such enterprise finds its most potent manifestation in the context of castration of the male victim. The abstract emotional scars affecting the community owing to the single individual bodily experience is enormous.

If at one level castration implies biological emasculation of that individual it can also be seen as symbolic emasculation of the group to which the victim belonged. For Sivakumaran, 'this is particularly pronounced in an ethnic conflict where the castration of a single man of the ethnically defined enemy is symbolic appropriation of the masculinity of the whole group' (Sivakumaran, 2007: 274). Such individually administered sexual violation of a male member of another ethnic or religious community is, thus, a proof not only that he (the victim) is a lesser man but also that his ethnicity and religion is a lesser ethnicity and religion (Sivakumarn, 2007: 274–5; Zarkov, 2001: 78).

Fear of loss

The fear of losing the genitals is perhaps one of the worst fears that a male can ever encounter in the context of a conflict. Although well concealed and protected it can in fact assume the location of strategic attack in an armed exchange.

Unsurprisingly given this strategic value, immobilising the male enemy for temporary or longer periods of time by attacking his genitalia has a long history. According to some studies it was a favoured method of combat among some enemy soldiers when they found themselves face-to-face with the enemy. Such was the widespread use of this strategy during the First World War that it gave rise to the circulation of slang D.S.O. (dick shot off) (Love, 2007: 92).

One cannot be entirely sure if the enemy opponent targeted the genitals of the person standing on the other side of the divide (through the barrel of his gun or bayonet) for gaining a tactical advantage, pursued it as part of a coordinated strategy or employed it for personal perverted pleasure. There exists little or no eyewitness accounts or personal testimony to evaluate these three probable reasons. However, some military personnel the author interviewed about this particular aspect of 'targeting' the male genitalia in combat situations, confirmed that a soldier may be guided by one of the above reasons or a combination of two or three reasons in any given context of armed encounter. Whatever may be the dominant motive on the part of the aggressor there is no denying the fact that from the male perspective the very vision of his genitals being severed from his body in a combat situation renders him immobile. For instance:

...one Californian policeman discovered during riots that militant men dropped their weapons much faster if he pointed his guns at their genitals rather than their head (Love, 2007: 92).

Although this strategy might appear novel in the late twentieth century United States, it was nonetheless a throwback to similar practices going back to the eighteenth and nineteenth centuries. Some states in the American federation actually permitted the castration of black slaves if they rose up in revolt against their master/planter or were found to be a threat to the white womenfolk. The psychological fright associated with losing the genitals over losing life was so pervasive that it was effective in subduing the male black against any possible thought of revolt.

The purpose of actually enforcing castration, or even merely suggesting it to the enemy, is to turn a potentially lethal opponent docile and non-militant.

Think for a moment of the cinematic rendition of such fear. In *Goldfinger* James Bond is tied to a table while his enemy is projecting a laser beam that cuts through the thick metal centimetre by centimetre. The objective is to slowly oversee the progress of this beam all the way up to Bond's genitals. On the surface the purpose of the villain would appear to be simple: to induce the all-powerful and invincible James Bond into complete submission through a novel torture technique. At the subliminal level the message is: a man's primary identity is linked to his genitalia. Sever it from him and you reduce him to nothingness.

Harming the opponent male's genitalia and thereby enforcing a successful conflict outcome is not limited to cinematic depiction of a villainous tactic. In a refugee camp in Kampala, Uganda hundreds of male survivors of sexual violence from the civil war in neighbouring Congo in 2011 came up with stories and evidence that reinforces the linkage between male genitalia as primarily masculine identity and specific violent undertakings by the enemy to disrupt and rupture that identity.

These survivors were not simply raped and asked to give oral sex to queues of soldiers but they were also 'forced to penetrate holes in banana trees (that run with acidic sap) with their sexual organ. They were made to sit with their genitals over fire. Ordered to drag rocks tied to their penis. And if that was not the end of the brutality, this particular organ of theirs was penetrated with screwdrivers and sticks' (Storr, 2011: 7).

Why such assault on a particular part of the body? Are these cases of 'penis envy'? Are these acts of deep vengeance? Or are these simply instances of perversion of the highest order?

It is not possible to track down the perpetrators of such crimes and ask for motivations. Hence with the wisdom available to us within the framework of cross-interpretation of various scholarly positions we can infer the following conclusion. While at the outset targeting a particular part of the enemy's organ may appear simply a form of deviance, an anomaly, and a clear evidence of paraphilia, there could be several layers of explanation.

Such aggressive responses leading to visible physical injuries over and over again alert the aggressor to a finite resolution of the conflict. By subjecting this cruelty the perpetrator is likely to ensure a sense of power and enhance self-esteem (Love, 2007: 424–5). As the argument goes, 'people experience violence differently, depending on their primary identity markers' (Shepherd, 2010: 77). Hence subjecting a specific group of individuals to a particular framework of violence creates the condition for sending out a specific message. It is a regulatory schema. Such undertakings seek to use the enemy's bodily experience as a site to inscribe and expose an asymmetrical power relation.

War, Hollywood and disembodied personhood

Each culture and civilisation has invested a good deal of time and energy exploring the place of the male body in the context of wars. As we noticed in the introductory chapter of this study, such particularised understanding surrounding the body often served as the basis for its subsequent treatment when captured and brought under the subjugation of the victor. Our preceding analysis in this chapter also indicated how violators' preferences have contributed to the imagery of the male body and the specific processes of violation it undergoes in armed conflicts and wars.

Our examination of this issue, i.e. sexual violation of the male body in armed conflicts and war, however, is only partial. Our ability to theorise about this phenomenon is dependent on the availability of verifiable empirical evidence. Since there exists a culture of silence with regard to the treatment that the perpetrator enforced on the body of his/her captive as well as self-censorship on the part of the owner about the violation that his body received in such encounters much of the subtle discourse and activism around it remains unexplored.

Therefore, in carrying on the inquiry into the body in conflict narrative, evidence of some weight is to be gained from an examination of its representation in other mediums—such as cinema. Issues of homoeroticism, homosexuality, male sexual violence against captive male prisoners and such although underexplored in academia, are themes that have nonetheless been explored in the visual media. Exploring such events in the vocabulary of cinema has two advantages. First, since cinema is considered a fictionalised form of story-telling, the events portrayed in it allow the audience to entertain the issue voluntarily and from a distance. Second, it follows that it brings out into the open an issue that had hitherto been kept away from evaluation in the public domain.

I have chosen three titles to provide a rounded argument on the treatment of the body in various conflict locales and across cultures. The films in question are *Lawrence of Arabia*, *Merry Christmas Mr Lawrence* and *Mississippi Burning*.

My reasons for choosing these three films are guided by two key impulses. First, they remain true to the theme of inter-communal conflict and war leading up to visions of sexual violence against the captive male body, and as such, fulfill my first intellectual objective. Second, while they are enacted in the backdrop of conflicts and war these three are unique in the sense that they cover separate cultural, geographical and historical settings. If anything this selection tells us that this is a theme that can be found across frontiers and divides, and the nature of the treatment of the body varies according to the intensity of the conflict concerned. They thereby provide us with a distinctive grasp on the issue.

Now let me begin with an assessment of *Lawrence of Arabia*. The story about the real life protagonist Thomas Edward Lawrence's rape remains controversial to this day.[7] While on a campaign to liberate the Bedouins and other assorted tribes in the Arabian Peninsula from the domination of Turks, Lawrence was captured by the Ottoman soldiers in Deraa, (modern-day Syria) on 2 November 1917. In *Seven Pillars of Wisdom*, Lawrence recalls that he was captured, interrogated, whipped and raped by the *Bey*, the local Turkish military commander in Deraa (Lawrence, 1962: 450–6). Recollecting this violation, Lawrence would write 'that night the citadel of my integrity had been irrevocably lost' (Lawrence, 1962: 455).[8]

In David Lean's presentation of Lawrence's story in *Lawrence of Arabia* we encounter his arrest, beating and an allusion to sodomy on T. E. Lawrence's tied up body. While from a surface assessment the beating and torture would appear to be routine—as is normal in the course of a conflict when an enemy leader is captured—on deeper introspection we find different shades to this treatment. The captor at first confuses his captive to be a Saracen (famed for their fine physical attributes). His pale body raises erotic fantasies in his torturer. Eventually, for his captor, Lawrence's body assumes the character of a sexual trophy. The heightened political tensions during the period and the all-round conflict provides the perfect cover for the violator to engage in his particularised forms of violence without having to worry about the consequences.

Therefore, while subjecting his body to humiliation and sexual violation, the violator succeeds in the twin objective of punishing the enemy as well as satiating his own sexual desires and fantasies. Given that in certain Oriental cultures sodomy and rape of male captives had a long established history, Lean takes liberty in highlighting that facet without feeling the need for any censorship. On the whole that particular scene in *Lawrence of Arabia* puts under the spotlight a subculture in which such abuse is used to break the sprit of the prisoner, humiliate, dominate and feminise the victim.

Merry Christmas Mr. Lawrence (Nagisha Oshima, Dir., 1983) brings to the fore the classic ambiguous homoerotic longing experienced by both the captive and the captor. It problematises 'the fictioning of the "the body" as the legal location of "the person"' (Cohen, 2008: 113) in the context of the enemy-enemy relationship. With that it highlights the complex mutual homoerotic attraction as well as revulsion towards this feeling (owing to the societal mores) that can be found in times of war between male participants from the opposite sides of the divide. The captor is weighed down by the captive's pansexual persona.[9] He is both discomfited by the presence of this captive and is drawn towards him (there is a subtext of repressed homosexuality on the part of the captor). But what makes this unconsummated desire particularly profound is the manner in which both the captor and the captive react to each other's body and the soul that resides within it.

In this particular instance, the homoerotic disposition of the captor (Captain Yonoi/Ryuichi Sakamoto) towards his British prisoner of war (Maj. Jack 'Strafer' Celliers/David Bowie) leads to a new interaction between the body of the captor and that of the captive. Yonoi, although attracted to Celleirs, nonetheless sees him as an evil spirit (capable of stirring his deep homosexual desires).

Aware of the mutuality of attraction the central character, Celliers, does the unexpected and reaches out to his captor Captain Yonoi and kisses him on both cheeks in full view of the battalion of Japanese soldiers and their British PoWs. Although conscious of his own homoerotic fixation the captain finds it impossible to accept the sexual advance of the captive's body in such an open manner—a direct insult to his own *Bushido Honour Code* of heterosexual purity. He reaches out for his ceremonial sword *katana* against Celliers, but is unable to kill his prisoner and collapses under the pressure of the conflicting emotions. The new camp commandant, who replaces Yonoi, is not stirred by any latent homosexual emotion. He demonstrates his heterosexuality by ordering the burying to death of Celliers out under a tropical noonday sun.

The film is also crucial in terms of underscoring the taboo associated with homosexuality within an ultranationalist and conservative culture of warfare. Particularly worth stressing is the opening scene in this visual narrative in which a Korean soldier is condemned to commit *seppuku* (a form of ritual suicide by disembowelment) after having been found in an 'improper' (homosexual) relationship with one of his captors, a Dutch PoW. Two opposite narratives emerge from this war-time experience.

Although the Korean soldier's body is contaminated by his physical actions, by committing *seppuku* he is allowed to rise above the failings of his body and attain a degree of respectability through the sacrifice of the body. No such reward, however, is forthcoming for the body or soul of the Dutch PoW. Forced to witness the *seppuku* along with the rest of the prisoners and the contingent of Japanese soldiers and officers, this character bites his tongue in the midst of this commotion and dies of suffocation.

The Dutch PoW is a victim twice over. First, he is victimised by his captor: his body becomes the repository to fulfill his captor's lust and desire. On balance, it is of course worth asking whether the victim had consented to such treatment of his body or not. We (the audience) are not privy to such knowledge. Perhaps the victim had consented to such a treatment of his body. But given the fact that he was a prisoner it would be a mistake to entertain the thought that his acceptance of this sexual interaction as an indication of active consent. Put simply, as Michel Foucault's analogy of prison and/or Primo Levi's depiction of 'the camp' would instruct us, a captive body has very little sovereignty over such decision making.

Second, after undergoing the forced or otherwise sexual domination by his captor, the victim is coerced to witness the whole *seppuku* of his captor. He is not allowed to undergo a similar self-sacrifice. While his captor has an escape route from his self-enacted humiliation, the victim is denied any such route. While the captor dies of bravery, the captive dies biting his tongue and eventual suffocation. The death of the victim it would appear is a result of 'shame'. Put simply while the captor's body dies of honour and becomes an object of future remembrance, by contrast, the body of his counterpart, the victim, awaits no such reverence. The victim's body is forced to die of shame and dishonour and thereby his personhood forfeits any future martyrdom or honour.

On another level *Merry Christmas Mr Lawrence* underscores the overall masculinity and femininity debate surrounding the body and the cultures in question. There are obvious sexual tensions and overtly homoerotic tendencies that can be found in the culture of the captors (the Japanese/Oriental). The way the enemy deals with these emotions is both revelatory as well as unsettling. There is an underlying tension between the cultural demands placed on the captor and his own inner desires towards the captive. The captor is stirred by deep homoerotic urges. The PoW camp provides the perfect cover to ingratiate this urge in the captive's body. Yet culturally sanctioned regulatory principles on superiority and inferiority, and purity and impurity stand in the way of his (the captor's) endeavor. These cultural frameworks both restrain and imprison his desire. Unable to express this sexual desire the captor ends up channeling his frustration by ordering brutal physical violence on the PoWs.

In Alan Parker's *Mississippi Burning* (1988), set at the height of race-riots/civil rights movement in the United States, the audience is presented with an incident where a black Mississippian kidnaps the town's white Mayor, who is known for his association with the white supremacist Ku Klux Klan. Now standing as a self-styled redeemer of past oppression the vengeful black man threatens the gagged and bound Mayor that unless he reveals the names of the conspirators in the murder of three civil rights activists in the region he is going to castrate him.

To make his point, the black kidnapper pulls down the Mayor's trousers and brandishes a razor blade.

At this point the kidnapper takes time to narrate the horrifying experience of a black youngster castrated by the Klansmen not so long ago. Now with the tables turned the black kidnapper says he intends to do the same to the Mayor. For the brevity of the argument let us go through the brief interrogation.

The conversation:

Agent Monk: You. I'm gonna tell you a story. A kid named Homer Wilkes lives 30 miles north of here. He'd just taken his girlfriend home and was walking along the road. A truck pulls up beside him. Four white boys took him for a ride. Now Homer, he hadn't done anything, except be a Negro. They took him to a shack, a regular old shack like this one. Then they took out a razor blade.
[*shows him a razor blade*]

Agent Monk: Ragged old razor blade, like this one. They pulled down his pants, they spread his legs, and they sliced off his scrotum.
[*shows him a coffee cup*]

Agent Monk: Then they put it in a coffee cup, like this one. Mayor, do you know how much you bleed when someone cuts off your balls?
[*throws the cup at him*]

Agent Monk: HUH! When they found Homer, he looked like he had been dipped in blood up to his waist. He was barely alive when they got him to the hospital, and he can barely walk now.

According to the director Alan Parker in this film he was 'trying to reach an entire generation who knows nothing of that historical event; to cause them to react to it viscerally, emotionally' (quoted in King, 1988). At another level, however, this short event in the three-hour-long film sends out a particular message. Such depictions purport to keep the viewer's emotional sensors constantly on the edge.

Freedom, it is often stated, 'is meaningless without ownership and control over one's own body' (McGuirre, 2004: 908). What *Mississippi Burning* highlights through its depiction of sexualized communal violence in the segregated southern United States (Klan ideal versus the black man's body) is that (a) the Negro's sexuality was not his preserve; (b) such bodily violence served as signposts of the social order; and (c) the impunity of the violator was socially sanctioned.

To use Franz Fanon's analogy here the basis of this violence has its origin in fear as well as a feeling of inferiority. The white man harboured deep anxieties about the Negros' sexual organ (vis a vis his own): 'What it can do to his (Whiteman's) woman' (Fanon, 1967). Hence it had to be undermined. The backdrop of racial inequality, which sanctioned subjection, and control of the slave's body, therefore, provided an easy occasion to enact these forms of violence. Hence the subtext of *Mississippi Burning* is the battle of the Negro/African American male over the possession of his sexuality. Agent Monk's confrontation with the Klan leader as well as the allusion to the past sexual violence against the black youth can be regarded as the demonstration of the Negros' resolve to take the physical and sexual ownership of his body back from the oppressive white supremacists.

Critics might take issue with my use of Hollywood to underscore a critical point. How can a Hollywood film, whose primary intention is to entertain, illuminate real life sexual violence? However it cannot be denied that by presenting certain facts as fiction Hollywood has forced the viewers and the general public to at least be aware of such aspects of conflict. In the absence of visual records of real-life events such a medium helps bring home the reality of the horror of sexual violence.

Message board

There is no denying the fact that 'the human body has been a potent and persistent metaphor for social and political relations throughout human history' (Turner, 2006: 223). Reflecting on it over four hundred years ago Locke posited 'the body, as well as the soul, goes to the making of a man' (Locke, 1694). The body's potential to act as a sounding board; a living organism capable of disseminating a certain message can hardly be underestimated. As an organic whole 'the body is at once the surface for any discursive inscription as well as the site of resistance to any such inscription' (Foucault, 1978; Butler, 1993). It can be a surface in which certain social messages can be inscribed (Featherstone, 2006: 233).

Little wonder then in an armed conflict or war the physical body attains such discursive potential.

The importance of a violated body as a framer of a certain narrative and a vehicle capable of disseminating that information is a truism that is hard to escape. In his work *In the Penal Colony* Franz Kafka designates the body as a writing surface—a surface able to receive the law or as in our case the violator's readable text (Kafka, 1984). The cognitive role of the body comes alive when it mediates in the dispersal of certain knowledge. War prints its mark on the body of its victims. Such marks 'act as an obstacle to forgetting; the body carries the traces of a memory printed upon it; *the body is a memory*' (Taylor, 2002: 142–3). A violated body and a public knowledge surrounding it are problematic indeed. These are written leftovers (Debrix & Barder, 2012: 127). It conditions the mental construct of everyone around the person that comes in contact with it. It not only defines the precariousness of the violated individual but the community of which he is a part.

It is hard to pinpoint when exactly societal norms came to view it as such. Turning to some religious texts, however, we find a clear and sustained engagement in the demarcatory interpretation surrounding the role of male genitalia, its sacredness and its loss following its exposure or violation. Judeo-Christian bodily ethics were so sensitive to the sacredness of the body that they instituted its mere exposure in public or nakedness within forbidden codes of sexuality (Cover, 2003: 56). In the main it invested two sets of roles in the male genitalia.

First, as the fountainhead of procreation (both literally as well as symbolically as vehicles for the continuation of the given race), following the injunction to 'be fruitful, and multiply' (Genesis 1: 28). Second, it reserved the right of access to the divine by a given follower depending on the physical condition of his genitalia. 'He that is wounded in the stones, or hath his privy member cut off, shall not enter into the congregation of the Lord' (Deuteronomy 23:1). If one were to take away a single message from this analogy it would be something like this: male genitalia must remain intact and unblemished, it must be protected (Cover, 2003: 55–6).

Unsurprisingly in those societies and civilisations where the genitalia has such intertwined sacred and profane dimensions, a violated body stands for a particular condition. It mirrors the impotency of the victim and by default the powerlessness and impotency of the community that it represents. Given the symbolism and heavy meaning associated with it, a violated body is a critical mouthpiece for the violators' objective. His transgressions and the bodily experience of that of the victim ultimately become a vehicle for communicating the former's intended message—ethnic, political, religious or otherwise.

While on the one hand the victim is aware of his bodily representations and the loss of those faculties should there be some form of defilement, the violator on the other is party to this knowledge and therefore intent upon introducing it to a permanent state of disruption. Thus begins a narrative of resistance and infringement. The violator is guided by the understanding that a captive body or a body acquired during the chaos of war provides an unparalleled opportunity in such experimentation. The body of an opponent, then, is a perfect object for colonisation. For the ideologically inspired the living self of the enemy is an invitation to reconstitute an image, a narrative.

If one were to return to the earlier question of eliminating the body versus allowing the body to retain life but with a certain message inscribed on it, then we are faced with this particular reality: for the perpetrator the living body carrying such a message can be of much more significance than that of a dead one. It is an effective and indispensable medium; it is a moving living vehicle capable of sending out long-term signals to everyone around him.

A body that has not been violated is a sovereign object. Even if the body has gone through physical punishment at the hands of the enemy the owner still retains a segment of independence and autonomy—a sovereignty that is associated with the soul. Even in situations when that body is imprisoned the owner retains and expresses his sovereignty through the presence of the untainted soul.

Making that body undergo sexual violation, however, snuffs out the sovereignty or autonomy of both body and soul. The victim, while still in possession of the physical self, has lost something invaluable and irreparable. He will never be the same again. No amount of cleansing will take away that stigma. It will stick to the soul like gum on the tarmac.

From the perspective of a violator the body that has retained its untainted character is a threat; it is a constant reminder to the violator that the owner of this body is 'free'. The would-be violator and the victim are aware of the existence of this autonomy. Therefore, the perpetrator is guided by the assumption that following the violation people will reflexively evaluate the bodies of such victims and respond with a relatively accurate and coherent response.

Conclusion

This chapter was primarily a discursive exercise in thinking through the relationship between male genitalia and conflict dynamics as well as the violator's overall administration of the victim's body.

There is a radical and binary interdependence between the male body and the context of the conflict. Because of its liminal position between sanctity and profanity in the discourse surrounding sexual violation it has a very significant strategic value. Our examination of the male body illustrates the intricate narrative of armed conflict and war. Hence, it represents an important point of departure in order to understand the complexities surrounding the questions about identity, sovereignty, nationalism and individual prejudice and perversion. Simply put, the reality of war is not just politics by any other means, but the politics etched on the body (McSorley, 2010: 7).

If the male sexual organ represents the masculinity, virility, and the spirit of resistance, it is the destruction of that organ or rendering it incapable that holds the key to his diminished presence. Putting that body through sexual violation irreversibly alters the state of the person. This mode of violation invades the intimate self of the victim and his dignity. Hence, however valiant that particular individual might have been in his fight against the enemy, upon his body's sexual violation at the hands of the opponent his body and consequently his very identity is consigned to infamy. Put simply this undertaking represents a rupture in the sovereignty that resides in the individual.

Since there exists an inalienable co-relation between the body of an individual and the society he inhabits, this mode of violation further gives rise to complex meanings and symbolisms. There is no escaping from the fact that there exists something called 'affectivity' of a violated body. Metaphorically at least an invasion into the bodily self of an individual amounts to the violation of the society as a whole (I discuss this in greater detail in chapters six and seven). Violation of an individual body enforces collective shame upon the community to which the victim belongs. That being the dominant reading this enterprise becomes an all the more attractive proposition for the aggressor in some conflict settings.

If violation of the adversary is designed to enforce an individual as well as societal transformative process it is vital that this undertaking receives closer scrutiny. The next chapter aims to examine that process. Within the framework of biopower, I evaluate the overall politics behind such violation and the outcome.

2

BIOPOWER

Sexuality is one of those primary forces whose sovereignty over man is assured by man's firm belief in his sovereignty over it.

Rene Girard, *Violence and the Sacred*, 1977: 34.

Conflicts and wars can have multilayered subjective explorations. They can be studied from the perspective of ideology, economics, identity, territoriality, power relations and ultimately the most fundamental of all—the place of living beings in this overarching narrative. From a phenomenological perspective, armed conflicts and war raise two fundamental questions: first, "how does war manifest itself in the life-world (Brighton, 2011: 101)?" Second, what are its contingent outcomes? According to a particular group of scholars, armed conflicts and wars are nothing but representations of biopower. In their view if one were to strip away all the exteriors of such conflicts what one ends up with is just one core principle: the ways of looking at and treating human life in such contexts. Put simply all other issues that were at play in these conflicts are only incidental and pale in comparison to the overwhelming debate surrounding human life.

Issues surrounding the place of life in general and the treatment of the body in particular in armed conflicts and war can be studied under the subject heading of what one might call biopower. Biopower, as originally defined by Michel Foucault, refers to 'a set of mechanisms through which the basic biological features of the individual human being is projected into a political strategy or a general strategy of power' (Foucault, 2007: 1).

Biopower is power over life. It is situated and exercised at the level of life. Biopower is a strategic coordination of the power of the violator in conjunction with the authority of the regime to extract whatever power is left in the potential and would-be victims. In addition, at the heart of this debate surrounding violation and biopower resides the issue of autonomy and forced disenfranchisement of that once considered inalienable autonomy. Such undertakings, I argue, undermine the body's normative functions a site of the sovereign.

War necessitates killing. Killing is what soldiers and combatants are trained to do (Morrow, 1993: 50), 'killing one's antagonist is the ultimate conflict resolution technique' (Pinker, 1998: 434–5). But killing fails to establish a sustained power relationship that is at the heart of this enterprise. Biopower, then, is most effective in situations where it succeeds in establishing a unilateral power relation over a living antagonist. It is the ability to 'control the conduct of others' that is most potent in the context of biopower. For Foucault it is a form of power exerted by 'acting subjects' upon 'free subjects' (Foucault, 2000). It is the subjectivisation of a given body and reconfiguring it to the forces of long-term power and subjugation.

It is the utilisation of 'bare' life to the process of a nefarious design. In order for biopower to be articulated fully the 'other' must be recognised and maintained to the very end as a subject who acts and responds to a particular kind of exertion. If the aggressor or perpetrator kills the potential enemy in an instant then there is no true representation of the biopower. Biopower focuses on an anatamo-politics of the human body (Rabinow & Rose, 2006: 196). It is most effective when individual bodies are targeted through disciplinary practices and power (Foucault, 1991; Debrix & Barder, 2012: 9).

In the view of critics like Butler and Agamben, there is a close kinship between such biopower and conflict conditions (Butler, 2009; Agamben, 1998: 3). The violator is acutely aware of the effects that his or her actions will have on the victim following his violation. This is an exercise that is not so much about the 'end of the victim's life, but the enactment of a given human condition itself' (Cavarero, 2007: 43–4). It is a managerial tool in the hands of a power-holding authority, determining questions of life and survival (Foucault, 1978: 137). At its most general biopower attempts to intervene upon the vital characteristics of human existence (Rabinow & Rose, 2006: 196–97).

If 'the *having* of a body personifies a person; then it is "the body" that makes the person' (Cohen, 2008: 119). What happens, for instance, if that given body is altered through sexual violation? Does the person in possession of his body maintain the same personality? Perhaps not! Alterations of the bodily condition through biopolitical designs would imply transformation of that individual's personhood. It seeks to impose a circumscribed condition on that living body. Violation implants 'a mode of conduct' into victim's body and its correlate soul (Rabinow & Rose, 2006: 198). The person living in this body is 'fully conscious' of his altered being. By acting directly on the victim's physical being the violator etches a narration to which the former is forever enslaved and condemned. This new conditionality reinforces the fact that he/the violated is 'incurably lost' (Agamben, 1998: 138).

The motifs of such biopower are not that hard to imagine. The victim's life/body sits at the heart of this biopower/biopolitical 'design and operations' (Debrix & Barder, 2012: 7). The violator is like one of those Amazonian beetles that inject their victim with venom, keeping them alive but rendering them permanently damaged. In this context the human violator seizes life as the object of its specific exercise. Through his/her actions the violator here processes the life of the violated and modifies it for a future purpose.

In the ultimate analysis biopower, as is explained within the context of sexual violation, is the condensing of strategic relations into relations of domination. It is the purpose and intention of the violator to elicit a certain kind of response, reaction and effect on his subject. Examined within this framework, the violated enters into a long-term power relationship with the violator. Thus the power exercised is both unilateral and ever controlling.

Towards a theory of violation

In his seminal essay *Necropolitics* Achille Mbembe meditates on questions of power, politics and war. He asks how sovereignty is exercised from the perspective of the more powerful over the less powerful. In particular he asks:

Under what practical conditions is the right to kill, to allow to live, or to expose to death exercised? Who is the subject of this right? What does the implementation of such a right tell us about the person who is thus put to death and about the relation of enmity that sets that person against his or her murderer? (Mbembe, 2003: 12)

Taken together, power, politics and facets of conflict can be explained in terms of biopower. As Mbembe puts it, 'Imagining politics as a form of war, we must ask: What place is given to life, death, and the human body (in particular the wounded or slain body)? How are they inscribed in the order of power?' (Mbembe, 2003: 12).

Further, under what condition is the right to sexually violate another body to be permitted? The impenetrability of the question is a nagging one. Why does the torturer decide to violate rather than kill? What does the implementation of such undertaking tell us about power relationships? These are questions that cannot be easily answered. The complexity of these questions weighs far more than that of Mbembe's. Viewed from a distance Mbembe would appear to be dealing with the question of rights exercised within a conflict, which has some legal basis. Put it a little differently, in a legalised war or a conflict the right to kill the opponent is sanctioned by law. Or both parties to the conflict are very much aware of the outcome prior to their engagement. They are conscious of the fact that if they find each other in an arena of conflict and if one of them has an inferior fire power or in a weaker position the superior's sovereignty in the domain of right to kill is a given.

But do we have any such precedence in the context of right to violate? The clearest and most unambiguous response to this question is 'No'.

Having said that, one cannot escape from the truism that although it has no acceptance in the legal or conventional doctrines of armed engagement a given individual, group or powerful party in certain contexts might engage in this practice.

Although unconventional, such acts can be argued to be as much as a means of achieving sovereignty over the vanquished as killing them is. Mbembe asks when a particular actor is engaged 'in forms of killing how is that action inscribed in the order of power'? (Mbembe, 2003: 12). While the violation of the opponent's body did not entail any general approval it nonetheless established a private sovereignty of the oppressor over the oppressed or the victor over the vanquished. Or, to use Debrix and Barder's analogy in a slightly different context, 'if this form of violation belongs to the state of exception, it opens up the possibility for the violator of creating a spatial domain where the victim's body and soul becomes an object abandoned to the full arbitrary force of the sovereign power that resides in the violator' (Debrix & Barder, 2012: 32).

While establishing this private sovereignty that initially remained as an undisclosed knowledge between these two parties alone the victor was consciously as well as unconsciously sending a subliminal message to that particular individual and community to which he belonged. The content of that message was simply the fact that the sovereignty of the victor is total and cannot be challenged. Given that such exercise of private sovereignty eventually becomes a part of the public knowledge, the oppressor while exercising this form of sovereignty would appear to have a long-term objective.

The central question that Malcolm Potts and Thomas Hayden in their seminal study *Sex and War: How Biology Explains Warfare and Terrorism and Offers a Path to a Safer World* (2010) ask is: 'Why do we humans, remarkably social animals with extremely large brains, spend so much energy on one thing—deliberately and systematically harming and killing other members of our own species?'

In situations and contexts where the regime associates the living body with political threat it focuses its attention on controlling that body. The binary questions as to 'What can a body do?' and 'What can you do to a body?' perpetually reside at the heart of that regime's thinking. It can corrupt the masses with ideas of subversion. It can destabilise the authority. Left unchecked the person residing in this body can in theory usurp the power of the regime. When confronted by these reckonings the regime looks for ways to counter this body. The conventional method through which the regime can face up to this body would be to eliminate it. However, there are practical difficulties. The number of bodies or entities that the regime has to kill in order to maintain its authority sometimes would run into hundreds and thousands. It may find such an undertaking hard to enforce for various reasons.

Systemic sexual violence against a section of the male populace assumes importance when the regime in charge of governance feels that the challenges coming to its powerbase cannot be thwarted by conventional use of its power. The regime might feel if it expresses restraint it would be seen as weak and if it uses extreme military force it may end up discrediting itself and thus lose authority. Since achieving absolute control through minimum bloodshed is its supreme objective the regime concerned might take recourse in exercising this particular form of biopower. Now let us situate this argument in a real life empirical context.

This is the story of a nameless victim. Let us call him Shiraz for the sake of convenience. This story was narrated by Afshin, a shopkeeper from south-west Iran who was Shiraz's friend. Shiraz was arrested and repeatedly raped by the Iranian police. Shiraz's crime? He was in an opposition political rally over Iran's disputed presidential re-election in June 2009:

> We registered him under a false name and with somebody else's insurance. The nurses were crying. Two of them asked what sort of beast had beaten him up like that. He was a broken man. He told us not to waste our money on him, and that he would kill himself (Poorgiv, *The Guardian*, 1 July 2009).

It was only when this nameless victim had received his first clandestine medical attention following his ordeal that he was able to narrate his story:

> It was on Saturday or Sunday that they raped me for the first time. There were three or four huge guys we had not seen before. They came to me and tore my clothes. I tried to resist but two of them laid me on the floor and the third did it. It was done in front of four other detainees (Poorgiv, *The Guardian*, 1 July 2009).

> They said, if you do not come to your senses we will send you to Adel Abad (another prison in the city of Shiraz) to the pederasts' section so that you receive such treatment every day (Poorgiv, *The Guardian*, 1 July 2009).

At a general level Shiraz was punished in a particular way owing to his opposition to the government. At another level, however, the undertaking of punishment through sexual violation at the hands of the police was undertaken to disseminate the narrative of the regime's unquestionable authority and power. If they had used conventional methods and had just beaten him up or at worst killed Shiraz then the remit of their authority would have been very limited. However by exerting a particular form of power (bipower of violation) they succeeded in not only removing Shiraz from any future political opposition but also in disseminating a reign of terror and anxiety among the masses through Shiraz's experience.

If biopower is a strategy for the governing of life its attractiveness lies in its ability to transmit distress among a wider spectrum of populace. Following its application, it is meant to break individual spirit, community cohesion and social bonds.[1] It effectiveness can be found in its ability to prevent the coming together of individuals and groups and offer any resistance to the regime.

Once the regime realises the effectiveness of such biopower it may move a step further and insitutionalise it. Jailed opposition political activists held in Iranian prisons have regularly spoken of the regime encouraging criminals inside these premises to rape the former. In fact some have gone so far as to suggest that Tehran regularly gives out condoms to the potential violators to mass rape jailed civil rights and political activists (Dehghan, 2011).

Similarly, during the civil war in Syria armed forces and paramilitaries loyal to Assad went about using a wide array of violent techniques against detained men that included penetration of their bodies with foreign objects, groping, forced nudity, beatings to the genitalia, electric shock to their male organs, genital trauma and finally rape (Merger, 2012).

According to Human Rights Watch, the Sri Lankan government in its attempt to quash Tamil separatism used all manners of sexual violence against Tamil boys and men belonging to both the civilian and militant stratum for prolonged periods of time. It used rape and other forms of sexual violence against:

…suspected LTTE [Liberation Tigers of Tamil Ealam] members or supporters to gather intelligence during the fighting and immediately after the conflict ended in May 2009, as well as to obtain information about any remnants of the LTTE since then, whether in Sri Lanka or abroad.[2]

That there is a strategic dimension built into such biopower undertaking is rather obvious. Torture and violation can be used when the power in whose name it is carried out is unstable (Scary, 1985). As a form of preventive punishment these campaigns not only have the ability to crush the morale of the victim forever but also succeeds in sending an instructive general message across the restive citizenry. As a mode of social control it is most effective in deterring would-be opponents of the regime from voicing their protest against the latter. It guarantees to instill fear in the opponents towards the government. It makes effective able-bodied male political opponents politically neutered and physically very afraid.

When I asked what he feared most, an opponent of Bashir al Assad's regime (let's call him Nemi) seeking refuge in England said he was not afraid of death. He was ready to fight. But he was 'mortified' by the thought of being sexually violated by paramilitaries loyal to the regime. Examined closely this statement would appear somewhat puerile. For how would one fear a particular physical harm more than the fear of death? Is not a damaged or abused body better than a body that is dead due to such an encounter in an armed conflict? Is not escaping death a far better condition than death itself? What Nemi was attesting to was the 'stigma' of such violence, which stuck to you like a 'bad smell' for you and those around you to smell.

As we shall see in chapter six in our assessment of victims' takes on such events the central objective of such undertakings is to shame, disgrace and dishonour the victim. Given that sexual violation of the political opponent facilitates achieving these three objectives in one go 'it is very much favoured as a weapon against the protesters and political prisoners. As a weapon of war it is a means to an end'. For Potkin Azarmehr, an Iranian-British blogger who has covered many of these incidents, 'by killing protesters, the government makes martyrs of them, but by raping them and allowing them to live, it makes them shunned in society' (quoted in Sadeghi, 2009). The violated bodies are festering wounds (both metaphorically as well as literally). They are a living testimony to the powers of the regime. Similarly it is a constant reminder to the owner of the body and the society that he inhabits concerning the impotency of their very being.

Such biopolitical enterprises or manifestation of biopower could also be construed as methods that seek to establish the virility of the regime over the impotency of the dissident. As we saw in the previous chapter the violated body has the potential to become a message board for the violator to announce the latter's supremacy and sovereignty over the victim and the community he belonged to. In a political context, the regime concerned finds it hard to ignore these obvious and intrinsic advantages. According to Shirin Sadeghi, a former journalist with *BBC* and *Al Jazeera*, such regime-sponsored abuse 'is also about marking these victims as defiled human beings—it's like a scarlet letter of social isolation against them, to deny them the community support and strength which they need to move past those memories and not to be defined by them' (Sadeghi, 2009: http://www.huffingtonpost.com/shirin-sadeghi/the-rape-of-taraneh-priso_b_233063.html, last accessed 25 July 2014).

Whereas some regimes may try and dissociate themselves from the remits of biopower or undertake it clandestinely, there are some who may openly declare their support for this method. What is more they may go so far as to instruct and encourage its various administrative and governing organs such as police and law enforcement agents to carry out such violation. Take Zimbabwe under Robert Mugabe's rule. Between 2002–2008 when there was a low intensity civil war in the country (Chan, 2003) Mugabe's regime frequently used rape as a weapon of war to silence its male as well as female critics (Hoad, 2007; Bastick, Grimm and Kunz, 2007: 13). It was particularly successful in making the most of these strategies while riding on the back of another culture more peculiar to Zimbabwe.

Some societies consider homosexuality as the 'whiteman's disease' (Dollimore, 1991:346). Since Zimbabwean society considered homosexuality as an aberration and was overtly hostile to anyone practising it, the regime found a ready-made market to tarnish the image of its political opponents.[3] It undertook the task of exposing the gay male body as a social problem. Having sexually violated many male dissidents the regime presented them to the masses in order to further diminish their standing in society. This was a process that aimed at complete marginalisation and eventual political death of the opponents to the regime (Hill, 2003).

Viewed within the context of biopower it becomes evident that this was an enterprise in the administration of life. It had its basis in 'strategies for the governing of life'. Had Mugabe killed those particular opponents he would have made martyrs out of them and in turn created a vicious opposition against his regime. However, by strategically sexually violating constituencies that he considered a threat to his rule he not only succeeded in banishing them from the overall political process but also managed to cap any sustained future opposition. By homosexualising the opponent's identity through forced rape and other forms of sexual violation he further alienated them from the mainstream society that was inherently homophobic.

Hence sexual violation of the enemy resulting in rape cannot be understood as 'just' a deplorable side effect of war provoked by soldiers' sexual frustration. Rape is raw biopower and literally a biopolitical weapon of war. As an exercise in biopower it is primarily intended to condition the enemy/victim's moral and physical context.

The overwhelming narrative to emerge from the discussion so far introduced us to the fact that it is the authoritarian governments, dictatorships and regimes with little or no respect for democratic principles that easily gave in to the temptation of using forms of sexual torture and violence against perceived enemies both within the state as well as those outside it. But this is only part of the narrative. If these regimes used such methods as incidental excesses linked to the self-preservation or promo-tion of the regime's interests some of their liberal democratic counter-parts may elevate such methods as part and parcel of an ideology of sub-jugation. For Lazreg 'in situations of political crisis, genuine or imagined, the avowedly democratic state reaches deep into its reserve of pure power, breaking loose from the usual restraints on its capacity to eliminate resis-tance through the infliction of physical pain' (Lazreg, 2007: 253).

In this context it is worth mentioning that the use of sexual violence against male dissidents as a policy undertaking to silence political oppo-sition is neither new nor is it limited to authoritarian non-western regimes. The British colonial administration in a last ditch attempt to hold on to Kenya in the face of a violent nationalist uprising resorted to systematic sexual violence and public castration of male independence fighters to keep the nationalist movement at bay. Mr Paulo Nzili an octogenarian victim testified in the High Court in England in July 2012 (some six decades after the incident) how he was taken to Embakasi prison camp where "he was publicly castrated with a pair of pliers normally used on cattle" by the prison officer Mr Dunman (Taylor, 2012: 9).

According to Mr Nzili's statement:

"I was taken to an open area in the [prison] camp where Luvai [Mr Dunman the British prison officer] stripped me of my clothes in front of all the other detainees."

"Kwatanehi was told to pin me to the ground. He was a very strong man."

"He pulled my right arm violently from behind me, through my legs which caused me to somersault over onto my back."

"They tied both my legs with chains and Kwatanehi pinned down both of my hands."

"Luvai then approached me with a large pair of pliers which were more than a foot long and castrated me" (http://www.bbc.co.uk/news/uk-2279 7624 last accessed 20 October 2014).

Similarly, take the French combat methods against the Algerian resis-tance in the 1960s. The French army, in order to avoid the legacy of defeat in the Second World War and in Vietnam, followed a policy of extreme violence in Algeria. In fact both French politicians in metropolitan France and the French officer corps viewed victory in Algeria as a necessary con-dition to overturn the humiliation of the past. Regaining lost honour, therefore, meant the use of both conventional and unconventional torture methods against the resistance. Recent studies show while the French army was relaxed in its use of sexual violence against the women of Algeria it was also not averse to the use of such violence against Algerian men (Lazreg, 2007).

Branding and appetitive aggression

An authoritarian regime is not the only one to use biopower of sexual violence to secure a victory against its opponent. An individual, group or even a community with a deep sense of insecurity may impose aspects of sexual violence against its male enemy to feel secure and powerful. In such contexts, exerting forms of cruelty and violence on your enemy can become an end in itself.

As one recent study dedicated to understanding the mechanisms motivating cruelty in contemporary armed conflicts and war has demonstrated, 'seeing the victim suffer can be a sufficient reward for violence, irrespective of secondary rewards like honour, status or material benefit' (Weierstall, 2013). In individually or communally mediated biopolitics of sexual violence, experiencing the suffering of the 'other's' body is considered a reward in itself.

Reflecting on the relationship between ordinary individuals and their association with irrational behaviour in times of conflict Elias Canetti writes, 'in war, the simple man, who does not see himself as anything special in peacetime is offered the chance of a feeling of power' (Canetti, 1979: 21). This craving for exercising a faculty that is usually denied in normal circumstances spirals out of control when the protagonist finds himself in an atmosphere of intense hate and anarchy. This context, when accompanied by an innate desire to do harm, leads our protagonists to do the abominable and that which is outside the norm. Put simply, out of utter rage and a smouldering thirst for vengeance, human beings can behave in a way that is utterly inhumane (Weierstall, 2013).

Upon closer introspection we realise these individually or group-mediated undertakings of violence are basically expressions of deep hatred in the face of the perpetrator's own impotency to address a particular issue concerning his enemy. Since the time of evolution of human life, male genitalia have featured prominently in the discourse on power and dominance. In some cultures in the context of communal competition and rivalry the sexual organ of the male body invokes constant debates about

power and potency. Some of these debates are open and many are subliminal. Within a given culture or racial type this may be confined to
such harmless debates about size, strength or virility. In the context of
intra-group, intra-ethnic or intra-racial interaction, however, this debate
may take many complex and at times dangerous turns.

When presented with an opportunity, radical groups incensed by years
of hatred might easily engage in punitive practices. Their sexual violence
might then be aimed at appropriating the masculinity of the victim. It might
manifest in situations when the violator feels it has a chance to redeem
himself by forcibly taking away the masculinity of his male victim.

Note, for instance, stories about Christian mob violation of their
Muslim counterparts during ethno-religious strife in Nigeria and the
Central African Republic (between 2012–2014). Here the killer mob specifically targeted their victim's genitalia before putting him to death.[4] In
one incident the Christian mob 'cut one Muslim man's genitals off and
put them in his mouth'.[5] Communal riots (for example, between Hindus
and Muslims in India, as we shall see in chapter four) have often provided the perfect occasion for the outpouring of repressed desires, prejudices and resentments. If we dissect the motives behind this communal
exercise of biopower we are confronted with very unsettling answers.

On occasion such violation provides a sense of virility to the killer
mob. Like some Stone Age tribes that dismembered their victim's body
before cannibalising their enemy's genitals, or some modern-day African
rebel leaders who carried off with their victims' genitals in order to
enhance their sexual and battle prowess,[6] the Christian and Hindu mob
that perform such acts in these conflicts display a clearly defined polit-
ico-erotic imagination. These were occasions for collective empowerment.
Although not articulated the mob seemed to be guided by this underlying desire.[7] Thus it cheered and jeered at the victim before he bled to
death. The mutilation served to infuse a sense of potency to the violator(s).

Yet the dominant questions that loom large in this interrogation are:
How do you brand your enemy? How do you differentiate between individuals who look like you, talk like you and dress like you? For administering questions of violation in a conflict is only possible when you are
clear about your enemy's true ethnic and religious identity. How does
one go about identifying those markers that distinguish him from his
enemy and thus enables him/her to engage in this premeditated offence?

In the past, in many cultures, it was sexual imagery which often dis-
tinguished one group from another. While its prevalence is blurred in

modern times, it makes its appearance from time to time during periods of extreme communal or inter-ethnic strife. Given this inheritance, little wonder the revelation of a culturally/religiously branded body and the consequent introduction of biopower find a ready propagator in such conflict settings.

As David Rieff's succinct analyses of the atrocities in the Balkans suggest, for the enemy looking for his targets it is never that difficult to clearly identify his would-be victims.

For a Serb militia or mob wanting to unleash their perversion and particularised forms of sexual violence the situation demanded a simple act of de-clothing. In Rieff's interpretation: 'The easiest way for Serb fighters to find out whether a prisoner they had taken was Muslim was to make him drop his trousers (Muslim men are circumcised and Serb men are not). From there, it was too often only a short step, psychologically, to cutting off his prick' (Rieff, 1995: 107).

Improvisational power/experimental violence

The Department of Psychology at the University of Konstanz, Germany has long immersed itself in a project that is 'dedicated to understanding the mechanism motivating cruelty' especially in the contexts of armed conflicts and war. Its work can be summed up in this single sentence: why do wars throw up incidences of extraordinary inhumanity by its human participants? We may have to seek answer to this through a brief analysis of the process of human behavioural evolution.

German/British sociologist Norbert Elias' influential study *The Civilising Process* argues that in Western Europe into the sixteenth century forms of cruelty and torture provided experimental entertainment for the powerful nobility and the masses flocked to such public spectacles of violence in order to satiate their visceral curiosity (Elias, 1969). Elias goes on to suggest that over time social regulations and emphasis on etiquette put a hold on this craving. However, at times the conditions of conflict and war unhinder the self-regulating psychological restraints and lift those barriers, which had originally removed people from that yearning.

War provides the opportunity for individuals, militias and the machineries of the state to use the body of the enemy as an exploratory site capable of providing insights into specific bodily reaction and elicit an external experience (Peninston-Bird, 2003: 32). Violence in such contexts takes an experimental turn. It is constructed. People assemble in a particular place to do a particular thing. The body of the enemy or opponent becomes the subject of an external gaze (Peninston-Bird, 2003: 32). They stage a particular act and wait for the outcome with a certain sense of curiosity, not being aware of what the end result would look like.[8]

In his acclaimed work *Maximum City*, Suketu Mehta narrates the incidences of a killer Hindu mob in the western Indian city of Bombay. The said mob has just doused petrol on a hapless Muslim street vendor and lit a fire. Later one of the killers describes the physical reaction of the body undergoing the process of killing: 'A man on fire gets up, falls, runs for his life, falls, gets up, runs' (Mehta, 2005: 43). In this undertaking there is a certain instrumental calculation. Prior to this venture the mob is not aware: How does a man on fire react? What actually happens when he is put in a certain condition? What does the spectacle look like? How far can the victim go in terms of his agony and struggle to fend off the certain imminent death? And so on.

Such deep-seated perverse individual or mob inquiries belong to a specific domain. It is called appetitive aggression. It is committed solely to fulfill a knowledge gap and in the process receive a certain pleasure out of the suffering of the victim. As the Konstanz team found out from interviewing nearly 2,500 former combatants from various contemporary conflict locations, about a third of these expressed that 'to some extent the nature of their violence and resultant struggle of the victim was personally satisfying, emotionally arousing and linked to a certain excitement' (Weierstall, 2013).

One of the earliest recorded cases of such experimental sexual sadism inflicted by the Serb militias against hapless Bosnian Muslims goes back to the peak of the conflict in 1992. A Muslim refugee from Gbosanski Petrovac in the relative safety of a UNHCR camp mentioned to a field officer in charge, that during his ordeal his Serb captors had forced him to bite off the penis of a fellow captive (Rieff, 1995: 167).

The fourth and last body of evidence relating to this paragraph of the Indictment concerns Fikret Harmbasic and chronologically follows immediately after the attacks on the above three victims. After G and Witness H had been forced to pull Jasmin Hrnic's body about the hangar floor they were ordered to jump down into the inspection pit, then Fikret Harambasic, who was naked and bloody from beating, was made to jump into the pit with them and Witness H was ordered to lick his naked bottom and G to suck his penis and then to bite his testicles.

Meanwhile a group of men in uniform stood around the inspection pit watch-ing and shouting to bite harder. All three were then made to get out of the pit onto the hangar floor and Witness H was threatened with a knife that both his eyes would be cut out if he did not hold Fikret Harambasic's mouth closed to prevent him from screaming; G was them made to lie between the naked Fikret Harambasic's legs and, while the later struggled, hit and bite his genitals. G then bit off one of Fikret Harambasic's testicles and spat it out and was told he was free to leave. Witness H was ordered to drag Fikret Harambasic to a nearby table, where he then stood beside him and was then ordered to return to his room, which he did. Fikret Harambasic has not been seen or heard of since. (Prosecutor v. Tadić, Case No. IT-94-1-T, Opinion and Judgment, 206, 7 May 1997, quoted in Lewis, 2009: 12).

Violence as performance

These forms of violence, as we have discussed, take place both in secret and in the open. Often times the violator undertakes this mission against the body of the victim as part of a performance act meant for his own consumption and the consumption of his in-group, fellow soldiers, camp, the military and above all nation. The violator, if he or she is directly par-ticipating in the very act of committing such violence or giving orders and watching it at a distance, is constantly reminded of the fact that his or her actions are going to be assessed in one way or another. Thus it becomes crucial for the violator to perform in a particular manner that both shocks and enrages his audience at the same time.

Now let me open it up a little. In the first part of this performativity, the violator while in a position of strength imagines himself as a colo-nial in charge of the coloniser. This role-play implies s/he has to live up to the traditional understanding of the coloniser's task, that is to impose, forcibly if necessary, his/her authority without any boundaries on the col-onised. Since the prerequisite in this framework is for the violator to act and behave in a certain way, s/he enacts his/her will upon the victim in a given manner that fulfils that role's requirement. Put simply the viola-tor while undertaking his task of violation was performing a given role, which was part of a pre-conceived narrative.

The second part of this performativity has to do with the public spec-tacle. The violator, as we have seen from several examples, may be under-taking his actions in full view and glare of the public (in this instance his/her fellow soldiers). There may be a mechanical device in place to record the events while the torturer is engaged in his/her torture. The objective in this particular occasion is to make the violator or torturer's actions a part of the public consumption. If that is so, the violator (apart from his/her private entertainment in the very act of violence) is also engaged in disseminating the event of a performance.

The 'violator as the performer' framework in turn gives rise to several imageries. From a power relationship perspective even if the violator's companions are colonials, not all of them are capable of colonising the coloniser. The violator is performing a role that other colonisers would like to undertake. S/he is doing what his/her fellow soldiers or comrades dream of doing but somehow lack the courage to carry out. In this undertaking there is an element of challenge for the violator—for s/he is doing something that is going to irreversibly alter that person and put him or her in a socio-psychological plane from which there will be no return. But while engaged in that very act of violation the violator is making a statement—that you and the larger society may forever condemn me for what I am going to do or doing but I stand above you all for having the courage to do it.

Therefore, if the enterprise of violating the captive enemy is a representation of biopower of performance it also seeks to highlight the performer's class act that goes beyond 'the camp' (immediate environment of violation). Just like the way the suicide-bomber or assassin puts his or her performance in a carefully choreographed visual representation in the public domain (internet or *Al Jazeera*), the violator by taking photographs or making a video diary of his/her victims' plight is establishing an image of himself/herself as a truer performer for whom performance and reality are both one and all.

Primarily it is an exercise in biopower in the sense that the action formalises a statement about the violator's own prowess over the victim. At the same time the violator through this very action is actively involved in dissemination of certain knowledge for public recognition. It purports to underline the fact that by doing the unconventional the violator is not only challenging the existing morality and law but also displaying his/her capacity and resolve to transgress those boundaries. By stepping away from the conventional and doing the abnormal the violator feels that s/he is superior from among the rank and file.

One might speculate that, for US soldiers in Abu Ghraib prison who subjected Iraqi male captives to sexual violation, their acts were not merely an expression of the coloniser's ability to establish his/her authority over the colonised; such undertakings were also very much performative. It was a form of 'rite of passage'—a performance that had to be enacted. It was an act that was meant to define the role of the performer as 'braver than every one of us'. It was a defining act that consolidated the image of the violator Private Lynddie Rana England as a supreme soldier.

In view of some critics this performativity was structurally twofold. 'There was the event, nude and crude, of violence against the victims, and there was the digital technology that reproduced it in images. The torturers were at once *performers* as well as true *violators*, alternating between mimicking torture and the real thing; indeed, they were adapting the real torture inflicted on the bodies and minds of their prisoners to the torture they were pretending to inflict for the camera' (Cavarero, 2007: 110).

This performativity aspect of the undertaking in Abu Ghraib is further reinforced when we closely scrutinise the video and still images that have since made their appearance into the public domain. These images provide evidence of:

a. (S) Videotaping and photographing naked male and female detainees;
b. (S) Forcibly arranging detainees in various sexually explicit positions for photographing;
c. (S) Forcing detainees to remove their clothing and keeping them naked for several days at a time;
d. (S) Forcing naked male detainees to wear women's underwear; ...
e. (S) Arranging naked male detainees in a pile and then jumping on them;
f. (S) Positioning a naked detainee on a MRE box, with a sandbag on his head, and attaching wires to his fingers, toes, and penis to simulate electric torture;
g. (S) Writing 'I am a Rapest' (sic) on the leg of a detainee alleged to have forcibly raped a 15-year old fellow detainee, and then photographing him naked;
h. (S) Placing a dog chain or strap around a naked detainee's neck and having a female Soldier pose for a picture... (Taguba Report, 2004: paragraph 6).

In Cavarero's opinion these 'photographs demonstrate, what prevailed was the pleasure of farce, the entertainment of horror transformed into caricature, a license to dehumanize on the part of willing actors in an atrocious pantomime' (Cavarero, 2010: 115). Another contemporary critic Slavoj Zizek shares this sentiment. According to Zizek 'recording the faces stupidly smiling beside the twisted naked bodies of the prisoners, was an integral part of a theatrical staging, a kind of *tableau vivant* which brings to mind a performance art in a theatre of cruelty' (Zizek, 2004). Yet in the view of some other critics, these 'documents are not just visual records but are themselves instruments for or acts of abuse' (Caton & Zacka, 2010: 204).

The biopower of sexual violence in the camp then is not only about the ability of certain individuals to enforce a form of sovereignty over their victim but it is also about the legitimisation of inhumanity in such contexts. For instance, when US Army Specialist Sabrina Harman was interrogated about her Iraqi prisoner who was 'placed in a box with wires attached to his fingers and penis' she is reported to have replied, it was 'her job to use the methods to keep the detainee awake' (quoted in Danner, 2004: 47). War, then, waters down what is acceptable and unacceptable in the domain of sexual abuse and violence.

Pornographic gaze

In the previous section we witnessed the individually mediated biopower at work. I argued, a given individual may engage in certain abuse and violence (a) to express his/her sovereignty over the victim; (b) to compensate for his/her own sense of inferiority; and (c) to win public approval surrounding his/her action. I also argued that these might at times belong to the domain of what one might call performative undertakings. However, for an action to be performative there needs to be an audience (captive or otherwise). If Abu Ghraib is an example of violator's performativity our knowledge surrounding it is handed down to us through the workings of a camera. It establishes the fact that our violator was not alone during the event—there was an audience.

As Butler inquires in her study, the photographs of Abu Ghraib 'presuppose a photographer—a person never shown in the frame' (Butler, 2009: 81). What is this individual's role in the overall undertaking? How do we assess his/her participation? What can we infer from his/her presence/absence from the overall representation of this horror? Since the person is the facilitator in disseminating these images and would appear to be present throughout the shooting these images we also need to assess and establish his/her performance.

Who was this photographer/photographers? Was s/he a participant? What was going on in the mind of this chronicler or chroniclers while capturing these horrendous images? Or, as Butler asks, 'Did [the photographer(s)] take them in order to expose the abuse, or to gloat in the spirit of US triumphalism? Was the taking of the photo a way to participate in the event and, if so, in what way?' (Butler, 2009: 81).

It's a grey area. We do not have any clear answers. What we have in this context is speculation. We can only infer. Perhaps suppose. We have very little to go on. Although we have these hurdles when we try to interrogate this capturer of the images, there is no denying the fact that the photograph was the fuse that might have enacted this cruelty. The production and reproduction of this violence is mediated through the photographer and his/her instrument. Again, for Butler, there is no avoiding the fact that there is a causal relationship between the acts of violence and the photographer.

Perhaps the camera promises a festive cruelty: 'Oh good, the camera's here: let's begin the torture so that the photograph can capture and commemorate our act!' (Butler, 2009: 83)

If so, the person in charge of peering through the viewfinder and pressing the shutter release button was working in unison with the violators in the foreground. The presence of this particular actor(s) with their machinery was very much a part of prompting, framing and orchestrating the act and therefore could be put in the larger troupe of performers:

The people taking the photographs exult in the genitals of their victims. There is no moral confusion here: the photographers don't even seem aware that they are recording a war crime. There is no suggestion that they are documenting anything particularly morally skewed (Bourke, 2004).

As one critic put it, 'we need something more like a psychology of group behavior, or, better yet, an account of how the norms of war in this instance neutralized morally significant relationships to violence and injurability' (Butler, 2009: 82).

If the key objective of such forms of violation is to shame the enemy, his culture and his future place in the larger society to which he belongs, then those capturing these images for private or public circulation would appear to be committing a far greater crime than those who are simply administering the violence and leaving it unrecorded.

In Butler's view:

The torturer knows that [recording the images] will cause the tortured shame; the photograph enhances the shame, provides a reflection of the act for the one who is forced into it; threatens to circulate the act as public knowledge and so as public shame (Butler, 2009: 89).

The use of a camera to maintain a profile of the victim in the process of shaming is a relatively new invention. It began in earnest with the civil war in the Balkans when Bosnian Serb militias and the military went about recording their victims' plight often with the full knowledge of the latter. This method was later adopted by the US military in its interrogation techniques and transported to such conflict locations as Guantanamo Bay in Cuba, Afghanistan and Abu Ghraib in Iraq.

In all these contexts the use of a camera to record the violence perpetrated against the victim had another crucial dimension. As one critic put it, the recording of the event and freezing the image for eternity serves as a powerful 'shame multiplier' from both the violators' and victims' perspective (Danner, 2004: 18–9). If the victim was shamed through such acts of violence as sodomy, forced intercourse or castration in private and without the prying eyes of the lens then perhaps he would have been able to reconcile with his shame to some degree in future. While an unrecorded humiliation and violation permitted the victim to keep his shame private and thus allowed him to lead a somewhat 'normal' life in a post-conflict setting such an option was not available to him if the event or experience was etched permanently in these modern methods of preservation—to be used and displayed at a moment's notice any time in the future.

It is the very memory of the events kept on record which has the power to haunt him forever. 'It is like being unable to shrug off a dirty memory,' commented one of the victims. In addition it is the fear that maybe one day someone he knows will get hold of the image or view it (as it is increasingly possible through the internet) and recognise his shame that constantly preoccupies him. It is like 'being violated again and again' were the last words of Hassan when our interview came to a close in a south Madrid café.

The lens, in the hands of the voyeur then, is not only allowing the torturer to multiply the shame of his victim but at the same time giving him the power to imprison his captive forever. The lens, in the ultimate analysis is the prison. It is an instrument of condemnation. A device that is capable of sending the victim into a permanent world of fear, shame, abjection, humiliation, self-loathing and possibly impotence, psychologically, politically and morally. For all practical purposes while capturing the images the lens (or the person behind it) is extending the humilia-tion beyond the time and place in which it occurred (Stemple, 2009: 61).

There were two sets of violator in Abu Ghraib. The first set of viola-tors were the human torturers. The second was the lens. One cannot underestimate the power of the lens as a critical component of this vio-lation process. As one of the soldiers later put it 'if there were no photo-graphs, there would be no Abu Ghraib… It would have been, "OK, what-ever, everybody go home"' (Sergeant Javal Davis/Kennedy, 2007).

Closing the circle

Biopower of sexual violence also works in the contexts of what I would like to call 'hierarchy of occasion'. As such biopower of sexual violence may be unveiled during a fleeting moment—when the chaos of conflict provides a momentary advantage in the power relations between two adversaries. Victims of abuse may become abusers if they finally get a chance (Kressel, 2002: 16). Therefore, while overwhelmingly an enter-prise of the powerful we may have an occasion when the victim, finding himself in a changed power hierarchy, would employ the same violence against his former violator(s).

Note, for instance, Harvey Hart directed a highly controversial play *Fortune and Men's Eyes* (1967/1971). Here we encounter the 'ideological evolution' of Smitty, the once heterosexual protagonist of the play (Brownmiler, 1975: 258). In the prison the resident evil King Rocco-Rocky has violated Smitty and forced him into sexual slavery.

Desperate to break out from his condition he beats down his violator when a chance presents itself. Logic would dictate that now since he is the undisputed leader owing to his past personal misfortunes, Smitty would proscribe any such violence from taking place. What we have here is a twist in the tale. One of Smitty's first acts as the new boss is to impose the same form of violation on the people around him. How are we to explain this paradox? Is it based on necessity or are its roots in vengeance? It may have something to do with exacting revenge as much as it is about instituting a strategy of authority that can only be tenable upon exercis-ing of such modes of violence. From a definitional perspective it may be described as acquired biopower of sexual violence. And, although rare there are examples of such acquired biopower of sexual violence in the annals of contemporary warfare.

For this study I succeeded in tracking down a former rebel leader of Guatemala's thirty-six-year long civil war in the country's second largest city Antigua. Col. Armando had a formidable reputation as a tough guerrilla fighter. He lived in a well-barricaded and almost fortified house. And rumour had it that all succeeding governments since the end of the civil war made sure he was well looked after and had full police protection. Now an ageing man, the best years of his fearsome past were far behind him. However, he also had a different sort of reputation—only known to a few close comrades-in-arms from his years in the jungle.

Our Colonel was notorious for exacting a strange form of revenge on captured government soldiers. He would not torture and kill them as was the practice and custom with several other guerrilla leaders in Rebel Armed Forces or Fuerzas Armadas Rebeldes or other left-wing terrorist groups of Guatemalan National Revolutionary Unity.

Instead he would order these captured men in uniform to perform various sexual acts upon each other in full view of his camp. And after a brief period of this performance he would order the more powerful of the two violated soldiers to castrate the other violated prisoner in the presence of his comrades. This gruesome performance would be ordered upon the new captives with the old surviving soldier participating in it. And then would begin the next process of sexual abuse and Russian roulette of castration. Clearly Col. Armando had developed an extreme form of sadism in his years in the rebel camp. But to his immediate friends in the camp Col. Armando was not a born sadist, this was something of an acquired passion. Like the character Smitty in *Fortune in the Men's Eyes*, Col. Armando had a reputation to keep. It was the only way he could demonstrate complete power over his adversaries. 'He cured himself of his violent neurosis by seeking out the bodies of his enemies to violate', commented one of his former comrades-in-war.

The story was that he was abducted by the paramilitary who were in collusion with the government soldiers while a young adolescent. And while in captivity he was repeatedly raped and sexually tortured by many of the guards and government soldiers. As was the case in the whole of Central America during the civil war years between the 1960s and the 1980s, once these captured civilians were released back into society (if they were freed at all) they joined the ranks of the rebels to exact their revenge. Armando's release and subsequent entry into the ranks of rebels was a part of those civil war dynamics.

While in the rebel group he rose swiftly owing to his ruthless efficiency and uncompromising views on administration of torture upon the captive enemy combatants. But what was incomprehensible to his immediate associates was his insistence on sexual violence on the captured enemies over conventional methods of torture. To many of his friends from the village (who later joined his guerrilla brigade and had no knowledge of his own personal experience in the hands of paramilitary) Col Armando was a normal kid with a regular girlfriend and apparently had no inclination towards violence, sexual or otherwise, in his teenage years.

Col. Armando through his actions occupied a territory of extremity. He yielded immense life-and-death power, yet he was not an elected leader and what is more was not accountable for his actions. This is not a psychological study. However if we were to examine the specificity of this behaviour, Col. Armando provides a very good example of victim-vengeance psychological repertoire. In crude terms, when an apparently 'normal' heterosexual boy or man is forced into homosexual violence he nurtures a sense of vengeance—not necessarily on his actual violator or enemy but all those who are somehow associated with his sense of victimhood. When this individual, damaged by his experience, finds himself in a situation of strength or position of power he may use the available opportunity to exact a form of sexual revenge that could be far worse than the one he himself had experienced.[9]

Furthermore, our protagonist, now occupying the position of victim-as-violator, did not display any hints of a confused and conflicted persona with deep unresolved problems with morality. For questions about moral perversity arise when a person accepts wrong moral principles (Morton, 2004: 109). If anything, Col. Armando's wartime decisions were clear, concise and always straight to the point of psycho-sexual humiliation of the captive under his command and eventual violation and violence. He was convinced of his ideological perversity. He actions demonstrate what might be regarded as retributive rage. For such characters:

… prey on the victim's emotional reaction to their power, perhaps because their anger comes from others having psychologically and physically abused them in a similar manner and they want to see their pain mirrored in the victim's face. This is their tool for revenge (Love, 2007: 427).

Col. Armando's was 'a good soldier' as even many of his adversaries commented. But the name Col. Armando made for himself or for which he is best known has nothing to do with his bravery during the height of the civil war. He was unique among his peers because he exacted a form of revenge that none of his fellow soldiers could employ upon their adversaries. From a victim's perspective, if anything, Col. Armando stands out as an avenger of his lost honour.[10] These are rare events, of course.

That powerful heterosexual men when sexually violated in custody would try to get even by employing the same tactics and methods when an opportunity presents itself is a theme discussed by Hollywood. Let us dwell on Tim Robbins' character in the multi-Oscar winning film *The Shawshank Redemption*. Here we have a straight married man who is forced into forms of sexual slavery while in prison. The Robbins' character tries to fight off his would-be violators vehemently. But he is eventually made into a gal-boy by one of the powerful men—a 'wolf'—as co-prisoner and narrator Morgan Freeman reveals. However, thanks to his association with the top brass in the prison he succeeds in exacting a violent revenge on his key violator in such a manner that he is 'left with a feeding tube in a hospital ward for the rest of his life'.

While Col. Armando could directly seek his vengeance by torturing his captured enemies in the civil war, the character of Tim Robbins succeeds in achieving that goal through indirect means. Also, while Col. Armando's form of vengeance was sexual violation far worse than what he had experienced in custody, the settling of scores of Tim Robbins with his violator we are shown is not overtly sexual—but the employment of violence nonetheless renders him physically (thus by extension sexually) incapable for the rest of his life.

In both these instances we are introduced to powerful heterosexual men who constantly feel repulsion towards their experience and would like to get over their ordeal through some form of revenge. Revenge ultimately serves as a form of catharsis for the violated. Although extremely rare, pre-meditated violation as catharsis makes its appearance in the public domain once in a while. Following the recently concluded Libyan Civil War (2011–2012), still images from an analysis of amateur video footage taken in the moments after Col. Gaddafi's capture appear to show him being sodomised with a pole or knife.[11] Were his violators his former victims? Were they exacting revenge on the now helpless leader for having ordered similar torture techniques while in power?

The examples given above relate to strong men exacting revenge. These are clearly occasions when the situation works in favour of our erstwhile victim. But what if the victim is not presented with such an opportunity?

What if he has less of a chance to exact his revenge on the abuser, viola-tor or his kind? What if the victim in question suffers from some form of latent homosexuality (for it is a fact that male-male wartime victims are always targeted when they show some signs of diminished masculinity)?

Inverse violation

Contrast the experience of Col. Armando with that of Jean Genet, the celebrated French philosopher and poet. What is the correlation? What is the commonality between these two disparate characters? Both have undergone severe male-male violation from an early age (albeit under dif-ferent circumstances and settings). While one grows up determined to avenge his violation by putting his captured enemies to violations of much more intensity that he himself had gone through the other ends up prais-ing his violation and even developing a fetish for strong males capable of such violation. What explains such contrasting behaviour?

It is a fact that the male sex organ resides at the heart of any aversion or adoration towards the violator from the victims' perspective. Just like our culture, some individuals may associate the penis with a supercharged symbolic value. As one critic has put it, 'its "thrusting", "forceful", "pen-etrative" nature been seen as the very model of active male sexuality' (Weeks, 2003: 51). When Col. Armando was putting his captured ene-mies through forms of sexual violation he was primarily undermining that symbol of male power. His aversion towards his violators led him to find ways of 'disgracing', 'degrading' or 'decapitating' that symbolic and actual source of male power and authority over another male in a semi-sexual context.

While that is one set of victim behaviour, another victim may enter into a form of adoration of the penis that has violated him. With this particular sentiment we come full circle with some victims' interpreta-tion of biopower. For Genet, 'a male that fucks another male is a double male'. A careful reading of Genet's *A Thief's Journal* (1949) and *Our Lady of the Flowers* (1963) that deals with the glorification of male-male vio-lation and several similar issues provides telling signs of a transforma-tion of a normal individual averse to the idea of being sexually violated by another male to his adoration of those violating him. So much so, Genet professes to see a compliment in the threat of sexual violence against his body (Brownmiller, 1975: 262). What is happening here? Is

THE LANDSCAPE OF SILENCE

the victim imagining their violator to be their protector, as is common with kidnapped victims experiencing Stockholm Syndrome?

In Sartre's interpretation, a male-male sexual violation from an early age can considerably influence the sexuality of the victim, potentially transforming that individual from a 'passive' to an active homosexual. While full of empathy for the victim he is nonetheless acute in calling the victim of such early childhood rape and the victim's adoption of subsequent homosexual identity as the formation of womanhood. For Sartre:

... an actual rape can become in our conscience, an iniquitous and yet ineluctable condemnation and, vice versa, a condemnation can be felt as a rape. Both acts transform the guilty person into an object, and if, in his heart, he feels his objectification as a shameful thing, he feels it in his sex as an act of coitus to which he has been subjected. Genet has now been deflowered; an iron embrace has made him a woman (Sartre, 1963: 79).

If Sartre is right, what we are witnessing is the psychological transformation of a heterosexual young man or boy (in Genet's case) to a homosexual following a prolonged period of constant childhood sexual violation and rape while in captivity. Mettray Reformatory where Genet was consigned to in his young adolescent years served as the context and location for this transformation.

If biopower of sexual violence is linked to an enterprise of establishing a permanent sovereignty over the victim's body and soul we see its full force in Genet. Brownmiller reminds us that Genet is not the only one to appreciate the 'deliciousness' of this male-male rape (Brownmiller, 1975: 263). In fact there have been several historical characters in the past that have expressed approval of their own violation and there will definitely be many in the future who would not mind celebrating their violation either in conditions of war or in a much more sober atmosphere of prison in peacetime. While that may be so it throws up an important line of inquiry: why do some victims end up celebrating their violation while others nurse a grudge and feel physically and psychologically damaged for life?

From a psychoanalytical perspective, Genet's confession of adoration towards his violator may have something to do with 'need to place oneself'. To paraphrase Fromm, sometimes a given experience becomes the defining character in some individuals' lives. From then on 'the individual leans on it, feels rooted in that experience, has his sense of identity as a part of it, and cannot see himself as an entity independent of that experience' (Fromm, 2002: 39). Whatever may be the specific reaction towards one's violator it is hard to ignore the overall power projection of such violence. If biopower of sexual violence is about creating a condition where the victim's identity is perpetually dependent on and defined by that event then s/he who enforced it in the first place succeeds in achieving that core objective.

Conclusion

While primarily an exercise in power, sexual violence against the male victim in armed conflicts and war purports to establish a mode of interaction that goes beyond the simple physical domination of the body. Owing to the multiple objectives surrounding biopolitics the body of the victim assumes the functional site of (re)production and mediation of political visions and divisions. Consequently, when appropriated by the violator the victim's body is consigned to specific socio-political and ideological experimentation.

Similarly biopower is about the seizure of sovereignty from a given body. In the context of sexual violence it goes a step further. It seeks to imprint a specific identity in the body. It is that force which subjugates life to a world of perpetual exploitative control. Its explicit function is to damage both the body and soul of the victim. Following its implementation it brings about a complete regressive transformation in the victim's personality and life. Once employed it weakens the victim's self-worth and self-image, smashes his ideological convictions and overshadows his future perspective. As an undertaking it is both subversive as well as malicious. It takes away from the individual the right not only to the protection of his/her life but the very essence of its sacredness. It is the absolute and unmitigated ability to strike on a life and rob its sacredness, which makes biopower of sexual violence so disturbing a force.

So far as the imposition of the biopower of sexual violence is concerned there is no clear binary divide on the gendered identity of its agents. It can be introduced both by male and female perpetrators. One abiding theme that remains paramount in this undertaking, however, is that both sets of perpetrators are motivated by what one might call the imposition of different models of sovereignty on their victim. Primarily it purports to humiliate, de-masculanise and strategically weaken the enemy male for good. Discipline and punishment are often its core objectives. In the next chapter I examine how extremist visions surrounding nation and nationalism often use biopower of sexual violence to silence any opposition to such projects.

3

IN THE NAME OF THE NATION

... war isolates aggressors from the truth of their own actions.

Michael Ignatieff, *The Warrior's Honour*, 1999: 177.

The centrality of the 'body' weighs heavily in both traditional as well as modern imaginations of the nation. In the political study of the body its various organs appear to have specific socio-political connotations throughout history. While the head may serve as the metaphor for the representation of the government, the heart may connote the soul force of that nation in the context of nationalism, national aspiration and a vision. Similarly, strong hands have always been associated with the physical power of that nation and the people it represents.[1] When we turn to examining the genitalia it invariably leads us in the direction of debates about potency, impotency, sacredness, pollution, virility, weakness, and so on. The male genital in this interpretation is the accessory tool used for the transfer of the nation from one generation to the next. It is a vehicle, an organ, literally and metaphorically in charge of overseeing the continuation of a people, an ethnicity, a religious group or a nation.

Consequently, as Turner puts it, 'Bodily metaphors have been important in moral debate about ... social disruptions. The division between good and evil has drawn heavily on bodily metaphors; what is seen as sinister is related to left-handedness, the illegitimate side, the awkward side. Our sense of social order is spoken in terms of the balance or imbalance of the body' (Turner, 2006: 224). Moreover it is long agreed within various disciplines in the social sciences that the body can and does intervene to confirm or deny various social significances (Gatens, 1995). Given the dominance of this line of thinking, in the view of some critics, unsurprisingly, 'our body has become the platform from which we see the world and also an object in that world which is seen by others' (Featherstone, 2006: 233).

When we evaluate the 'body' in the context of the nation we invariably come up with some enduring belief systems. A given classification of the body on the men's sense of their value to their nation and their self-worth is often dependent on the virility and non-contamination of their own body's physical purity (Peninston-Bird, 2003: 36).

Yet, equating the body with the nation is not new. Thomas Hobbes' reference to the 'body politic' in the *Leviathan* where he suggests, 'Man is not only a natural body, but also a body of the city, that is, of the so-called political part,' is an early example of this referential interpretation. However, we notice a full exploration of this concept in the work of Ernst Kantorowicz (1957). In Kantorowicz's interpretation 'the sacred body of the nation cohabits with the mortal body of the sovereign' as long as the monarch's body is physically alive. This, of course, raises two interlinked questions: Is the body-nation symbiosis limited to the sovereign alone? Or, can we locate other such associations?

In the context of civic nationalism where the sovereign is replaced by the citizenry the assumption is that the sacred body of the nation now resides within every citizens' body. In such scenarios it is primarily a co-terminous and co-dependent relationship. A healthy and unviolated male body is, therefore, *sine qua non* with healthy nationalism and national identity.[2] Consequently, the burden of responsibility or onus is on that individual citizen to protect the honour and sacredness of the nation through the maintenance of his own physical purity. This task or responsibility of protecting oneself and thereby protecting the nation assumes increased importance especially in the case of male citizens as they are considered natural defenders of the nation. Consequently, within this framework of interpretation male masculinity—body and soul, outward appearance and inward virtue (Mosse, 1996: 5)—is seen as co-terminus with the national self and national identity. Put simply, one who upholds these virtues upholds the nation—one who allows it to be damaged ends up damaging the nation in the process.

Furthermore, in the discourse surrounding nation and nationalism the male body has a purpose. It has a stated function. The body has to stay sacred. Sacredness of the body and national purity often goes hand-in-hand. A citizenry consisting of healthy, unviolated, and pure bodies are fundamental to a self-respecting nation. Such bodies, in other words, are indispensable to forging spirited nationalism and self-assured national identity; while it remains uncontaminated it can be the repository of a sacred vision.

This conditional relationship, however, has its obvious problems. From the perspective of the enemy of a given polity or nation, if the nation constitutes a body of citizens then it makes sense to contaminate one (or better still several) of these bodies with the expectation that such an undertaking would lead to the contamination of the entire national body politic. Consequently, by instituting this particular form of violence on that body the enemy not only alters the condition in which the owner of that body resides but also succeeds in proclaiming the banality of the nationalist political project that he and his community stood for.

Issues of personhood and the body are generally implicated in nationalistic expressions of violence (Taylor, 2002: 158). From the perspective of extremist nationalism, violation of the body of the male enemy is at once a productive break: this very act of transgression initiates a long series of outcomes guaranteeing the victim's complete and total dislocation. It sets into motion his enslavement. He is no longer an equal with the enemy. Violation allows the violator colonisation of the body-social identity. It facilitates the control over the victim's soul and thereby that of the nation. Consequently, a violated body (citizenry) implies a violated nation. It undermines the very foundation of the sacredness of nation, nationalism and national identity. It marks a departure from that inherent sacredness. Put simply, a violated body is an insult to the national imagination and national spirit. It is a failed project—an entity incapable living up to the expectation built into the idea of sacredness of nation and nationalism.[3]

From the violator's perspective the male body of an enemy can be seen as any one or several of the characteristics highlighted below:[4]

(a) as a biological reproducer or half-contributor of a member of a given ethno-national collective
(b) as a defender of ethno-national claims
(c) as a promoter of national boundaries
(d) as a representative of masculine power-projecting nationalism

(e) as an ideological reproducer of a specific (enemy) identity

(f) as a key constituent in a future political project.

Since these high-value roles are in direct opposition to the violator/enemy's own identity and power projections s/he feels it necessary to undermine it. As I shall discuss at length later in this chapter, while killing eliminates the possibility of that individual playing any of the above roles, sexual violation of that member belonging to a rival ethno-nationalist community ensures a far greater outcome.

In the highly emotional and competitive world of national virtue, national strength, and national character, where masculinity is invariably associated with unwavering physical strength and unsubordinated national identity, the violation of an individual male member at the hands of that nation's enemies implies emasculation of that nation once and for all.

Consider the imagery that the West Pakistani soldiers harboured in their mind when they went about ritually raping both men and women in their anti-independence drive in East Pakistan (now Bangladesh) in the 1971 secessionist war.

According to the Pakistani Lt. General Amir Abdullah Khan Niazi Piachi who was at the helm of this military undertaking, 'East Pakistan was "a low lying land of low lying people"' (see Rummel, 1997) and therefore the bodies of those inhabiting that space did not warrant equality with that of West Pakistani people. Thus they could be brutalised, violated, vanquished and, if need be, got rid of. Niazi who created the *Razakar* forces as his handmaiden for suppressing East Pakistan nationalism unleashed a campaign of sexual terror that became synonymous with the 'Rape of Bangladesh'.

Urdu-speaking West Pakistanis proud of their own particular variant of national identity were not the only ones or the first to undertake this form of sexual violation against their political opponents in an organised manner in the name of nationalism. In that gory twentieth century many other races and people appear to have engaged in such practices openly.

Focusing on a more recent conflict we find echoes of a similar undertaking. In the imagination of the ultra-nationalist Serb militias and military their Bosnian and Croat prisoner's body was representative of an 'evil nation'. Left to themselves the bodies of then enemy Bosniaks and Croats, the torturers felt, would go about further propagating this 'evil nation'. How was one to stop the imaginary as well as the actual spread of this project? Quite simply for the Serb ultra-nationalists this could be

achieved by rendering the body of his captive enemy incapable of producing that vital lifeblood which has the potential to spread the nationalism that the aggressor is fighting against.

It is worth remembering here that from the very outset the principle
of nationalism has almost indissolubly been linked, both in theory and
practice, with the idea of the use of violence against its supposed enemies (Howard, 1991: 39). Force, brute or refined, is what societies, nations,
and ultimately their histories are built upon (Netz, 2004: xi). Ability to
use that force or effectively withstand an outside oppositional force defines
a nation and its national identity. This being the inheritance, historically
neither individual actors nor states have cared for much when it comes
to controlling violent tendencies in the name of nationalism (especially
during times of national unrest and civil war).

Consequently what has happened is that while the state has organised
the use of violence in a specific order, individuals seeking to impose or
work for their own variant of nationalism have often operated outside
that demarcated zone which stipulates the kind of violence that is permissible and that which is not. In fact in the hands of the ultra-nationalist such force can lead to forms of violence that dehumanise the victim
completely. Once the perpetrator begins to attack his victim he notices
as well as takes comfort in the consequences of this degradation (Kressel,
2002: 172). Viewed within this particular framework, the use of egregious violence by the ultra-nationalist Serbs was nothing out of the ordinary. However, it is the specific manner of their undertaking against the
enemy's body executed solely for the propagation of their version of virulent nationalism, which demands introspection.

Since killing their prisoners outright posed various logistical and long-
term strategic challenges, the Serb militias and military systematically
went about damaging the male reproductive organ of their Bosnian and
Croat prisoners from the moment of their capture. If the body represented the reproduction of another life, the Serbs hurt the organ of that
particular body which facilitated that reproductive process. Hurting the
testes of the prisoner with blunt objects such as wooden clubs, kicking
with heavy boots, giving massive blows to it by a rifle butt were all part
of a strategy to institute 'irreversible ischemic changes in reproductive
cells caused by edema' (Loncar et. al., 2010: 198).

In a patriarchal system, an attack on the reproductive organ threatens
national reproduction because it makes survivors damaged goods (Allen,

1996; Skejlsbæk, 2001). Expunging the male body of its central function in the process of reproducing the nation (both metaphorically and literally) allowed the Serb perpetrators a sense of authority that they were desperately seeking. Moreover taking a wider perspective one could argue that, from the perpetrators' point of view, such wounded and humiliated bodies, although physically alive, were for all practical purposes dead political entities and by that stretch of imagination dead nations.

A full body without its reproductive organ is an organism of antiproduction (Deleuze and Guattari, 1985: 8). In the imagination of some Serb torturers, however, 'the internal death of reproductive cells' through beatings of the scrotum did not visually represent the death of that body-nation association. The prisoner's body had to show some external marks of the death of this natural reproductive capacity. Thus semi-castration and castration of the body assumed urgency is some Serb-held prison camps.[5]

Furthermore, one of the less known aspects of the Rwandan genocide was the systematic and indiscriminate emasculation of Tutsi males covering a whole range of age groups including those too young to reproduce. Such undertakings mostly involved the hacking of the Tutsi male genitalia by Hutu extremists. As with Bosnian Serb extremists, we might theorize that the Hutus who carried out these atrocities were guided by the imaginary that is the nation and its biological reproduction through male intervention. Their preoccupation with the reproductive system, and specifically with part of the body that produce fertility fluids, committed them to attack a particular part of the Tutsi male anatomy. These were primarily premeditated undertakings whose central objective was to sever (quite literally) the Tutsi male's capacity to reproduce and thereby put an end to any future generation of Tutsis in the Rwandan nation. In view of anthropologist Christopher C. Taylor, 'in order to convince themselves that they were ridding the polity of a categorical enemy and not just assaulting specific individuals, they first had to transform their victims bodies into the equivalent of "blocked beings"' (Taylor, 2002: 168).

These radical ultra-nationalist Serbs or Hutu extremists, however, were neither unique nor the first to treat the male reproductive organ of their enemy as a threat to their nation and national identity. They were merely replicating the imagination and methods of another extremist group from the not so distant past—the Nazis. While the Bosniak Muslims and Catholic Croats preoccupied the Serbs, the Nazis were by and large obsessed with the Jewish and Gypsy ethnicities and the nations they symbolised. In the Nazi worldview, Jews and Gypsies represented 'lives unworthy of life'. They had to go. Creating a German nation free of these two nationalities required their complete annihilation. While the Nazis embarked on that path earnestly at one point during their reign they also experimented with the possibility of castrating the entire Jewish and Gypsy male population in order to stem their future reproduction. This was, indeed, thought to be one of the best possible ways 'to deal with the Jewish Question and Gypsy Plague' (Fonseca, 1996: 273).

Once people commit their first evil act, often without much thought a new logic pushes them on toward more heinous undertakings (Kressel, 2002: 171). A certain Dr Horst Schumann, who had been active in Hitler's euthanasia programme, had investigated the effect of X-rays on human generative glands. In 1941 he came up with the idea of addressing the 'Jewish Question' by mass sterilisation. This proposition was instantly seized upon by Heinrich Himmler, the Commissioner for the Strengthening of the German National Character, who gave his personal support to the plans 'by making available suitable material in the Auschwitz and Ravensbrück concentration camps'. Following this high patronage, Dr Schumann:

… got hold of able-bodied Jews aged twenty to twenty four, and exposed their sexual organs to X-rays for fifteen minutes. Subsequently the men had to go straight back to work. Those who could not keep the pace because of the ensuing burns and abscesses were gassed. Two to four weeks later the remaining victims were castrated, so that their testicles could be dissected and examined under the microscope (Kogon, 1950: 153).

Combining his medical knowledge with his ardent nationalism Dr Schumann would place before the Nazi public domain the following recommendation in the aftermath of his experimentation on the hapless male concentration camp victims: '…if persons are to be rendered permanently sterile, this can be accomplished only by X-ray dosages so high that castration with all its consequences ensues' (quoted in Kogon, 1950: 153).[6]

Castrating the nation

'I am going to hang Saakashvili by the balls,' (*The Economist*, 2012: 42) Prime Minister Vladimir Putin was heard saying to his French counterpart Nicolas Sarkozy, during the Russian standoff against the

Georgians in August 2008 when Moscow and Tbilisi entered a brief but nearly disastrous border war. Putin was clearly incensed by the fact that Mikheil Saakashvili, the Georgian leader and president at the time had the courage to stand up to the mighty Russians. The brief border war was for all practical and symbolic purposes an affront against the superiority of the Russian nation. How could an underling, only recently part of the mighty USSR, dare to stand up against Russia, the successor state to the Soviet Union?

By engaging in an open fight against the Russians President Saakashvili might have been trying to proclaim the equality, potency and manliness of his nation Georgia vis-a-vis Russia. This was intolerable for Moscow. The Georgians, the theory goes, had to be expunged of this vain attempt to proclaim their manliness. Metaphorically at least, the best possible approach to extricate them from this public show of potency was to tell them that their leader is going to be drained of all his manliness when 'hung upside down by his balls'. Castrating Saakashvili, then, would serve the symbolic purpose of castrating the whole Georgian nation.[7]

'Manliness,' Bourdieu points out, 'is an eminently *relational* notion, constructed in front of and for other men' (Bourdieu, 2001: 53). From a definitional perspective and, externally at least, both the aggressor and the would-be victim are in equal possession of manliness. Both are endowed with a socio-biological definition of the body by being the natural possessor of male sexual organs. The aggressor or violator is eminently aware of this fact. How is he then to enact and establish his manliness over that of his captive? The aggressors' manliness, in other words, is dependent on the denial or expulsion of the manliness of his enemy. If he were to establish his own manliness over the 'enemy other' he can only do so by denying this inherited natural biological right of his opponent.

For so long as his enemy other is in possession of this identity the aggressors' manliness is far from paramount. Put simply, the enemy has to be expunged of his manliness—not necessarily his life (for taking away life prior to taking away his manliness is counter to the whole project of establishing the aggressors' unchallenged masculinity). The required objective here, therefore, is the opponent parting with his own masculinity. He needs to demonstrate that he is not only devoid of masculinity but also that his manliness is of no value. Presence of either of these faculties is an automatic threat to the aggressors' manliness and the nationalism he stood for.

Hence if the enemy male is castrated or forced to part with his masculinity by the aggressor it is because the latter not only took objection to his virility but also in some instances went a step ahead and took offence to the fact that he dared even to exhibit that masculinity. Note, for instance, this particular incidence involving Bosnian Muslim prisoners and their Serb captors. The aggressors here lined up naked their captives while Serb women from outside undressed in front of them; during this parade of sexuality if any prisoner had an erection, his penis was cut off (Carpenter, 2006: 94).

From the outset this undertaking has all the hallmarks of the declaration of aggressors' sovereignty. For these violators admitting and submitting to the Serb sovereignty not only meant recognising the former's political supremacy but also its extension into the victims' psychophysical thought processes and bodily behaviour. On the one hand those who were able to control their erection were automatically demonstrating their recognition of that sovereignty. On the other, those victims who failed against their natural urge or were not able to subdue their bodily reactions in that particular parade were seen to be defying the sacredness of the Serb female body and thus by extension the Serb sovereignty.

Consequently, within the framework of aggressive nationalism the aggressor by subjecting his captive(s) to such treatment is making a pronouncement that 'you are so cowardly, unmanly and devoid of an iota of potency that you cannot even have an erection when confronted by the sight of real life naked women'. Thus your cause is as good as dead and your physical being is abominable. Those who exhibited this trait of submission escaped punishment. By contrast those captive Bosnian Muslims whose body responded to a natural condition were easily identified as threats and meted out a form of exemplary punishment as to this will happen to you if your body and mind dare to express feelings of masculinity.

In such situations as contested nationalism and ultra-nationalist conflict sexual violence can function as a form of communication between hegemonic and subordinate masculinities (Alison, 2007: 85). Examined within the context of the violator's ultra-nationalism and the victim's inability to counter it as it is expressed during acts of sexual violence, there appears to be operating a concentric circle of hierarchy. Such nationalistic power relationships are reflected in a myriad of contexts.

Apart from reducing the victims' identity both physically and metaphorically to an object of femininity, through his (also potentially her) acts of violation the perpetrator enables his/her ethnic/religious/political identity to become more masculinised. It is very much a power play. This hierarchy is a declaration of masculine nationalism of the violator and reduction of another masculine national identity (that of the violated) into an inferior stratum akin to that of a lower stratum of feminine identity—where the latter is devoid of any such strength. It is a hierarchy of relationship where masculinised identities are ascribed power and feminised identities are not (Skjelsbæk, 2001: 226).

The enforcement of feminised identity also brings into discussion the very act of penetration, as penetration is 'masculine'. If that were so, a male victim receiving penetration either physically or in terms of crude objects (directly by the violator or through the commands of the violator) is in fact admitting that he is indeed submitting to the wishes of the violator. The violator who is penetrating has the base masculine power. The receiver is the repository of that power and thus by definition feminine. Male-male sexual violation in a nationalist context therefore is never about the hegemonic party wishing to be penetrated—for that would undermine the very basis of his virility and strength.

Expanding the nation

Power and violence in discourses surrounding nationalism express themselves most clearly in a politics of space (van der Veer, 1996: 259). In extremist ethno-nationalist projects the underlying conflict dynamics are always propelled by contest over control of that space. Moreover such projects are not only exclusive but also expansionist when it comes to narrating that space (physical, political, imaginary, or abstract). That being the core objective, hegemonic radical nationalists in deeply divided societies often take recourse in strategies that specifically seek to remove any competing claims to a given narrative of the nation.

In such contexts the extremists among that hegemonic nationalist project use all manners of violence if it guarantees that they will control or expand their national space. The Bosnian Serb nationalist project appears to have consciously embraced sexual violence against its perceived enemies as a mechanism to (a) push Bosnian Muslims and Croats out of the physical space they occupied; and (b) kill any nationalist ambition of the future generation by the physical emasculation of the enemy.

While staying close to the Balkan civil war and focusing specifically on the sexual violence of the Bosnian Serbs against their enemies we are confronted with the fact that this initiative was primarily aimed at pushing back the Bosnian Muslim nation. In fact, the Bosnian Serb extremists wanted reports of their brutal methods to spread among the non-Serb population in order to induce people to flee their homes and relinquish claims and titles to the physical territory they held. Consequently, the more savage and humiliating the Serb ultra-nationalists were, the more intimidating an impression they left and the greater the chances were of their occupying new territories (Kressel, 2002: 16).

Organisation of a specific brand of nationalism is not only about the control of a given physical space; it is also about populating this space with a certain kind of people. If nations are understood to contain 'different alleles of the same gene competing with each other, and the ones that are carried by the more reproductively successful individuals have a greater probability of being replicated in the population's next generation' (van den Berghe, 1978: 402), the scene may then be set for a specific variety of socio-biological purge by the most powerful over the weaker.

But where does sexual violation of non-Serb men in Bosnia fit into this narrative? We need to take a backward glace into history to locate the answer to this specific question. In the name of national homogenisation the first task that many victorious cultures and nations of the past were engaged in while consolidating their authority at home or conquering a new territory elsewhere was to systematically annihilate the reproductive male population which could range from any male between the ages of ten to seventy. Then this victorious power would go about raping the vanquished women and selling them to servitude whereby the male genetic line of that particular nation would be cleansed from the face of the earth.[8]

Interrogating the question of nationalism and a hegemonic community's resolve to keep it pure and uncontaminated, one critic argued 'history always repeats itself and that someone is always a Jew' (Kressel, 2002: 13). Meditating on the Bosnian Serb violence against its hapless male victims we notice this old barbaric strategy of the past at work.

If 'nation' signifies a 'specific body of citizens', for the ultranationalist Serb militias and army during the Yugoslav war of the 1990s the conflict was an occasion to engage in propagating a specific gene in order to oversee the emergence of a specific biological nation. Carlson says that the Serbs systematically used sexual violence against Muslim men and boys in order to preclude future procreation (Carlson, 2006). Crudely put, it was an exercise in the imposition of a specific socio-biological order that sought to deny non-Serbs access to their nation.

Punish and discipline

Although there was no attempt to call it so, in a broader sense, conditioning the captive enemy male's body to this process of humiliation could be argued as punishing the form of nationalism the victim stood for or was associated with. These very actions could also be construed as one dominant victorious nationalism dishing out punishment on the defeated. If punishment is the central objective in this undertaking it raises some difficult questions. For instance, for Hobbes:

[H]arm inflicted upon one that is a declared enemy, falls not under the name of punishment: because seeing they were either never subject to the law, and therefore cannot transgress it; or having been subject to it, and professing to be no longer so, by consequence deny they can transgress it, all the harms that can be done to them, must be taken as acts of hostility (Hobbes, 1839: 300).

Furthermore, Hobbes makes a critical distinction between punishment and the random use of violence. He argues that punishment can only be applied in those situations when the victim is already in a 'condition of political obedience'. The authority that inflicts the pain through punishment is aware of this fact and thus applies it as a corrective or a form of social control.

A punishment, is an evil inflicted by public authority, on him that hath done, or omitted that which is judged by the same authority to be a transgression of the law; to the end that the will of men may thereby the better be disposed to obedience (Hobbes, 1839: 297).

If that is so, one could infer that the perpetrator of sexual violence considers the victim as still being a member of his/her overall political vision; considers the would-be victim as a natural violator of the political order that the perpetrator represents; or believes that by inflicting such violence s/he can bring about a transformation in that individual, leading to a declaration of complete obedience to the prevalent political order.

Political discourses of the body frequently view it within the context of command, control, discipline, obedience and subjugation. Using the work of Michel Foucault within the discourse of competing nationalisms one could argue that employment of sexual violence against men invokes aspects of punishment and discipline in specific contested social space. In such contexts, Foucault argues, disciplinary power 'functions to the extent that it isolates a space, that it determines a segment. Discipline concentrates, focuses and encloses. The first action of discipline is in fact to circumscribe a space in which power and the mechanisms of its power will function fully and without limit' (Foucault, 2007: 44).

Many nation states, private individuals and desperate communities regularly take recourse in these Foucauldian corrective measures to lash out against their opponent. At times these undertakings are part of a never-ending cycle of revenge. As psychiatrist John Mack puts it, 'ethnonationalist groups that have been traumatised by repeated sufferings at the hands of other groups seem to have little capacity to grieve for the hurts of other peoples, or to take responsibility for the new victims created by their own violent actions' (Mack, 1990: 125). In the context of contested nationalism or competition over space between the distinctly divided communities, the most powerful of the two always ends up taking recourse in particularised forms of violence in order to maintain its hegemony. What is more in these specific instances the use of egregious violence is not seen as something morally invalid but legally permissible and just.

The ultra-nationalist Bosnian Serbs were not the only ones to have engaged in such practices. We may have instances when a hegemonic state imposes an extreme disciplinary or corrective measure on part of its citizenry that resists its authority. In other words, a 'nation state in its attempt to protect its depleting sovereignty may organise itself in such a way that it became a source of torture and insecurity for the very citizen it sought to protect and care for' (Kazi, 2009).

In the contemporary context, nowhere is this imagery more profound than places and people in the midst of separatist conflicts. Take for instance, the Kashmiri nationalist struggle in the Indian administered area. Here, in the disputed region, the Indian army regularly conducts 'penis treatment'. Under this initiative suspected militants, Kashmiri freedom fighters and opponents to Indian rule undergo a prolonged period of electric shocks administered into their male organ (Peer, 2010). Rendered impotent, the victims are then returned to their society.

A routine form of torture? Or, does it have any other subliminal message? When spoken to, one of the regular soldiers responsible for this clandestine undertaking responded by saying, '*Haraaamzadon ko bataana hey azaadee mango to kya milta hey*—'We need to teach these arseholes what you get for demanding independence.' The use of such violence from the violators' perspective is both disciplinary and more importantly necessary. It carries a clear and obvious normative message intended to deter any future Kashmiri subversion against the Indian 'body politic'. As Inger Skejlsbæk has argued, 'in order to disseminate fear and demonstrate control over a restive separatist civilian population sexual violence is often considered most effective' (Skejlsbæk, 2001: 222).

Examination of this particular violence also allows us to delve into a more fundamental discourse on nationalism and violence, whose main protagonists are both individuals and crude ideas often working in unison. Evaluation of the violators' conception of violation posits that the greater the control over the opponent's body (beyond the obvious physicality) the greater the value of that nationalist enterprise. Over time such punishment-control contexts assume mainstream acceptability, leading to subservience of the individual conscience to the extremist nationalist ideology of the state.

Now let us focus on the second aspect of these discipline-seeking actors, in this case individuals and groups. True in the context of competing nationalism, disciplinary power is primarily held in the hands of the state and its security apparatus although it may at times be used by free radicals when they feel there is a necessity to impose it privately. In such situations there may be very little or no ideological reasoning behind this undertaking. Privately undertaken these violations are at best privations of single individuals. What is the psychological process that triggers such undertaking flimsily identified as nationalistic fury?

Hutus who went about killing their Tutsi victims during the Rwandan genocide as we discussed earlier would at times employ horrific sexual violence against their Tutsi male counterpart. The violator in such situation was guided by two sets of rulings. While his killing mission was sanctioned by an organised ideology imposed by a faraway leadership the employment of sexual violence against his male victim was guided by the violator's private grudges and imagined inadequacy. The Hutu male who oversaw slow sexual torture of his victim or employed it himself was enraged by envy, jealousy, frustration and deep anger.[9] He was jealous because the Tutsi had a wife who was far better looking than his own; he was frustrated because his victim was sexually active while he was not.

The perpetrator prior to administering such violence had gone through what one might describe as a process of psychological preparation. His undertaking was an expression of the violator's utter contempt for the enemy, a contempt born of real and imagined wrongs of the past and present (Kressel, 2002: 39). It was an exercise in scaffolding a fragile self-respect that the violator possessed. It was as if the violator found a deeper meaning in this specific undertaking and his self-respect was bolstered by this action. Ultimately while exacting revenge in the name of the group to which he belonged or the nationalism he identified with the violator was actually redeeming his own inadequacy vis a vis his enemy.

Nationalism of the sadist

Nationalism is about love of the nation, and this is often a self-sacrificing love (Anderson, 1991: 141). The dark underside of this self-sacrificing patriotic love, however, is rooted in fear and hatred of the 'Other', and this is often expressed in sacrificial terms (van der Veer, 1996: 250).

Such being the foundational narrative, unsurprisingly during periods of crises in nationalism, this backdrop can lead ultra-nationalists to seek out outsiders from their midst, impose upon them a stereotypical image, and eventually vent their frustration and anger on that branded group.

Just as there are stereotypes of the nation in terms of the history, racial characteristics or cultural practices, there are stereotypes of enemies (Breuilly, 1982: 50). Armed conflicts and wars are fertile grounds for the construction and dissemination of certain stereotypes. That people from another culture or race are a 'threat' and thus can rightfully be sacrificed in one way or another assumes heightened meaning during such conflicts.

The 'Other' now occupies the site for all those aspects of identity that the aggressor considers unacceptable and threatening. The 'Other' is considered to be in possession of what some critics have described as autonomous 'territories of the self' (Goffman, 1959) which can be invaded by specific rituals of violation (van der Veer, 1996: 259). Unsurprisingly when exposed to this virulent narrative masquerading as nationalist ideology the very physical body of the 'Other', now the enemy, becomes the repository of the violators' specific design:

They were hitting me, as well as others, in the testicles, using metal hampers, metal bars, kicking with the boots. My testicles were swollen, the size of large oranges ... Serb torturers would beat us, step or jump on us until they tired out. They were deliberately aiming their beatings at our testicles saying 'you'll never make Muslim children again' (ICTY, Oral Proceedings of Bosnia and Herzegovina, CR 2006/06, 51).

Or, take the case of Jimmy McCartan from another theatre of conflict. A Catholic man of twenty-one from Northern Ireland, Jimmy in his Sunday best had gone to a wedding in Hollywood, in the east of Belfast in 1972. Once in the hotel, where the reception was held, Jimmy McCartan went to the bar. In the bar he was spotted by a gang of Protestant paramilitaries belonging to the Ulster Defence Association (UDA), who called him an IRA man. McCartan sensed trouble and asked the barman for a safe passage from the place. The barman opened a back door and let him out. But once outside the UDA gang pounced on him.

Jimmy McCartan's body was found the next morning by a football pitch in East Belfast. His body bore 250 cigarette burns. He was mutilated. 'They had cut him, uh, down below' (Remnick, 1997: 77). Protestant paramilitaries beating up their victims, killing them through a slow process of torture at the height of the troubles in Northern Ireland was not new. What was singularly unique and different in the case of Jimmy McCartan is that his killers had mutilated his genitals while McCartan was alive. What was going on in the torturers' minds when they were cutting up Jimmy McCartan's genitals? Was it some form of homoerotic masochistic ritual? Was it perversion? Or was it some simple dastardly fun?

Some three decades later when I brought this and other similar incidents up with some of the former Protestant paramilitaries the responses were uncannily similar to several others from different trouble spots around the world. 'This is what you get when you and your kind want to break us up' was the standard answer. 'Break us up' here meant undermining the separate political identity of Northern Ireland as part of Britain and not Ireland.

Jimmy McCartan had the bad luck of having a wrong identity marker and had strayed into the wrong neighbourhood. He was not political. He did not proclaim any separatist nationalism. Why then was he treated the way he was treated? It is proposed in some circles that increase in wartime sexual violence is rooted in biology—it's higher because of a putative link between the aggression necessary for combat and the male sex drive (Jean Wood, 2006: 323). Were the Protestant paramilitaries using McCartan's body as the site for employing their higher sexual aggression? Were they not inspired by their own specific version of nationalism to exact revenge on McCartan and the nationalist aspirations he represented? The answer could lie in both sets of explanations; for, 'rage and violence turn irrational when they are directed against substitutes' (Arendt, 1970: 64).

Sri Lanka provides the backdrop to some of the worst conflict-related violence in our times. The long running civil war that raged there between 23 July 1983 and 18 May 2009 is primarily known for the number of war dead. The quarter-of-a-century long conflict saw some 80–100,000 conflict deaths and a million displacements. However, the less known aspect of this conflict was the existence of 'camps' that perpetrated Bosnia-style torture on the inmates. As of now it is not clearly established how many of these 'camps' really existed. Similarly, given the complex nature of the violence we will never know the exact number of male victims who underwent forms of sexual torture in these camps.

The conflict generated all manner of violent activism on the part of the rebel LTTE and the government soldiers that one would find hard to imagine. While there were many reported and unreported events of sexual violence against rebels, government soldiers and civilians, one particular event that occurred early on in the conflict and provided impetus to both the government side and the rebels for such undertakings in future was the 1983 riots in the Welikada prison in Colombo.

The prison held hundreds of LTTE supporters and some guerilla leaders. In the first wave of the riot government-sponsored assailants massacred some thirty-five inmates on 25 July 1983. Two days later, the assailants barricaded two supposed LTTE guerilla leaders, Ganeshanathan Jeganathan and Sellarasa Yogachandran, in the gaol, wrenched their testicles from their body, and gouged out their eyes with iron bars before stabbing them to death (Anderson et al., 2007: 448). The event, although widely publicised, was never properly investigated.

While the assailants later claimed that they were instructed by government officials to attack and kill the captive political prisoners what is puzzling is the manner in which Jeganathan and Yogachandran were tortured prior to their killing. Why did the assailants wrench the testicles out of their victims' bodies prior to their killing? We may seek the answer in the killers of Jimmy McCartan. In both cases sectarian, ethnic as well as religious differences separated the violators from their victims. For the violators these differences posed a threat to their autonomous hegemonic identity. Since their victims stood for and were identified with a form of separatism their violators had to locate symbols of that nascent autonomy in these individual bodies and put them through this ritual violence.

The sectarian and nationalist issues that contributed to a certain group of male violators to unleash their sexual fury on their victims are not gender-specific. Although men are overwhelmingly the violators on such occasions we cannot limit ourselves to the view that it is only men who perform such acts of violence. As our knowledge about various conflict situations becomes more acute and intimate we realise that this understanding needs an overhaul. For a complete and rounded interpretation of this issue we also need to explore the role of women in this investigation.

According to some critics 'women fighters [nationalists] face similar social pressures within armed and rebel groups that men do and when guided by a specific ideological trait or faced with specific circumstances are likely to commit similar forms of violence' (Cohen, 2013: 386). So, the fact that women can sexually violate men needs to be confronted. Earlier in chapter two, while discussing Abu Ghraib violations, I referred to the female participation in the violation of their enemy male captive. But let us broaden the discussion and enquire about the nature of female violation. Female-male sexual violation in such scenarios may consist of a whole host of actions and undertakings. This may include sexual humiliation—by forcing the captive to take off their clothes and parade them naked (as we encountered in the case of Abu Ghraib); it can also take the form of sexually taunting the victim; it may involve sexual prodding of the male private organs; may lead to mutilation of sexual body parts of the victim; and in the worst instance lead to forced male vs. male rape between two victims. All these undertakings conclusively suggest that women can physically violate men without physically exposing themselves.[10] Also, as we shall see, nationalist conflicts very often draw in and prompt women to embrace the role of the violator.

A cursory glance at women's participation in such undertakings would suggest that they are as brutal as their male counterparts in violating their victims. A glimpse of this brutality can be located in the post-war history of Eastern Europe.

After the end of the Second World War, Josip Broz Tito's partisans unleashed abominable horror on Hungarians and Germans in Hungary while accusing them of collaborating with the Nazis. In one such instance, the violators were exclusively women. The victims on this occasion interestingly belonged to an order of Catholic priests in a monastery in Vojvodina in Southern Hungary. Their fault? They had done little or nothing to prevent the torture and killing of Serb civilians by Nazis and their collaborators in the region. Incensed by the supposed anti-nationalist actions of the priests and fuelled by the spirit of Serbian nationalism these partisan women of Vojvodina tied up the priests and 'tore off their testicles with pincers' one by one and bled them to death (Andereson et al., 2007: 247). Staying near the same theatre of conflict, but half-a-century later, we have documented evidences of 'a Serb woman in her twenties repeatedly and savagely beating young Bosnian Muslim men on their genitals in full view of the camera' (Kressel, 2002: 17). According to other reports their intervention in this nationalist war was twofold: 'women participated in sexual torture in camps, both facilitating rapes of enemy women and engaging in acts of violence against male detainees' (Bastick, Grimm and Kunz, 2007: 117).

Some years after the genocide new facts emerged that validated the argument that many Hutu women actively encouraged their men not only to kill, but sexually mutilate their victims (Nowrojee, 1996). Similarly, during Hindu-Muslim communal violence in Bombay in 1993, Hindu 'women were seen distributing bangles to men (a symbol of timid femininity) who did not participate in such violence. Moreover some women went so far as actively assisting Hindu men in the gang rape of Muslim women' (Hansen, 2001: 123).

Notwithstanding the gender difference of violators, one abiding issue that runs throughout these three evidences is the reason behind such undertaking. A simple killing in these particular instances would have served very little purpose. By wrenching the testicles out of the Catholic priests in Hungary, or from Tamil prisoners' bodies when they were alive, and by slicing off Jimmy McCartan's genitals the violators were making a statement to the violated as well as to the ethno-religious and sectarian groups to which the victims belonged. For the violator such violation operated along a simple binary divide that made his victim stand out. 'You get this because you are'—Catholic, Tamil, Hungarian, Muslim or black and so on goes the violator's logic while introducing such abominable horror on the victim.

'We made their kind and their cause impotent' retorted one of the ex-paramilitaries when quizzed about the rationale behind that particular form of violence. While no such response could be elicited from those assailants who sexually mutilated the LTTE political prisoners Jeganathan and Yogachandran, it is not hard to ascertain the motive of violators. Taken together in these instances the violators were rendering their victims as well as whatever political cause they represented or stood for impotent physically as well as metaphorically.

While outwardly they may appear as freak incidents, one cannot deny the fact that there were specific motives behind the violence perpetrated. Sometimes we need the resolve and emotion to acknowledge an act in order to pin it to a meaning. These were motives which could have been very rational and might have been inspired out of logical thinking. The desire to inflict harm, pain and misery on another individual is summoned easily in some deeply divided societies with groups competing against one another over some abstract principle or idea.

In the end, within the context of extremist nationalism sexual violation of the male body provides complex sets of meaning. When the perpetrator or the aggressor reaches out to his prisoner or captive in the form of sexual violence, s/he is guided by three sets of general desires (Sivakumaran, 2006). In the first instance, the body of the victim serves as a perfect objective for the former's emasculation/feminisation vis a vis the aggressors' demonstration of extreme masculinity or masculine nationalism. Second, by forcing the victim into forms of sexual violation the perpetrator seeks to build an image of homosexual identity for the victim and the autonomous culture, religion or nationalism he belongs to. Third and finally, in some armed conflicts the targeting of male sexual organs as an object of violation (castration) may function as an attempt to prevent the male from future procreation,[11] thereby symbolically annihilating his community's competing national narrative. What binds these different modes of undertaking like glue is an idea and an ideology. To quote Norman Cohn, 'however narrow, materialistic, or downright criminal their own motives may be, such men cannot operate without an ideology behind them. At least while operating collectively they need an ideology to legitimate their behaviour, for without it they would have to see themselves and one another as what they really are—common rapists, opportunistic thugs, and sadists' (Cohn, 1967: 263–4).

Legitimisation

For Carl Schmitt the political is an exceptional moment of decision, which simultaneously institutes both a violent enemy-friend distinction and the autonomous authority on the part of the decision-maker to refashion the nature of the political (Schmitt, 1966). The recognition of an 'us' and 'them' divide reinforced by an exclusionary political belief might lead to a legitimisation of such violence.

Similarly, Steven Pinker, one of the most influential public intellectuals of our time, reminds us, 'war is not universal, but people in all cultures feel that they are members of a group (a band, tribe, clan, or nation) and feel animosity toward other groups' (Pinker, 1998: 509). In the imagination of some groups this animosity needs to be nurtured and sustained in order to provide a sense of self-worth and grandeur. When this form of jingoist identity preference guides a people's imagination, extremist nationalism is easy to evoke. Jingoist or military nationalism seeks to engage in an exercise of boundary building and conferring of enemy status to those who are outside it. Consequently, the participants in this variety of nationalism embrace an 'adaptive logic of coalitional aggression and the cognitive mechanisms necessary to support it' (Pinker, 1998: 513).

If the enterprise of nation and the ideology of nationalism is the explanatory framework behind this violence it is crucial to inquire how the community to which the victim belonged addresses this question of nationalism under attack.

Each autonomous nationalist community has symbols of identity. Equally importantly it has set rules on transgression and shame. According to one critic, 'some revolutionary nationalists and genuine communists cannot tolerate taints of homosexuality. For it undermines their warrior ethics of liberation ... [it] is an accelerating threat to their survival as a people and as a nation' (Clarke, 1983 quoted in Dollimore, 1992: 346). Most nationalist communities where one of its male members has experienced transgression at the hands of its rival nationalist group tend to disown the victim of such experience from its ranks. For some critics, 'nationalism favours a distinctly homosocial form of male bonding' (Anderson, 1991; Moses, 1996). "Typically represented as a passionate brotherhood the nation finds itself compelled to distinguish "its" proper homosociality from more explicitly sexualised male-male relations, a compulsion that requires the identification, isolation and containment of male homosexuality (Parker et al, 1992: 6)." Thanks to this exclusive imaginary, the victim, because of his misfortune, suddenly finds himself as an outsider and unceremoniously disowned. This process of disowning is a product of several interconnected emotions. The victim is blotted out from the political imagination because: (a) his experience is grotesque; (b) his presence degrades and undermines community identity; (c) his violation discredits the collective's nationalism and national character. The victim's personal experience makes an uncomfortable reading in the nationalist imagination, which the community would like to forget; for the victim now casts a long shadow. His very presence or mention in any context is an affront on the sanctity of the community's nationalism. He is a burden. He serves no useful purpose. Hence he has to be purged from any future nation building exercises.

This being the dominant perception, the narrative of nationhood conveniently edits our victim, his experience, and the political reality surrounding the event. Interestingly this conscious attempt at forgetting becomes an officially agreed policy undertaking by some nationalist communities whose members had gone through the process of sexual violation in intra-state or inter-state nationalist wars.

This is best exemplified by the coverage of sexual victimisation of Croats and Bosnians in the Croatian mass media. It is now well established that thousands of male members of these two nations were sexually tortured, abused and killed by ultra-nationalist Serbs during the Balkan wars of the 1990s. However, when it came to acknowledging and reporting these events, the Croatia mass media censored it heavily.

An investigation into the Croatian press from November 1991 to December 1993 found only six articles addressing the sexual abuse taking place in the civil war compared to over one hundred about other forms of torture experienced by Croat men, and more than sixty about the rape of women (Zarkov, 2001; OCHA, 2008: 13). Interestingly the only visible male victim of rape and castration in the Croatian press during this period was the mention of a Muslim man. Since Bosnians were Muslims and Croats were Catholics that particular form of violence experienced by the victim fell in the domain of Bosnian not Croatian identity or nationalism. If that form of self-denial was not enough, the Croatian press went about repeatedly highlighting that Serbian men were homosexual sodomists who went about raping Muslim men.

As Dubravka Zarkov argues, any news about such violence had to first pass through the filter of nationalism (Zarkov, 2001). Reporting the sexual abuse of Croatian men at the hands of Serbs in the Croatian media amounted to a cultural and national disgrace. Admission of such violence amounted to denigrating the masculine identity of their individual selves and the invincibility of Croatian nationalism. The post-war Croatian nation simply did not have the appetite or will power to humiliate itself further by acknowledging the experience of some of its male victims. Therefore, Croatian victims or those who entertained the thought of publicising such abuse suffered by their compatriots in the mass media or otherwise were considered at best mindless and at worst traitors to the Croatian cause and Croatian nationalism.

According to Zarkov, the collective need to lie and sleepwalk into a world of make believe had to do with defending and promoting the Croatian nation. The press and the public had to engage in peddling the symbolic virility of the Croatian nation represented through power, masculinity and, above all, heterosexuality of Croatian men in order to shore up the cause of Croatian nationalism (Zarkov, 2001). Thus the male victims had to be sacrificed for the collective.

One could argue modern nation state and the accompanying nationalism has always been virulently homophobic and hence the exclusion of male victims. Note, for instance, Norman Mailer's "phobic logic" in his influential essay *Truth and Being: Nothing and Time* where he suggested the triadic relationship between nation-civilisation-heterosexual men. According to Mailer, "as a civilisation dies, it loses its biology. The homosexual alienated from the biological chain, becomes it centre (Mailer, 1962)." Our victim, owing to his experience, then is by definition a homosexual, an unnecessary appendage who needs to be expunged from the national narrative.

Remaining on the issue of nationalism and national identity in the context of male sexual violation, there is another often overlooked issue that is equally serious and complex. For instance, while one community can enter into a form of self-denial about the rape of its male members by an enemy nation in order to protect its national identity and image from being tarnished, another community may use such events to further aggressively increase and legitimise its virulent nationalism. In other words, inter-ethnic rape is more political than other kinds of rape in the war-zone (Skejlsbæk, 2001: 219). The former Yugoslavia, again, provides the backdrop to this particular line of argument.

In the 1980s a Serb living in the now independent state of Kosovo named Djordje Martinovic reported rape by the dominant Kosovars. In due course he was admitted in a hospital in Pristina and received treatment for removal of splinters of glass in his anus. During this period Martinovic claimed that Kosovo Albanian men had sexually tortured him and had raped him with a glass bottle (Bracewell, 2000: 563).

Subsequent investigation revealed that the alleged victim had violated himself by putting a bottle in his anus. Serb nationalists, however, picked up this false story for propaganda purposes. Soon enough a petition signed by Serbian intellectuals proclaimed the (falsified) violation of Martinovic as an attack against the Serb nation (Bracewell, 2000: 573). The ultra nationalist Serbs were to argue that the rape of Martinovic was a metaphorical rape of the entire Serb nation and Serbs needed to rise up against the Kosovo Albanians to avenge this insult.

One is not entirely sure how much of this propaganda surrounding sham inter-ethnic sexual violation was responsible for the future rape of Bosnian men in the Yugoslav civil war. However, one cannot discount the fact that this particular claim was exploited very effectively by Serb nationalists to initiate a campaign of terror against all the former partners in the Yugoslav federation including the Kosovars. For some critics the rhetoric used in Kosovo was given a return by the Serbs and in a war which included acts of rape, the Muslim men were frequently targeted to prevent them from degrading Serb men as well as women (Diken & Laustsen, 2005: 115). If the Bosnian men underwent forms of sexual violation at the hands of Serb nationalists in the name of nationalism, it was because of them being inheritors of acts and deeds that took place over many centuries when Muslims were supposed to have violated Serb men and women (Ignatieff, 1997; Judah, 1997).

It becomes apparent, then, that within the discourse of nationalism our victim is victimised twice: once physically for being the representative of a particular political narrative and again subsequently when the political system to which he originally belonged denies him his identity.

Yet, a balanced assessment of such practice would suggest that both the individual victim as well as the collective are complicit in this cover up and peddling of an alternative reality. The victim is as much to blame for assisting in this forgetting exercise as the state or the nation concerned.

As I highlighted in the introduction of the book, the self-censorship of the victim in many ways assists the nation to conveniently ignore the episode and move forward. For a nationalist imagination this makes perfect sense. Both for the victim and for the nation he belonged to, recalling the episode amounts to 'shame' and disgrace; an experience which both would like to push out of the public domain, as neither want to keep their selves colonised by this memory for it casts a long uncomforting shadow on their past, present and future. In the end both end up in a complicity of silence. There may be exceptions to this general rule, however.

Violation and martyrdom

Defeated nations occasionally deal with past violations of their members in unexpected ways. While the overwhelming majority likes to keep the experience of its violated members safely at bay, a few communities and nations actually use the occasion to rebuild and bolster their sense of identity. Initially uncomfortable with the reality surrounding the victims' experience the collective may use the episode to shore up its nationalistic aspirations and construct an autonomous communal identity. In the annals of sexual violence against men there are a number of examples where the violated victim is turned into a symbol—a martyr for the collective.

While such martyrdom is not easily conferred upon all victims it is not always very clear what the reason is behind such conferring. The 'true' motive of those celebrating the martyrdom of their victim/hero is not always clear.

A simplistic answer provided by those who come to express this reverence towards the given victim is the uncomplicated fact that the person concerned bore his victimhood with pride. He stood for an ideal dear to the collective. More importantly unlike our countless victims he did not hide from the stories about his violation. In other words his grief was as much private as public. We have an absorbing interpretation of that in the personality of Saint Sebastian in the historical/religious tradition of Christianity. Sebastian, who was killed in the year 288 AD, was a high-ranking Roman soldier. He fell out of favour with the power of the then Roman Empire for courting and embracing Christianity (a banned religion at the time) and for protecting Christians from Roman persecution.

The entire story of Sebastian, his exploits, his suffering at the hands of his enemies and his eventual martyrdom, like so many other examples from early Christian history, is without any real basis in fact. What we have instead is a complex set of subtexts, narratives and legends that draws upon archetypes current at the time. In this maze of accounts one narration that is constant and runs through all descriptions of Sebastian's life is his supposed help for persecuted Christians for which he earns the wrath of the high Roman authorities. For this betrayal he is tied to a pole and then shot with arrows by his fellow soldiers until he falls to the ground like a porcupine/hedgehog and is clubbed to death. It is this story of martyrdom (standing up for Christianity during the early years of its consolidation) which subsequently earns him sainthood.

While there is unanimity concerning the manner of his death, what is interesting is the alternative interpretations of events leading up to Sebastian's final fall from this earthly life. One of the most provocative, striking and acutely relevant representations of Sebastian's victimhood comes to life in the 1976 production and release of a British film *Sebastiane* by British writers/directors Derek Jarman and Paul Humfress. The complex narrative of this film revolves around the life and times of a group of nine Roman soldiers inhabiting a remote island in the far-flung frontiers of the Roman Empire.

Sebastian is on exile in that remote island by the orders of emperor Diocletian (third century AD). While inhabiting that space he becomes an object of lust and fascination for his fellow soldiers for both his earthly physical beauty and for his ideology/faith which forces him to refuse combat with his fellow soldiers (Christians don't fight). While it does not appear blatantly obvious, Sebastian nevertheless is an enemy of the empire and the ideology and faith (pagan) it stands for. Hence he needs to be vanquished. So begins a series of sadistic and sadomasochistic sexual advances towards Sebastian by his fellow soldiers and notably their leader Captain Severus. Although an outcast (for not following the imperial orders to persecute Christians) as well as an outsider (for his pro-Christian beliefs) Sebastian refuses to give in to the sexual advances and demands of his fellow soldiers.

This refusal to comply with the wishes of the victorious or those at the top of the power hierarchy is seen as a further affront against the regime. Even the high representative of that regime Captain Severus, who is smitten with his own intense homosexual desire to violate Sebastian, is refused such advances by our victim. Eventually Severus's monumental failure to sexually violate Sebastian (for he wants this encounter to be mutual in a true Classical homoerotic fashion) ultimately forces him to channel his frustration and anger in ordering Sebastian's death by shooting of arrows by the fellow soldiers.

The temperate yet forceful interpretation of *Sebastiane* in Jarman's hands suggests an alternative but probable version of events leading to our central character's violation and eventual martyrdom. This new way of reading Sebastian's life, as through the eyes of the violator, suggests a mode of victim-violator relationship as has never been told before.

Read from the perspective of sexual violence, Sebastian's sufferings would appear to encompass the entire community of the violated through the ages. The agonising pain on his face following the shooting of arrows from Diocletian's soldiers into his earthly body is at once the representation of the collective pain of almost unimaginable vastness. If one were to exclude the traditional association of this suffering of Sebastian with the defence of Christianity and transpose it to the secular domain then he would splendidly fit into a modern-day martyr refusing to bow to the pressure of the violators and choosing death instead.

This martyrdom, however, comes at a price. Just like the way Severus and his band of soldiers were smitten with the desire to violate their victim for his striking physical beauty, generations of painters, writers and poets have tried to entertain the same desire lust and passion. That Sebastian is an erotic figure meant for violation by other men was not only confined to the life and times of Saint Sebastian. We do not know for sure how Sebastian looked in actual life. What we have are a steady stream of paintings dating from the mediaeval age. If the images of the renaissance artists Antonio Pollaiuolo (1431–1498) or Guido Reni (1575–1642) are any indication, Saint Sebastian had a physical figure that can be equated with the sensuousness of a languid Greek god.

Unsurprisingly it is that sensuous beauty (without Saint Sebastian being homosexual or gay) that forced his adversaries to his violation. No one best describes this homoerotic desire to violate Saint Sebastian better than the celebrated Japanese author Yukio Mishima.

In fact in his autobiographical novel *Confessions of a Mask* (1958) Mishima writes of a young man who has his first ejaculation upon seeing a portrait of Saint Sebastian (1615) by Guido Reni:

A remarkably handsome youth was bound naked to the trunk of a tree. His crossed hands were raised high, and the thongs binding his wrists were tied to the tree. No other bonds were visible, and the only covering for the youth's nakedness was a coarse white cloth knotted loosely about his loins... Were it not for the arrows with their shafts deeply sunk into his left armpit and right side, he would seem more a Roman athlete resting from fatigue... The arrows have eaten into the tense, fragrant, youthful flesh, and are about to consume his body from within with flames of supreme agony and ecstasy. The boy's hands embarked on a motion of which he had no experience; he played with his 'toy': Suddenly it burst forth, bringing with it a blinding intoxication... Some time passed, and then, with miserable feelings I looked around the desk I was facing... There were cloud-splashes about... Some objects were dripping lazily, leadenly, and others gleamed dully, like the eyes of a dead fish. Fortunately, a reflex motion of my hand to protect the picture had saved the book from being soiled (Mishima, 1958: 37).

For critics such as David B. Morris, in Mishima we notice the pain of the victim (Sebastian) change its meaning. Instead of empathy towards his suffering Sebastian is being elevated to a private militarised homo-erotic vision. What we have here is an obsession this image provokes in the body. And, in the best of ancient Japanese tradition the martyr Sebastian enters into contact with *shudo* (the Way of Boy Love) (Morris, 1991: 131). Hence the violated becomes a perpetual object of eroticism and violation.

This mode of receiving erotic pleasure through the sufferings of a third person immortalised in a painting, story or photograph is not an isolated event. Note, for instance, Georges Bataille's admission of receiving 'intense erotic pleasure' following his exposure to a set of pictures depicting the slow execution of Fou-Tchou-Li, a Mongol guard convicted of murder-ing Prince Ao-Han-Ouan in 1905. In fact, Bataille goes to great lengths to publicise his views on such public depictions of violence by bringing out his controversial work *The Tears of Eros*.[12] According to some critics 'for Bataille, the images do in fact open up an exciting disorder of the senses, a conjunction of grotesque murder and sexual delight' (Taylor, 1998: 30).

Why do some men find this visual imagery erotic? Why did Mishima find the martyrdom of San Sebastian personally fulfilling? The answer that one seeks in general and about Mishima in particular could be located in some of the commentaries made on Bataille. For scholars like Kate Millett who has spent a good deal of time and energy dissecting the inner recesses of such perverse behaviour (as is the case with Bataille's discourse on the Chinese execution), such a disordered response has to do with 'deeply rooted obsessions among Western men with the Orient as the place to perform and enjoy sadism' (Millett, 1994). If that is so, what we are witnessing in Mishima is a reverse process at work—the Oriental masculinity seeking erotic pleasure from viewing sadistic images of vio-lation of an Occidental man.

Once we move beyond these attestations of personal sexual gratifica-tion through certain images we are confronted with the larger questions of martyrdom that are usually associated with these violations. True, pub-lic martyrdom for their sexual violation in theatres of conflict is rarely con-ferred on the victims. According to one critic, in the cultural memory 'the victims of rape are not included in the public rite of mourning over the lost war, they are not admired as "heroines" and do not receive any compensation'(Schmidt-Harzback, 1992: 43, quoted in Seifert, 1996: 38). Even when they are instituted by the *vox pupuli* or by some regime it is for other reasons. While conferring these martyrdoms the instituting authority tries its best to gloss over the sexual violation of the victim(s) and tries instead to highlight some other aspect of the victim's character. If that were not enough the general public for whose emotional consumption these martyrs were introduced in the first place want a particular price for recognising or being asked to recognise this martyrdom of the victims.

We do not have, as yet, another powerful contemporary example of a male victim of such violence who has been canonised into a secular or temporal martyr following his victimhood. What we have, instead, is the conferment of such titles on an entire generation of female victims of such violence. It is estimated that in the 1971 civil war in East Pakistan over a million women (and many men) were ritually violated by the occupying West Pakistani army. As I have mentioned elsewhere in this study it was a clear and fully-fledged attempt by an occupational force to use rape and sexual violence to subjugate and silence secessionist nationalism.

According to many contemporary accounts of the time, barely a household existed in East Pakistan (now Bangladesh) which did not have a woman who was raped by the West Pakistani army. In a traditional Islamic society where the honour of women is held very highly indeed, such violation led to a collective communal shame. As a result, most of these violated women who were repeatedly raped and often made pregnant (to introduce a future generation of Pakistanis in this society lacking in strength and courage so the argument went from the violators' logic) were often abandoned or sent away from their homes to hide the shame that they had brought upon the household for having invited violation owing to their sexuality.

In a highly imaginative (dubbed by some as visionary) move the then prime minister of the country Sheikh Mujibur Rahman declared all female rape victims national heroines (Brownmiller, 1975: 83). For Rahman and his government these violated women were true freedom fighters for they had courted the wrath of the powerful enemy and had been brutalised in the process. Following this announcement by Rahman the shaken and suffering masses of this nascent nation easily bought into this vision and vowed to accord this status without any rancour or reservation.

In solidarity with these living martyrs many idealistic men of the country came forward expressing their willingness to rehabilitate them through marriage. But the sentiment stopped with that expression of willingness. When the government actually asked these men to enter matrimony an overwhelming majority of them wanted the state to compensate them for agreeing to take home a violated/damaged/shameful woman. According to a report at that time the demands of the Bangladeshi men willing to marry one of these 'martyred women' ranged from the latest model of Japanese car, painted red, to the publication of unpublished poems (quoted in Brownmiller, 1975: 83).

While a few actually managed to receive the status of martyrdom owing to their suffering, they rarely succeed in gaining the full appreciation of the community. Helena Khan's fictional assessment of this status suggests that to be labeled as a *birangona* (the brave woman), which elevated the violated to a 'special' place in the national narrative, was in reality to be given a crown of thorns. Official recognition of their suffering, the decision to confer a certain societal status, or pinning the label of heroism ultimately 'isolated them and destroyed their ability to survive in the nation' (Khan, 2013). In fact their newfound status as martyrs/heroines became an object of shame for people from whose families these women originally came. Having a martyred heroine openly carrying the marks of enemies' sexual violence became a source of permanent humiliation. Thus they ended up disowning these heroines.

Conclusion

A given body or assembly of bodies have always worked as a vehicle of representation and dissemination of a particular political ideal and ideology.[13] This mode of representation eventually leads to the imagination of a nation. But the nation by its very definition covets homogeneity. It is an exclusionary idea that advantages one group over another. It is this emphasis on exclusivity that ushers in an atmosphere of distrust and conflict where one group tries to unseat another from the national narrative by using all available means.

If nationalism is an emotional mix of blood and belonging (Ignatieff, 1994) in the eye of the violator, the enemy male in nationalist conflicts symbolises a repository of 'defiance', 'a threat', or 'evil', which ought to be subjugated. The undertaking, therefore, is the unveiling of destruction/deconstruction of the culture of the enemy. Disembodying the enemy's national aspiration through damaging his body is often the supreme objective of masculine nationalism. By emasculating the body of the enemy it succeeds in emasculating the sacredness of that nationalist vision. This, in turn, initiates the destruction of elements of consciousness at the individual as well as communal level.

Given this understanding, unsurprisingly in the context of competing nationalisms, in ethno-religious conflicts the body of the male opponent or enemy serves as a canvas on which the violator etches some of his/her most graphic and scrutable messages.

Sexual violence in war is a product of regulatory schema. Conceptualisation of such violence cannot and should not be analytically separated from their wider economic, military, political, organisational, and strategic contexts. The use of sexual violence entails political effects that are different from the use of other forms of violence (Skejlsbak, 2001: 219). Examined within the political economy of nationalism sexual violence is a means to strip men of their political and nation-making assets. It is the national and political value placed on a given individual or group of individuals which often provides a permissible condition for the violator(s) to embark on those specific undertakings.

This being the reality, punishing the victim for the perpetrators' own twisted nationalistic vision, personal woe and unmitigated sexual frustration all contribute to this visceral undertaking. In such context there often exists a 'convergence between particular regimes of vision and the accompanying violence' (Virilio, 1989; McSorley, 2012). The victim is punished both collectively (for the cause of nation, nationalism and such) and individually (for personal sexual deprivation, jealousy and anger). Little wonder then with the 'narcissism of small differences' perpetually on the rise, that more and more victims are subjected to this treatment in the name of ethnicity, religion, nationalism and, above all, the nation.

4

THE TORTURER'S SOUL

Man has a thirst for evil.

Georges Bataille, *Oeuvres Complètes*, III, 1990: 42.

We have, so far, spent a considerable amount of space analysing the 'victim's' bodily and mental disposition following his exposure to this particularised form of violence. It is worth bearing in mind that such undertakings are always a collective act. It always involves two individuals, that is the victim and the violator and, at times, a collection of individuals. Given that it is a collective act the process of violation is bound to have some effect on the violator(s). It becomes imperative, therefore, to ask what does the violator as an individual feel in relation to this experience? Does the violator go through a similar transformative process, as is the case with our victim?

One does not always have the requisite tools to probe the violator's true state of mind prior to and during such violation. The objective phenomena associated with the consequential effect of forced sexual violation for the perpetrator of this act is less precise.[1] The violator rarely comes up with a confession. Moreover, since such actions are undertaken at times on the spur of the moment, are predatory, opportunistic and mostly occur in a geographical area that is far away from the violator's original place of residence, the latter simply vanishes after instituting and administering this very act.

Also, unlike his or her victim the subjective external physical manifestations of this violence are rarely present on the violator. Even in those

107

instances where the violator (let us say) was physically involved in raping his victim it is hard to acquire a coherent picture of the violator's
physical and mental condition afterwards. Yet it is imperative that we
prepare a repertoire that explains, albeit tentatively, the politics and psychology behind this undertaking.

For Walker, 'the linking up of sexuality with cruelty and humiliation,
either inflicted or suffered, is less difficult to explain than would at first
sight appear'. And, he continues to argue, 'in a mild degree, pain and suffering, whether witnessed in others or experienced in themselves, can for
many people of a neurotic temperament evoke a pleasurable psychic state'
(Walker, 1952: 127). Normally such a temperament is tamed by social
norms, but in conditions of conflict such norms do not always exist. Put
simply, our violator, on this particular occasion, is operating outside what
one might call normative constraints.[2]

We notice a similar interpretation in Georges Bataille when he reflects
on the extreme erotic impulses of us humans. According to Bataille, 'eroticism is the "extreme emotion"', which opposes the human to the animal.
The animal is ignorant of death and law:

... for an animal nothing is prohibited—thus it is driven into its sexuality by the
blind instinct of its organs. When we meditate on human beings then we realise
that we are the only *morbid animal* caged in prohibitions we refrain ourselves
from channelling our extreme impulses. But there are occasions when this refrain
is abandoned in order to seek out 'a calculus of pleasure' that instigates the individual to fulfill his extreme erotic desires that belong to the genre of sexual violence (Bataille, 1990: Vol. X, 593).

Violation of the other in one form or another, then, is a pleasurable
state of affairs that affects some individuals intensely. This form of objectification of life, in the view of some critics, is nothing but 'transgressive
sexuality'.

Furthermore, according to Bataille, 'being' increases in the tumultuous
agitation of a life that knows no limits (Bataille, 1985: 172). By borrowing
an interpretation of Susan Sontag from another context we realise that:

... sexuality remains one of the demonic forces in human consciousness—pushing us at intervals close to taboo and dangerous desires, which range from the
impulse to commit sudden arbitrary violence upon another person to the volup-
tuous yearning for the extinction of one's consciousness, for death itself ...
Everyone has felt (at least in fantasy) the erotic glamour of physical cruelty and

an erotic lure in things that are vile and repulsive. These phenomena form part of the genuine spectrum of sexuality ... (Sontag, 1994: 57).

In normal parlance one may term such desires 'depraved'. But it is very much an objective reality in some situations and contexts. As John Glenn Grey reminds us, 'men who in private life are scrupulous about conventional justice and right are able to destroy the lives and happiness of others in war without compunction' (Grey, 1970: 144). If that were so, one would not be far from the mark to suggest that an element of sadism and masochism exists in most people. While it remains controlled in normal circumstances this emotion can be unleashed during times of chaos and loss of order. According to Sontag, 'few people regularly, or perhaps ever, experience or get a chance to fulfill the full spectrum of their sexual desires' (Sontag, 1994: 57). Circumstances where the normal is absent and anarchy is the order raise in men and women dangerous desires, close to taboo.[3] If one were to 'explain the linking up of the emotion created by suffering with sexual activity' (Walker, 1952: 128), as Walker does, then some of the wartime sexual violence against men can be partly explained away in this particular framework.

True, one is never privy to the mental condition of the perpetrator when s/he undertakes his or her mission of sexual violence against the male victim. But with the psychological tools available to us one could argue that some of these undertakings may have their basis in a certain degree of personal sexual self-fulfillment. Or, worse still, it may have been undertaken to compensate for the torturer's own sexual inadequacy or character disorder. By borrowing from general psychological interpretations of such deviant behaviour (if this belongs to that genre, that is), one could argue, 'offenders in such contexts are individuals suffering from character disorders, and these consist in faulty relationships between Id, Ego and Super-Ego' (Honderich, 1984: 96).[4]

Condemning the victim to a certain sexual torture or witnessing this cruelty from a distance as a visual spectator are likely to have a demonstrative effect on the violator, leading to a form of personal fulfillment. Hence the undertaking of a clearly set-out programmatic series of transgressions of ascending severity upon the chanced enemy may actually be deeply fulfilling for the transgressor. The eyes here extract a surplus value from the spectacle of suffering (Deleuze and Guattari, 1984: 211).

While such engagement from a distance counts for one variety of fulfillment a direct participation in imparting such violence may have its basis in the fulfillment of another set of desires. In such direct involvement the violator invests his/her body for the revelation of what Bataille called 'being'.

Although a post-conflict society or a society in peacetime may view such undertakings as 'vile' and 'repulsive', upon closer scrutiny we realise that it may have been firmly anchored in a clearly defined objective framework. This transgressive sex with steady interchangeable victims, in this particular instance, can be interpreted in two explanatory frameworks. At one level it explains Bataille's interpretation of the violator's need to reach out to his 'being' (Bataille, 1985)—fulfilling a desire that was not otherwise available or denied to the violator in peacetime.

On another level it is moored in what Sontag interpreted as 'a primal demonic urge that pushes individuals to embark upon initiating actions that are taboo' (Sontag, 1994)—descending into a world of non-conformity where everything is permissible. Viewed within the personality theory of offending, these are primarily offenders whose instinctual drives for immediate gratification have not come under control (Eysenck, 1964; Honderich, 1984).

Examining it closely we are also confronted by the fact that such behavior, although unique in the annals of contemporary wartime sexual violence, nevertheless cannot be discounted as freakish or unnatural. As is explained within the framework of the 'personality theory of offending', at times 'the individual's behaviour is determined completely by his heredity and by the environmental influences which have been brought to bear upon him' (Eysenck, 1964: 177).

If this is a valid explanatory theory, then consider the practice of *Jujubi* (which is ingrained in peacetime traditional West African magic and witchcraft, that calls for such perverse undertakings), and the subscription to such a belief system by the violators could be argued to have led to such predatory transgressive behaviour. It is now well established that several rebel commanders and self-styled generals of armed groups during the civil war in Liberia (1989–2003) actively sought out young male victims to violate in order to strengthen their *Juju*, sexual and physical virility.

The pleasure principle

Conversations around the excesses of such violence in Liberia provide one set of explanations. But West African witchcraft-led, drugs-laden, predatory practices cannot be our only focus in assessing the violator's intentions and the effects of his actions on his own body and soul. We ought to broaden the discussion into what I would like to call a secular perspective.

If one were to examine various recorded events over the past few decades on violators' behaviour it would appear very often that the violator orders such violence on the enemy captives but is not directly involved in it. Evidence that has emerged from various 'camps' testify to the fact that to a large degree the active acts of rape are undertaken between enemy captives or prisoners. Interestingly, one common attitude that one encounters while interrogating the violator's behaviour is his attempt to dissociate himself from the homosexual acts between his victims. The violator, in this instance, while he forces his victims into performing homosexual acts, nonetheless likes to identify himself as a heterosexual. He would like his victims and co-violators to believe that he feels revulsion at any homosexual act.

If that were the case our violator would appear to be heterosexual and has the least interest in such activities apart from inflicting the maximum amount of pain on his victims. However, this mode of interpretation is problematic. For example is the (male) violator ordering this violation completely free of homosexual tendencies? One could argue that while at its core this undertaking may be a political project there is no denying the fact that some violators receive some personal pleasure from the violation. Apart from the obvious power dimension, the latent homosexuality of the violator needs to be put under scrutiny. Both Herbert Marcuse (1974) and Dennis Altman (1993) are in unanimity that, while the violator may argue otherwise, those individuals engaged in male-male sexual interaction directly or indirectly are simply playing it out in order to realise their own hidden unfulfilled desires. Perhaps the presence of the rank and file prevents the violator ordering such violation from engaging in homosexual acts himself. In the view of Marzena Sokolowska-Paryz, 'when putting on a uniform, men are transformed into soldiers' (Sokolowska-Paryz, 2012: 22). Direct sexual violation for obvious reasons requires the taking off of or discarding the uniform and exposing the naked body. This in turn would imply the breaking away from war (at least for the duration of the violation) and becoming one and the same with the victim.

That being the underlying imagination, many potential violators order their violations to be carried out through a third party. While the uniform prevents some violators from directly taking part in this undertaking, this does not necessarily mean the violator who gives the order from a distance is insulated from the process of violence and is unable to gain personal sexual gratification and pleasure. Although one cannot discount the power dimension in some conflict locations such undertakings may be directly linked to the violator's desire to fulfill some private fantasy. Witnesses to violence may actually be a contributing factor to their own sexual arousal. For 'men', it is argued, 'who do not commit acts of sexual aggression generally find depictions of such aggression more arousing' (Kressel, 2002: 38).

However it is imperative that we dissect and closely examine this issue of fantasy and desire from both a theoretical and philosophical perspective before we embark upon their manifestation in an empirical context. According to some critiques fantasy and desire are interrelated like two sides of the same coin. Fantasy in other words is a 'real' desire, which, because of societal prohibition, seeks an unreal, but realised enterprise (Scruton, 1983: 130). In the view of Roger Scruton:

....the subject of a fantasy really does want something. This is brought out by the fact that, in the case of sexual fantasy, the sexual experience may be pursued through the fantasy object, and attached to it by a definite onanistic activity. The subject wants something, but he wants it in the form of a substitute (1983: 130).

Therefore, one could argue, our subject, the violator, wants something (he has the desire to violate another man). Ordinarily he is not allowed to do so owing to a host of factors most important of which is the taint of homosexuality should he decide to enact it (in the knowledge of the society). Consequently, the desire that is born of sexual fantasy seeks an occasion and victims that both lie outside the societal scrutiny and protection. The loss of order and the prevailing anarchy of war provides perfect cover and opportunity to translate these private desires and fantasies into experienced realities. Such actions, in being prohibited, compel the violator to an excess bordering on the unreal. In the view of Scruton 'a fantasy often seeks to gratify itself, not in the delicately suggestive, but in the grossly obvious, or explicit' (Scruton, 1983: 129).

It is rarely talked about, but some conflict locations in our time actually became synonymous with such fantasy-led recreational violence. Returning to the topic of Liberia, again, we are faced with the fact that the civil war there spawned some of the worst male-male combat sexual excesses in our time. It was almost like characters from deviant violent comic strips stepping out into the real world with their phantasmagorical and obsessive cruelty.

Furthermore, the hapless male civilians in such situations become the substitute and immediate surrogate objects to satisfy those private deviant fantasies and desires. Hence the majority of rebel leaders who manned thousands of checkpoints across this fractured country routinely subjected the male passers-by to strip naked and pretend to have sexual intercourse with the bare ground. At other times these militias often forced their male captives at gunpoint to engage in sexual intercourse with their mothers, sisters and daughters.

There were several underlying motives (refusal to co-operate with the armed factions, hesitancy when asked to take part in the fighting and so on). However, by and large, if one were to believe the confessions of the former rebel commanders and foot soldiers now dotting the visual media (*Youtube* and so on) such undertakings were primarily executed by the perpetrators in order to realise their private fantasies and receive some private gratification in the process.

Habitual aggression—a matter of faith

I have, so far, outlined facets of male-male sexual violence, which were primarily occasional. On most of those occasions both the violator and the violated found themselves at a critical juncture, which somehow triggered an occasion for those particularised forms of violence. While it was played out against the background and backdrop of a mutual hatred towards each other, the more powerful of the two participants dictated the nature of their interaction. Following the actual occurrence of that violence, however, both tried to escape from that given episode—either through self-censorship or non-admittance of the event. And for the external observer, to a large extent, the whole episode remained overwhelmingly ambiguous due to the lack of engagement with the event either by the violator or the violated or, in some instances, by both.

While the above is generally the case we are also faced with a scenario where the aggressor not only celebrates his involvement in the violence of the past but also openly declares his intention to engage in such acts in future. How is one to comprehend this behaviour, which does not fit the norm? The answer may lie somewhere in a repertoire of psychological, cultural and, above all, historical explanations.

There is no document of civilisation which is not at the same time a document of barbarism (Benjamin, 1986). Yet, for Freud, civilisation is built on the renunciation of powerful sexual/carnal drives—while the individual or group life is geared towards the satisfaction of instinctual desires, the social situation and surroundings (which Freud calls 'reality') prevents engagment in those practices that can offer those satisfactions (Freud, 1930). The world that the individual or the group inhabits does not allow or puts restrictions on the fulfillment of those desires for two interrelated reasons. First, any individual or group mediated effort to achieve those desires can lead to social tension. Second, satisfaction of unlimited aggressive sexuality is likely to lead to substantial destruction of the society. Put simply, for Freud, the society that the individual inhabits restricts individual desires and drives that seek sexual satisfaction in various forms. And in the process it denies its members what they really want (Freud, 1930: 278).

What happens when individuals are taught this form of social control? Does it eliminate their desire(s)? Do individuals find other ways of fulfilling those instinctual satisfactions? Or do individuals and society at large over time find themselves in an evolutionary progression where the need for fulfilling those satisfaction(s) becomes redundant?

Freud does not propose that this framework of self and societal censorship is a permanent condition. Or, to put it differently, there is no evidence to suggest that having learned to control their deviant desires individuals eventually succeed in getting rid of those wishes. For Freud, there is no escaping the pervasiveness of individual desire to achieve those satisfactions. Limited by social mores and forms of social control the individuals merely build a particular reality or 'civilisation'; escape to, or take refuge in, a fantasy world; or end up learning to control their desires (Freud, 1930: 278).

If, for Freud, it is the civilisational impulses and social control that prevents individuals from engaging in private spheres of public violence, for Norbert Elias 'it is the state that is the ultimate machinery of control when it comes to civilizing individual impulses of violence'. The phrase that sums up Elias's theory in a nutshell is 'social constraint towards self constraint' (Elias, 2000: 365–79). The 'civilizing process' of the state, as Elias called it, is made possible when the organs of the polity enter into a perpetual political control that inculcates the behaviour of a habitual self-control over the violent impulses of individuals. In addition, for

Elias, since forms of personal, group or societal violence are delegitimised by the state and looked down upon by the society at large these constituencies enter into a form of habitual self-constraint over impulsive action. In addition, such self-constraints are also made possible with the emergence and advancement of the 'threshold of shame and embarrassment' (Elias, 2000).

Forms of social prohibition and individual censorship against seeking out particularised forms of desire and their fulfillment, however, lose their controlling power during extreme social conditions. The chaos-ridden society is less conscious of individual duties and the societal proscriptions. A society undergoing severe upheavals—owing to the prevailing chaos—may provide a window of opportunity to individuals to engage in and fulfill the desires and satisfactions that were otherwise proscribed.[5]

An example of this excess and abandonment of inhibition is the practice of cannibalism. As is generally understood, cannibalism seems to 'contradict common moral and ethnical beliefs on what is acceptable in conflict and war scenarios and what is not' (Weierstall, 2013). During the First Liberian civil war (1989–1996) many rival gangs did not only engage in the indiscriminate rape of boys and men from the opposite side but went a step further and openly practised what can be described as ritualised sexual cannibalism.

The unfortunate male opponent when caught or captured had to part with his genitals. Having chopped off the genitals from the living body of the victim his captors then either kept them as a talisman or at times devoured them in the belief that by procuring the genitals of the enemy they were indeed receiving their power. This newfound power they believed would allow them victory on the frontlines of combat and remove any battle-related obstacles that lay ahead.

General Rambo, one of the countless warlords that the conflict spawned did not have any qualms about boasting of such deeds. As a self-confessed cannibal he proclaimed, 'I was an ambassador of war,' and the cannibalising of male genitals of the opponent was simply another undertaking in his war effort.

Joshua Milton Blahyi aka General Butt Naked, (in)famous for his antics on the battlefront where he usually went charging at his enemies stark naked, was a step ahead of General Rambo in terms of insane ruthlessness. The self-styled General and his militias, called the Butt Naked Brigade, not only devoured the enemy's severed genitals but also drank the victims' blood. This ritualised cannibalism was alleged to have given Milton Blahyi and his militias 'special powers', made them 'invisible' on the battlefront and rendered their bodies 'bulletproof' against enemy arsenals (Ellis, 2007).

While such practices may appear to be excesses in the chaos surrounding civil wars, riots, communal clashes and inter-group skirmishes with ethno-religious overtones, they often provide an easy outlet and, at times, an 'ideological excuse for the participants to engage in extreme sexual violence against their victims' (Brownmiller, 1975: 114). As an appendage one could also argue that the loss of temporary social control precipitated by these conflict situations induced these violators to lower the guard of self-censorship that was in place throughout their membership of the society.

If the individual and the society are to be described as actors then both are participating in transitory mutual co-acting. It is a collective. As a collective during this prevailing chaos they are less conscious of their original duties and obligations, and engage in a mutual acceptance of each other's temporary failings. As soon as the overall chaos that had gripped the society subsides it becomes conscious of its proscriptions. Hence we have the likes of General Butt Naked, who has become a penitent former warlord and evangelist in the aftermath of the civil war in Liberia and who openly admitted his failings on camera.[6] A perpetrator of such crimes repenting for his crimes openly, of course, is an extremely rare event.

The barbarity and horrors of the Liberian civil war cannot be dismissed as freak incidents with tribal overtones as some would like us to believe. Notwithstanding the private confession of a penitent warlord we ought to remember that the permissive condition that facilitates particularised forms of sexual acts and sexual violence against a given group (which would otherwise be proscribed) is not limited to some specific conflicts. Surprising as it may seem, some sophisticated societies with a long history of the rule of law and democracy can be found to be equally complicit when it comes to such ritualised violence. This is particularly so in the case of India where such atrocities find their ample manifestation during Hindu-Muslim communal violence (often described as riots) in India.[7]

The psychodynamics of radical Hindu sexuality towards Muslim men is such that even when there is no actual engagement in such violence and violation, the former constantly engages in an everyday linguistic violence against the latter. To paraphrase Seltzer's analysis of serial kill-ing (Seltzer, 1998: 1) and use it in this particular context, 'there is almost a deep felt need to violate the enemy "other" on a constant basis which is almost addictive where private desires and public fantasy cross'. Hence we have the constant use of verbal imagery of such violence, the public approval and fascination with it, and its actualisation whenever there is a window of opportunity.

The marking of this particular constituency as 'legitimate violated sub-jects/bodies' as we shall see in the following paragraphs serves a symbolic as well as psychological purpose. Here complex socio-religious differences are reduced to simple physiological variations. In the Bourdieuan sense the symbolic violence in such communal contexts is 'censored but euphe-mized' it is a form violence that is very much part of daily hegemonic practice, but of 'disguised and transfigured' form (Bourdieu, 1977: 171).

In the worldview of radical Hindus the Muslims inhabit a distinct sex-ual-spatial identity. The way the male Muslim's sexual body is organised affects the perception of its rival Hindu counterpart. It projects a per-verse and excessive sexuality onto its Muslim 'Others' (Gopinath, 2006: 135). The male Muslim body (owing to circumcision) is not analogous to that of the body of the Hindu. Within this radical rhetoric 'the coun-terpart to the chaste Hindu male is the Muslim male polygamist or rap-ist'. In a spatial imagination of the purity and distinctiveness of the land of Hindus these male Muslim bodies are regarded as an affront.[8] Therefore when defining the Muslim male as *kattu* or *landya* (circumcised pricks) the attributor is not using derogatory and offensive language in the every-day sense of the term but declaring the alienness of the possessor of this male masculinity (Hindus do not engage in ritual circumcision of the male or female bodies).[9]

The second psychological/symbolic aspect of this repertoire of violence is much more complex. While our anti-Muslim radical Hindu is certain of the externality of the male Muslim body, he also harbours a deep-seated inferiority complex in relation to the circumcised organ of the Muslim. Thanks to more than one thousand years of Islamic rule he is in possession of the knowledge that plenty of Muslims violated Hindu women during their conquest of the subcontinent. For the radical Hindu, at a subliminal level, that conquest and violation by the Muslim men of Hindu women is representation of the latter's sexual prowess.

In the contemporary context, for the radical Hindu, a Muslim is still a sexual threat. Although he (the male Muslim) may not be in possession of actual power and authority to control the Hindus he nonetheless is in possession of a distinct sexual power. Just like the Fanonian interpretation of the non-black/white reductionist view of the male black/ negro to his penis (Fanon, 1967), the radical Hindu identifies his male Muslim counterpart with this particular faculty. The circumcised organ of the Muslim, therefore, is a menace to Hindu masculinity and pride. The possessor of this sexuality needs to be vanquished. If one could bring about the fall of this enemy by attacking his primary sexual identity (circumcised penis) all the better.

During Hindu-Muslim communal riots prior to targeting their victim, Hindu radicals ritually defame the Muslim in custody. In most instances it involves asking the victim to display his circumcised penis and then douse kerosene on him or chop his penis off. While putting the victim through such ritual sexual violation his aggressors are not going in to the details of examining the culture that he belongs to, the civilisation that he represents or his inherited history; for, in most instances, the violators share the same racial, cultural and civilisational attributes that our victim possesses. The entire exercise, however, surrounds his slight physical difference—presence or absence of the penile foreskin.[10]

Evaluating these actions in a Freudian psychoanalytical conception one may like to argue our aggressor while condemning our victim to these particularised forms of violence was letting out his repressed desire. As I highlighted earlier, for Freud, civilisation legislates which sexual behaviours are permitted—the perverse is forbidden. But during social chaos, as is found in times of communal riots, these controls are less severe, allowing our aggressor or violator to engage in the forbidden. Hence the theory that these acts could very well be homosexual rituals when men in groups desire each other, yet are ashamed of their urges, and so they satisfy themselves by convening at a common target (Rosenblatt, 1983: 64).

In any event, the violence that is meted out to our victim during these communal riots is as much communal as sexual. The radical Hindu in such instances would perhaps actually like to engage in sexually violating his victim but is constrained by some remaining iota of social control that we discussed earlier and ends up ritually humiliating his victim while always keeping himself at a safe distance. Equally importantly given that such sexual violations are public spectacles and therefore likely to become a part of indelible public memory, the violator feels restrained from engaging in his private desires of sodomy and so on.

While for Norbert Elias the shame of being observed while committing a crime or act of violence that society does not approve of can dissuade that individual or group from enacting that particular act, in some other contexts a feeling of inferiority or private shame about one's own identity can push the protagonist to commit proscribed violence (Elias, 2000).

Alongside our actual aggressors are another group who would have liked to participate in those particular orgies of violence but did not have the opportunities to engage in them for various reasons—such as distance from the location of violence, fear of direct participation and so on. While not direct participants, this group nonetheless valorises such undertakings and feels that he is a part of the collective that achieved this (gory) feat. It is almost like a repressed longing finding an outlet at a distance. These secondary violators play an instrumental role in legitimising such undertakings. And by doing so, they succeed in giving expression to a hitherto unmet desire.

Note, for instance, the pamphlet that members of the Hindu extremist *Bajrang Dal* distributed following the anti-Muslim riots in Gujarat in 2002.

Narendra Modi you have fucked the mother of *miyas*. The volcano that was inactive for years has erupted. It has burnt the arse of *miyas* and made them dance nude

(quoted in Fernandes, 2006: 282).

The content of this celebratory pamphlet has several different levels of detail. It is apt, therefore, that we dissect it. The protagonist Narendra Modi was the chief minister of the province of Gujarat, India in 2002 when Muslims were subjected to indescribable violence. More than one thousand Muslim men, women and children were violently murdered of which many were ritually violated. By overseeing this carnage against Muslims Modi's government, in effect, was giving vent to the collective radical Hindu craving to violate the Muslims.[11]

The reference to 'volcano' has a double entendre here. While on the one hand it may simply refer to the upsurge of Hindu bottled-up anger against Muslims, on the other, 'eruption of volcano' has a strong sexual symbolism referring to the prowess of Hindu masculinity. The association of erupted volcano and burning of Muslim 'arse' is quite simply the reference to Hindus using their hitherto powerless organ to sodomise the Muslims. And the last part of the victory song 'made them dance nude' could be argued to mean committing Muslims to a state of extreme fear of violation which has sent them helter skelter.

Whatever ambivalence (linguistic or otherwise) might have been there in framing the radical Hindu psyche in the earlier passage is abandoned completely in the next couplet. Note the explicit expression of predatory sexual undertaking against the Muslims.

We have untied the penises, which were tied till now without castor oil in the arse we have made them [*miyas*] cry.

(quoted in Fernandes, 2006: 282).

The declaration above is as much a self-admission of a new sexual revolution taking place among the Bajrang Dal cadres as it is a desire to penetrate and sexually violate the Muslim male. While the language of the second stanza is abominable it is nonetheless crucial in terms of its return to a hitherto absent overall objective. It is an unequivocal and unambiguous admission on the part of the radical Hindu constituency to have engaged in acts of male-male sexual violence. It is admitting to the fact that it has used its sexual power to penetrate the Muslim male literally, symbolically and metaphorically in the crudest possible manner. And in the process contributed to, and left behind, a painful agonising experience to its victims.

While that is so, there is no denying the fact that the statement under scrutiny has also layers upon layers of meaning. While predatory sexual violence is the overall narrative, at another level the underlying reference here is about the escape from the conventional social mores or social control that the civilisation (as Freud would term it) has put in place. The riot, then, is the context, which at once made possible the venting of radical Hindu anger, facilitated sexual violation of the enemy by its male members, and much more importantly, liberated our protagonists from the shackles of civilisation.

If that is so, the riot doubles up as an event (to subvert and control the Muslims) and an occasion in the sense that it allows those radical Hindus partaking in it to engage in and fulfill their own private homoerotic violent desire(s). The central figure or protagonist here is the Hindu phallus. In the Lacanian framework it (the phallus) is the 'signifier'. Here the signifier, has 'an active function in determining certain effects in which the signifiable appears as submitting to its mark by becoming through that passion the signified' (Lacan, 1958: 284).

THE TORTURER'S SOUL

Reflecting on the previously quoted hate pamphlet some observers have argued that its contents were not only an incitement to sexual violence but were also 'suffused with anxiety about Muslim male sexuality' (Nussbaum, 2007: 187). Furthermore, for some critics, this evident preoccupation with sexual organs reveals a 'dark sexual obsession about allegedly ultra-virile Muslim male bodies that inspire and sustain the figures of paranoia and revenge' (Tanika Sarkar, member of the *Concerned Citizens' Tribunal* that investigated the events following the Gujarat riot, quoted in Nussbaum, 2007: 187).

Female as the male double

It is not only during communal flare-ups or civil strife that he seeks ways to violate his opponent's organ; it remains a permanent fixture of his daily existence, even during times of peace. In the absence of actual avenues (such as riots) to subvert and control the male Muslim sexuality his adversary(ies) fall into a form of everyday linguistic sexual violence.

Every conversation he has that in some way involves Muslims is suffused with a rich vocabulary of abuses and punishment methods that he would like the Muslim to go through. As always the choice of terms to describe the Muslims and the ways of dealing with them revolves around their penises and anuses. Here is a sample of those linguistic aggressions:

Kattu (the circumcised one); *Kattu ki aulaad* (son of the circumcised) *Kattu ki gaand maar do* (fuck the circumcised in the arse); *landya* (the circumcised pricks).

While such derogatory, obscene and offensive remarks may exist in all cultures where two antagonistic groups might use such language of subversion to intimidate the enemy, on closer inspection one is likely to recognise some disturbing undertones. While mapping this behaviour we notice a sentiment and desire that is at once punitive as well as sexually self-satisfying. Our radical Hindu male, if he had his way, would go about violating his Muslim counterpart at every available opportunity. What is the source of this obsession? What sustains this line of craving? A more relaxed interpretation of such behaviour would suggest that 'these are situations where men in order to prove their masculinity to one another will do anything' (Rosenblatt, 1983: 64), including engage in the previously described egregious violence. It is the absence of opportunity that forces him to engage in linguistic violence as a default position. This is, indeed, a common practice among individuals fired up by visions of a particular kind of violence. To paraphrase Žižek, it is the use of such language itself which pushes the violators' 'desire beyond proper limits transforming it into a "desire that contains the infinite" elevating it into an absolute striving that cannot ever be satisfied' (Žižek, 2008: 55).

There is no escaping the fact that Hindu radicals in India deploy sexual and gender ideologies that harness sexuality to the propagation of the community/group/nation (Gopinath, 2006: 136). Why so? A deeper analysis of this behaviour needs to be culturally specific and historically anchored if we are to understand with precision the basis of that psyche. To this constituency theirs is a repressed history of gendered and sexualised violence. Radical Hindu perception of their past is punctuated by a vision of continuous subjugation, intimidation, humiliation and, above all, sexual violation at the hands of their Muslim rulers and rivals. To make matters worse the Hindus, although numerically powerful, could do nothing to prevent this millennia-long control. Aided by an institutional political authority Muslim male sexuality became synonymous with wanton rape, abduction, easy procurement of women, ability to hold harems and so on.[12]

When a people or a group with memories of such inscrutable and very ancient animosities at the hands of powerful, aggressively masculine enemies finally assumes power, it tries to find ways to repeat their experience on their erstwhile enemy.[13] In such situations distant historical events become psychologically relevant and meaningful for their specific enterprise (Kressel, 2002: 18). In the view of some critics people with such an outlook invariably seek a counterculture of masculinity that emulates the perceived hardness of the aggressor of the past (Nussbaum, 2007: 1996).

In the context of sexual vengeance this is most conclusively demonstrated in the case of Russian sexual violation of German men and women following the Allied victory over Nazi Germany at the end of the Second World War (Brownmiller, 1975: 77). For Nussbaum, when there exists 'a prolonged sense of helplessness and humiliation as the result of real political events (to some extent also heightened and reconstructed by fantasy) self-hatred can easily turn outward' (Nussbaum, 2007: 189). Compared to the sexuality of male Muslims, Hindus often felt impotent, inadequate and in some ways helpless. In this narrative the actual sexual identity marker that divided the two was the absence of foreskin in the male Muslim and its presence in his Hindu counterpart. Thus he built up a sexual schizophrenia against his adversary and *kattu*, a subversive and underground term to describe his powerful double, became assumed as a common currency.

The rape of the circumcised phallus

In their everyday discourse, the radical Hindus rarely depart from their discussion about the sexual appetite of the Muslim man and the prowess of his genitalia.

He is extra virile as he contains a hyper amount of seeds of fecundity, as exemplified in Muslims having a larger number of children than their Hindu counterparts. Above all he is hypersexual, for he can legally possess up to four women. Seen alongside the Hindu organ the Muslim penis is not only much more powerful but it is also a threat to Hindu masculinity. It is a challenge: it can subvert the Hindu social fabric.[14]

In sum, the circumcised male Muslim sex organ feeds into radical Hindu male insecurity. Control over male Muslim sexuality would seem to lead to control over Muslims as a whole. Thus our protagonist is constantly pursued by the thought of subjugating that symbol of Muslim masculine strength: for the control of that organ leads to his own empowerment, which has so far been eluding him. However our would-be violator is prevented from enacting such acts by some fundamental constraints. Moral traditions and cultural taboos discourage such undertakings (Thornhill & Palmer, 2000: 173). Yet, as Freud suggests, those harbouring such insecurities are not fully able to control those impulses. Such repressed ideas are dynamic in the sense that they are forced into the unconscious, and because they have a motivating effect on human actions (Freud, 1930). These desires have to manifest in one way or another. Therefore, in the melee of communal riots such undertakings find a receptive audience and people are freed of the taboos that have restricted them so far. This endeavour is also facilitated by the fact that the society they belong to lowers its prohibitions and subtly condones such acts when the potential targets are members of the enemy group (Murphey, 1992: 21).

However, in such contexts in the absence of having the opportunity or the occasion to violate the male Muslim bodies directly (for various reasons) the radical Hindu uses the body of the Muslim female as a surrogate for his own personalised male-male sexual violence. In a psychosexual concoction that combines ego, unconscious, desire, sexual inadequacy and anger, the Muslim female vagina mirrors the male Muslim circumcised penis.

Since the (Muslim woman's) body only receives the circumcised Muslim penis, it is a repository of Muslim male sexuality. In such a context the body of a Muslim woman serves as a legitimate proxy for a Muslim man. The penetration of the Muslim woman's vagina by an uncircumcised Hindu penis therefore introduces a whole new narrative of power and punishment. It is both a causal and retaliatory sexual violence. It is a form of violence where men of one particular religious group get even with men of another religion 'through the convenient vehicle of a woman's body' (Brownmiller, 1975: 13).

By sexually violating the Muslim woman the radical Hindu male is taking possession of the domain of the circumcised male Muslim penis. This violence is a literal and metaphorical displacement of the Muslim male. By penetrating the Muslim woman with an uncircumcised organ he is pronouncing the superiority of his own sexuality over his adversary and releasing all the anxiety and frustration that he has been nursing against the Muslim circumcised organ.

This form of behaviour fits in neatly with the explanations of some social theorists that such sexual acts are 'not concerned with sexual gratification but with the deployment of the penis as a concrete symbol of masculine social power' (Sanday, 1990: 10). Moreover, as Ruth Seifert argues 'rape is not an aggressive expression of sexuality, but a sexual expression of aggression... a manifestation of anger, violence and domination ...' (Seifert, 1996: 37). Hence it is not sexual gratification the violator is after but his undertaking is an exercise in establishing his superior masculine identity.[15]

Aside from this milieu of empowerment at another level, the setting also creates a situation in which the enemy (Muslim men) are relegated to a context where they are labelled as incapable of proving their manhood in protecting their women (Salzman, 1998: 365). Rape of enemy women, therefore, symbolically demonstrates victory over enemy men, who have failed in this task (van Creveld, 2001: 34–7). At a communal level such violence informs the community that their protectors (the male members) are unable to protect themselves. And, if they are unable to protect themselves, how are they to protect 'their' women, and their community? (Sivakumaran, 2007: 269). Furthermore, for some other critics, such 'public endorsement of sexual victimisation means public defeat of the honour of the men: the loss of their public, status-focused face; the public admission of the loss of their bloodline; and the loss of their identity soil/nation' (Olijic, 1998: 190).

The takeover and occupation of the Muslim woman's body by male Hindus is often a brutal affair. These are often atrocities of a quasi-ritualistic nature centred on the femininity of the body: cutting off the breasts, slashing the body open with sword and introduction of nonporous metal and wooden objects into the vagina.[16] Although direct violation of the woman in communal conflict situations is the norm, there are times when the violator considers it below his dignity to penetrate his uncircumcised organ in her vagina or anus. In the radical Hindu nationalist imagination there exists a clear binary distinction between Hindu women and Muslim women. Their identity is placed in two diametrically opposite worlds: moral purity versus sexual impurity; legitimate versus illegitimate; the private versus the public and so on. In sum, while Hindu women represent sexual purity and sanctity, their Muslim counterparts are considered impure and prostitutes (Gopinath, 2006: 135). Consequently for our protagonist direct body-to-body violation or penetration of a woman that occupies such a lower status is a disgusting prospect: he does not want to 'dirty his penis with the contaminating fluids of the Muslim woman' (Nussbaum, 2007: 209). Given this understanding physical sexual intercourse, therefore, is replaced by artificial penetration.

Similarly, the 'mollification aspect' (Brownmiller, 1975: 97) that suggests the rioting mob or company of soldiers needing/requiring the woman's body out of some intrinsic male sexual urge is occasionally lost when a radical Hindu approaches his would-be female Muslim victim. The consummate hatred that he has been harbouring against the Muslim circumcised organ, however, takes another form of violation of the Muslim woman. Since she is the repository of bearing future generations of circumcised Muslim males she needs to be annihilated.[17] 'Fucking a Muslim woman,' therefore, just means killing her. Instead of murder necessitated by and following sex, 'the murder just *is* the sex' (Nussbaum, 2007: 219).

From former Yugoslavia to Rwanda and Central African Republic to India, wherever these horrific violations took place these undertakings were often carried out by people or mobs who were known to their victims.

Examined closely, such radical deviant behaviour would appear to militate against the age-old injunction, a code of honour, which proscribes public sexual violence against people known to the violator. If anonymity between the violator and the victim is a fundamental factor in introducing such violence—for an anonymous victim can be stripped of his/her humanity easier than a known one—(Brownmiller, 1975: 88) on most of the occasions when Muslims are targeted for such violence their perpetrators are often known to them—they often belong to the same neighbourhood (Mehta, 2005).

The religiously inspired sexual violence against Muslim boys and men in such conflict settings is not specific to India alone. In some other theatres of conflict the ugliness of such enterprises were far more open and vicious. That for the perpetrators of such violence the sexual/reproductive organ of the Muslim male is a threat to the supremacy of the group or community that opposes it, was blatantly felt in the conflict in the former Yugoslavia.

Radical Serbs consistently made the Bosnian male genitalia their target of direct attack. In the view of some critics, 'here the central desire was to humiliate Muslims. To this end, they were equally wiling to treat male bodies as objects—cutting and mutilating them for sport' (Kressel, 2002: 39).

At a deeper psychological level, the Serb militia that forced its Muslim captives to undergo this excruciating horror harboured a deep sense of inferiority that was linked to its adversaries' fecundity. Just like the Hindu mob that associated Muslim fecundity with their male genitalia, the Serb militias felt the only way to undermine the Muslim identity at a symbolic as well as practical level was to degrade this instrument of propagation and procreation. While they liberally engaged in chopping off Bosnian Muslim male prisoners' testicles they also went about instituting the highest possible ways of self-abuse between the prisoners. According to one Bosnian Muslim prisoner:

I saw how Muslims were forced to bite each other's testicles off, their mouth filled with testicles and blood, ripped blood vessels sticking out of their mouths. Daily Serb torturers forced Muslim prisoners to (expletive) each other, to perform oral sex on each other, forcing these bestialities especially among family members, between a father and son. (Application of the Convention on the Prevention and Punishment of the Crime of Genocide, Bosnia and Herzegovina v. Yugoslavia [Serbia and Montenegro]). Oral Proceedings of Bosnia and Herzegovina (CR 2006/06) 51; also see Lewis, 2009: 13.)

These two narratives from India and Bosnia are united further if we make an overall assessment of the strategic outcome for the violator.

Essentially both are political projects that have several attendant objectives built into them. First, such acts force the Muslims to flee from one area to another following their witness to the horror inflicted upon some member of their community. Second, it exacerbates the demoralisation process that was already in place for being a minority surrounded by an aggressive majority. Third, it breaks up the community spirit of the victim group by forcing them to enter into forms of role reversal or partly abandon their outward identity markers. Fourth, it inflicts long-term psychological damage to the group spirit. Fifth, it consolidates the power of the perpetrator both in the medium and the long term (Bernard, 1994: 35–9; Skjelsbæk, 2001: 223).

The destruction of the self

Conversations around the excesses of such violence in ethno-religious conflicts provide overwhelming explanations surrounding power and vengeance. But there is one particular form of violence in such contexts that is harder to explain. This is forced incest between members of the victim community. As we discussed in relation to Rwanda and India, in inter-ethnic and inter-religious conflicts there are often instances of forced violation of one male member by another from the same group or within the family (Taylor, 2002: 169).

What is crucial is the motivational forces behind such indirect violation. Why our aggressor may force his captives to undergo forms of intra-family or intra-group sexual violation is complex. Such undertakings give substance to all sorts of symbolic and metaphorical explanations. One's initial reaction to such events is to put it in the category of deep psychological deviation. Yet, as we do not have any explanatory confessions of the aggressor behaviour we can propose some tentative assessments.

At the heart of this undertaking was a form of power play. In the first place, one could argue, apart from deriving some form of personal deviational pleasure through his actions the aggressor was condemning his victim to a form of moral failing from which he was unlikely ever to recover.

Very often such undertakings are ideologically driven. Through these actions the aggressors give meaning to various culturally held beliefs, which have political implications. Forcing your victims to perform sexual violation on each other relates to committing these individuals to a concentric circle of violence that symbolically expunges them from the national narrative. According to some critics such references exhibit 'the image of misdirected flow; for incest causes blood and semen to flow backward upon one another in a closed circuit of the family rather than in an open circuit between families' (Taylor, 2002: 169). The metaphor for forced incest here is in fact a call for an end to the regeneration of that family and its communal identity. It is also a proclamation declaring the illegitimacy of the victims' being and an invitation to withdraw from any claims or share in the nation.

Moreover, the victims' fate is forever anxiety-provoking for their community at large. These very actions, this act of defilement of one member of the community by another weighs heavily on the community conscience. Such actions with heavy moral implications impose a death-like experience on the collective.

For the group or the enemy who ordered this violation and oversaw it, the above outcomes were the very objective s/he was hoping to introduce into the community to which our conscience-stricken forced violator belonged. It had to be done in that particular manner in order to accrue the highest possible strategic gain. Objectively viewed, it is a form of strategic cultural cleansing of the most horrifying proportion. By enacting this particular form of violation the aggressor succeeds in not only destroying the families of his victim but also destroying the ethno-cultural and religious community of the enemy.

Brotherhood of guilt

Every violence is the culmination of a decision making process. Often times it is an individual who is in charge of this process. If that individual is found to be engaged in a specific form of violence that decision would appear to have had its roots in one or several factors. This decision to impose a specific violence may be conditioned by obedience to an extremist leadership, conformity to spurious values, ethnocentrism, stereotyping, prejudice, dogmatism, and intolerance towards the other and so on. But can one not imagine a scenario where the individual who is forced by the events to carry forward an order decides to revolt against the prevailing condition. What if he is weak in his resolve to undertake certain violence against the 'Other'? What if he refuses to be party to the mob violence? What if he is a conscientious objector to such violence?

Surprising, as it may seem, from the genocidal plains of Bosnia to the killing fields of Sierra Leone and riot-hit city of Surat in Gujarat to the prison camp of Abu Ghraib in Iraq we had rare voices from among the rank and file of violators who were repugnant of these undertakings. These were individuals who were either opposed to these evil missions or were forced to be a part of this decision making process. Our assessment of violator behaviour or psyche would remain incomplete if we did not examine the actions of these conscientious objectors.

As we are aware, not all US soldiers in Abu Ghraib were enthusiastic cheerleaders for the sexual violation of Iraqi captives. Many Liberian and Sierra Leonean foot soldiers have confessed to the fact that they were often forced by their commander to impose a specific category of violence upon their enemy against their own wishes. However the larger questions remain: Why did the group, commander or militia leader force them to be a part of these undertakings? What was the politics behind it?

The aggressor who forces those from among the rank and file to undertake or witness this violation is basically interested in enforcing a sense of guilt that he himself carries around. His prime objective in forcing his fellow members to participate in this enterprise of horror and the macabre is to enforce on them a sense of common and collective complicity. For he or the group he belongs to is aware of the fact that he (they) are conducting something that is criminal and therefore they wish everyone of their compatriots to share this burden of crime. Although the crime may have had its basis in an individual urge or desire that particular individual nonetheless wants to hang the responsibility of guilt around the neck of the collective. Clearly the instigator or initiators of this crime do not want one of their members to go around with a clean and clear conscience while the former finds accused of a moral as well as professional lapse in conduct.

In some other contexts forcing the conscientious objector to do something which the violator has done serves as a kind of rite of passage. Combat worthiness requires the mob, militias, and the soldiers to embrace a definite set of values that demands the display of a 'warrior masculinity'. It is the contingency of structure and demands placed by the immediate environment that give rise to and foster a certain deviant behaviour.

Reluctant or involuntary, once forced into this collective act of violation our violator foregoes any right to absolving himself/herself of moral or any other form of guilt. Thus from the aggressors' perspective such a group act of violation against the enemy is a necessary condition, for it not only establishes uniformity among the group but establishes a 'brotherhood of guilt'—moral, criminal and otherwise—from which there is little or no escape in future.

This sort of group initiation into a crime whose sole purpose was to force the reluctant violator into a sense of perpetual guilt was very much a part of the Serb militia group the White Eagles, known for its excesses of sexual violence against both sexes in the Yugoslav civil war. For some critics:

White Eagles made rape a gesture of group solidarity. A man who refused to join the others in rape was regarded as a traitor to the unit, and to his Serbian blood. Sometimes that impulse to bond with the male group became a kind of perverse inflaming energy inciting to rape. Lust is only a subsidiary drive. And sometimes, young men in war may commit rape in order to please their elders, their officers, and win a sort of father-to-son approval. The rape is proof of commitment to the unit's friendliness. A young man willing to do hideous things has subordinated his individual conscience in order to fuse with the uncompromising purpose of the group. A man seals his allegiance in atrocity (Morrow, 1993: 50, quoted in Diken and Laustsen, 2005: 124).

Once a part of this gory rite, our individual militia or soldier is forever trapped in a sense of guilt and shame the moment he appears beyond the perimeters of this community to which he has become a part of through his acts of violation. It is this knowledge of personal individual guilt which keeps the violator glued to the infamy of the group and he is unable to free himself either from his actions or the group to which he has become a member through his action. Following the end of Bosnian civil war Borislav Herak, a twenty-one-year old Bosnian Serb foot soldier who fought with the Army of Republika Srpska (VRS), was found guilty of thirty-two Counts of murder and sixteen counts of rape. In his confession he stressed the fact that 'he hated the raping and killing but claimed to have done it only out of peer pressure and fear' (Rodriguez, 1993).

True, the pressure to conform often pulls some of these characters the wrong way (Glover, 1999: 59). Citing the above example one could also describe 'peer pressure, authority and modeling as examples of the way in which the violent behaviour of individuals may be created, conditioned and consolidated' (Jacoby, 2008: 86). Yet it would be erroneous to argue that there were no conscientious objectors to such undertakings who refused to be a part of this orgy. What happens if a would-be violator rejects the demands placed upon him by the group? What if he decided to follow his own moral code rather than the order of his comrades or superiors? Was the violator not in possession of his free will: the will to choose rather than do something decided by others? Since such activity fell outside the laws of war, our violator could have said 'No' to this forced undertaking.

This is a question that Herbert C. Kelman and V. Lee Hamilton in their seminal work *Crimes of Obedience: Toward a Social Psychology of Authority and Responsibility* asked:

What do you think *most* people would do if they were soldiers in Vietnam and were ordered by their superior officers to shoot all inhabitants of a village suspected of aiding the enemy, including old men, women and children?...What do *you* think you would do in this situation—follow orders and shoot them, or refuse to shoot them? (Kelman & Hamilton, 1989: 172–73)

In Oliver Stone's 1986 Hollywood blockbuster *Platoon* one of the central characters Chris Taylor (Charlie Sheen) opts out from a killing spree of his captive Vietnamese civilians. He displays a breakthrough of conscience in the face of the utmost horror. This refusal to kill is an act of direct disobedience to his commander's orders. At a time and in a climate where killing your enemy or being killed was the norm, such refusal to participate and carry out this order was deeply troubling indeed for Taylor's fellow soldiers.

True, 'in war the moral resources—respect, sympathy and the sense of moral identity—are often neutralized, but even when they still exist, the trap of war can make them largely ineffective' (Glover, 1999: 156). This view is reinforced in the arguments of psychologist Susan Opotow who suggests that such events as war create conditions for moral exclusion. Once in this frame of mind the violator 'rationalises and excuses harm inflicted on those outside the scope of justice. Excluding others from the scope of justice means viewing them as unworthy of fairness, resources, or sacrifice, and seeing them as expendable, undeserving, exploitable and irrelevant' (Opotow, 2001: 156). For individual combatants these are occasions for expelling oneself from one's morality.

Yet, we see states of exception where private morality supersedes institutional orders of conformity. On these occasions we see individuals who instead of expelling that private morality are in fact wearing it externally for all to see. What Taylor was doing in the cinematic rendition of wartime lethal violence and atrocity was digging deep into his own well of morality. He was entering into a self-sanction against the institutionally sponsored culture of mindless violence. He was refraining from behaving in ways that violated his own private moral standards. He was at once able to see the dividing line between conserving his own morality and the loss of it. He was afraid/concerned that such impulsive behaviour or decisions (such as the violators were taking) taken in the thick of war would impact on his own self later on. For if he did as his comrades-in-arms did he would consign himself to a state of perpetual self-condemnation until the very end of his own life or physical self.[18]

Albeit rare, fortunately cases of conscientious objectors against such indiscriminate use of violence are not limited to Vietnam alone. In the civil war in the former Yugoslavia we have instances where Serb fighters refused to obey their commander's order to rape enemy civilian men and women. Sadly their refusal to consent to their superiors' demands often resulted in their execution at the hands of their fellow soldiers (Kressel, 2002: 17).

Moral disengagement or death of morality?

The craving to violate as well as the refusal to participate in such undertakings in armed conflicts and wars then represent a complex world of command and obedience, individual and the collective, but above all questions about morality and immorality. When there are these dualities as general rule it is the negative tendencies that prevail in such settings. According to some critics, in conflicts and war 'the moral psychology of a violator is bound up with the conflict between the weakening or overwhelming of the moral resources and the tendency for the violators' inhumanity to break through' (Glover, 1999: 113). Put simply the condition of disorder and the demands placed by the 'outfit' pushes individuals to lower his/her moral standards and engage in the ghastly and the horrific.

But we need to ask whether prevailing anarchy is the sole determinant in conditioning conflict-zone sexual violence. Are there other factors in play? Were violators not, on these occasions, acting out their own evil inside? Was it because in doing evil, they were 'genuinely exercising their freedom, asserting themselves, and controlling the situation they had created' (Kekes, 2005: 113–14)? Had they purposefully gone beyond both the moral and immoral like Joseph Conrad's Captain Kurtz in *The Heart of Darkness*? Or, is it that our violator was both moral and immoral at the same time?[19] How does one explain this duality? Or, the lack of it, as is the case with Captain Kurtz?

It is well known that we as human beings have managed to cap some of our violent emotions owing to socialisation. In other words if there were no social mores and values guiding us into the world of 'do's' and 'don'ts' plenty of us would probably be going about enacting the most vicious crimes imaginable. All societies recognise these principles and inculcate them into their members from a very early age.

Given the variety of cultures and nationalities our violators come from, it would be grossly erroneous to suggest that some cultures or societal values permit individuals to engage in such violence while others prohibit it. Cultural background is clearly not a trigger in explaining the violator's action and behaviour towards his victim. We could not, for a very good reason, condemn all the Germans as Nazis either during the Second World War or after the defeat of Germany. If this line of thinking has any validity one cannot commit all Serbs, Hutus or, for that matter, Americans to the status of torturers.

If we discount the idea that some cultures, ethnicities or religions are inherently evil (thus by extension those belonging to that culture or religion as being evil) then how do we go about explaining a member of that group's morality or lack of it (when s/he was engaged in that given enterprise)?

According to critics like Albert Bandura the perpetrator or violator, although s/he belonged to a certain cultural group, had a given religion and espoused the cause of his or her own specific nationalist vision, was not intent on damaging the image of his or her specific inheritance (Bandura, 2010). His/her actions were not aimed at projecting certain collective visions or standards. For what the violator was doing was abstaining from these identity markers and the 'do's' and 'don'ts' while violating his/her victim.

Accordingly 'selective activation and disengagement of internal control permits different types of conduct by persons with the same moral standards' (Bandura, 2010: 161). One could argue while our violator during his/her enactment of the crime is not governed by the same moral standards as a normal human being s/he is not abandoning those standards altogether. What s/he is doing is switching off from the normal everyday morality by 'selective activation and disengagement from humane conduct'. In other words our violator was turning on and turning off the general moral standards depending on the context.

Hence, while a violator's action is inherently evil one cannot say the same for the person engaged in such violation. Heinrich Himmler and

Franz Stangl the Nazi butchers, were therefore not completely devoid of morality but were using their moral faculties selectively. Franz Stangl, the SS camp Commandant in Treblinka, 'in white clothes supervising the daily murder of thousands people, enjoying his lunch of meat and potatoes with home-grown fresh vegetables, and having a quiet nap between herding naked men, women and children into the gas chambers and disposing of their corpses' (Kekes, 200 5: 51) was perhaps an ordinary individual meticulously following orders. Using the same yardstick one could argue that Lynndie Rana England (for the lack of a similarly acknowledged violator) was not inherently a person lacking morality but had turned off that faculty in her being for days in Abu Ghraib.

Such line of argument takes us back to the Eichmann trial.[20] It absolves individual responsibility surrounding such crimes and squarely puts the blame on the administration of which the individual violator or killer was a mere accessory—a cog in the wheel so to speak. Now let us put our case of sexual violence committed by US soldiers in Iraq and seek answers to the question of moral responsibility.

So far as his administration was concerned, the government of George W. Bush that oversaw the torture and violation at Abu Ghraib was in no way responsible for the happenings at Abu Ghraib. While distancing itself from the soldiers who wore the US armed forces uniform while carrying out the torture, the official view was these individuals were not representing the US army. They were acting independently. They were simply entertaining their own private passions. In other words, Abu Ghraib was the work of a bunch of criminals or 'a few bad apples' that acted independently and were far removed from any official policy on the treatment of enemy combatants in captivity (Rejali, 2007; Zimbardo, 2007; Einolf, 2008).

Conclusion

The guiding spirits of violation—when conducted in public—can be traced to the violators' own ideological predispositions. In situations where the violator and victim sit on two opposite sides of the ethnic, religious and/or ideological divide, the actions acquire a greater intensity. While initially these motives may be simply opportunistic in nature and character, at a later stage they metamorphose into a momentary, universal principle. Such actions from a violator's perspective may be in keeping with certain ethno-religious predilections, such as the Hindu fundamentalist view of Muslims or the ultra-nationalist Serb treatment of Bosnian Muslims. Hence, debasement, humiliation, emasculation and, at times, extermination of the victim after putting him through these series of acts was in line with the radical thinking.

There are, of course, a number of subsidiary aims that come into play in relation to the violator's behaviour. This may include a range of behavioural specificities starting from homophobia to suppressed homosexual inclinations. Following his or her actions does s/he find himself/herself within such frames of responsibility? We rarely encounter violators' expressing their remorse and regret concerning their own specific actions and behaviour. One is not sure whether the violator is tormented by his conscience. We do not have any public account of where the violator pleads for a form of forgiveness—divine, moral or otherwise—for the unspeakable suffering s/he had brought on his/her victims. However, so far as the exertion of this mode of violence is concerned, what is involved is not a state of mind but the nature of mind.

Clearly, in most instances, the violator was guided by premeditated malice. The explanatory force behind this specific action suggests that prior to undertaking this specific undertaking the violator had overcome moral barriers. On these occasions the violator, through various systematic forms of self-deception, persuaded himself/herself that his/her acts are really acceptable (Morton, 2004: 62). While engaging in such evil s/he was in 'violation of limits that protect minimum conditions of human well-being' (Kekes, 2005: 130).

In any event, as Michael Ignatieff reminds us, 'victory' (if the violator considers his/her actions to be one) 'encloses the victor in a forgetting that removes the very possibility of guilt, shame or remorse, the emotions necessary for any sustained encounter with the truth' (Ignatieff, 1999: 177). And, as we have seen in the case of some high-profile violators such as Radovan Karadzic, not only are they devoid of any compunction when the evidence of their crime is put before them but instead, defend their actions.[21] There are no second thoughts. No self-doubts about their past actions. No guilt trip. No room for such emotions.

5

THE LEGAL CONUNDRUM

Law condemns, not to punishment but to guilt.
Fate is the guilt context of the living.

Walter Benjamin, *Reflections*, 1986: 308.

Sexual violence against men in armed conflicts usually invokes an end-less set of questions about both the nature of violence and the retreat of the jurisprudence which facilitated the introduction of this violence.[1] Put simply, the presence and absence of legal measures to curtail such under-taking sits at the centre of such debate. It is, therefore, vital that one examines the juridical discourse surrounding such violence and how the former tries to address the latter.

Although fragmentary, prohibitions against sexual violence during armed conflict and war have been a part of international humanitarian law since the nineteenth century. In addition, many societies with their specific warrior codes have explicitly prohibited such undertakings. Yet, from our discussion in the previous chapters, it would appear, the cus-tomary international law or conventional domestic laws are either inad-equate or lacking when it comes to addressing the plight of male war-time victims of such violence.

If one were to assess the present canon of international law in order to inquire if it provides sufficient legal scaffolding for the protection of adult male victims of sexual violence in theatres of conflict, then one is presented with a rather ambiguous picture.

In its current incarnation international law provisions do not specifi-cally prohibit crimes of sexual violence against men in armed conflict.

While the emerging instruments that deal with sexual violence in armed conflict and war focus on the protection of women and children, including boys, they appear to exclude men from their applications (Mouthaan, 2012: 7).

Up until recently, while the customary international law demanded that crimes against humanity (such as wartime rape of civilians) be punished, there was very little effort to see this through. This was mostly due to the fact that international consensus regarded it as the duty of individual states and regimes to prosecute these crimes. Given that individual states had the power and wherewithal to oversee the prosecution of these crimes it was felt that there was no need for the international tribunal and domestic courts of third countries to enforce these legal strictures on another state. This mode of interpretation of customary international law, however, had its obvious limitations.

In the first place, sexual violence during armed conflicts and war in national legal jurisdictions had historically been marginalised as private domestic matters and not typically the concern of the state (Henry, 2011). Hence as and when there have been demands on the state to address such issues surrounding justice, the state has taken a back seat or absolved itself of its responsibilities. Understandably it is the failure of the states and regimes to implement the facets of law and fulfill their obligations in the context of crimes against humanity (and on occasions regimes actively promoting these crimes as was the case in Serbia) which led to the thought behind creating a much more powerful supranational body that can surpass individual states' sovereign power and can prosecute individual criminals and leaders implicated in such crimes. The objective was to end the era of impunity for those responsible for committing crimes against humanity (especially sexual crimes during armed conflict). The current International Criminal Court (ICC) can be said to be the result of such thinking and activism.

In the view of some critics, despite the conventions' and statutes' fine-sounding norms, none of them has provided an explicit definition of sexual violence as a war crime or as a crime against humanity in the true sense of the term (Zawati, 2007: 29).

Broadening the base

As we have seen in many contemporary conflict zones, sexual violence against boys and men does not always consist of penetration or direct physical contact. It can take the shape of specific orders for the captive victims to enact—walking naked, masturbating in front of female and male captors, being photographed naked and so on. Do these physically distanced enforced actions between the perpetrator and the victim constitute 'true' sexual crimes? In the above context, it is evidently clear that while the victim did not experience any direct physical contact with his violator he felt duly violated by these distant inflictions, resulting in his physical and mental pain.

In the view of some observers in the current context there is no universally agreed legal definition of cruel, inhuman or degrading treatment that can be successfully argued to be acts that constitute sexual crimes (Mouthaan, 2012: 13). Often it is this knowledge surrounding the legal loophole that encourages distant violators (like the ones in Abu Ghraib, Camp Delta, Camp X Ray and countless other such facilities beyond public scrutiny) to engage in their particularised forms of violation.

How could such undertakings be controlled or prevented in the first place? The responsibility to stem this should have three interrelated dimensions: at the individual level; command structure; and the state.

First, at the individual level, military personnel serving under any flag or rebels fighting for any warlord should be made aware of the rules of engagement in their specific conflict. There has to be some reckoning at the individual (soldier/rebel) level that any such undertaking conducted against the wishes of the captive by his captor constitutes crime. Since crimes of sexual violence can constitute torture under the provisions of current international law, the violators can be made accountable for their actions.

Second, the management in charge of the command and control should be held responsible for any acts of omission on the part of the personnel serving under his/her leadership. Thus, any lapse on the part of their personnel shall be regarded as a failing on the part of the leadership and thus the latter made liable to prosecution under the provisions of the ICC.[2]

Third, the overall responsibility for the controlled behaviour on the part of its soldiers squarely rests on the state. In fact, it is the state that is the key actor in either facilitating sexual violence against the captive enemies and civilians or making sure such violations do not take place at all. Existing evidence overwhelmingly suggests that often combatants engage in actions and activities that do not reflect the sentiments of the state. However, it must be acknowledged that a certain degree of permissiveness in terms of power projection against what the state considers enemies of its interests can prompt its soldiers/military personnel to disregard the rules of war.

The appalling behaviour of US marines in Iraq, Sri Lankan soldiers in their home country and ultra-nationalist Serbian soldiers in Bosnia are some cases in point. Therefore, the role of the individual state in this context can hardly be exaggerated. To ensure that such events do not take place or are perpetrated by its citizens/military personnel, 'a State must take reasonable measures to prevent torture, including sexual abuse from taking place, such as appropriate information about the prohibition of torture, including sexual violence, in the training of amongst others, military personnel even if abroad' (Mouthaan, 2011: 21).

The onus on the state to prevent the occurrence of such violations is so severe that some critics have gone on to argue that 'government officials at all levels may be held responsible if they failed to stop torture where it occurs' (Rodley, 2009: 100).

Guarding the guardians

So far as the merit of punishment goes, it proclaims the sacredness of the victims' rights. From a normative perspective, punishment also reinstates the core values of retributive justice. While retributive justice is fundamental in addressing the wrongs committed during the conflict it also serves as a framework of deterrent; a strong warning against all the potential and would-be violators (Bastick, Grimm, & Kunz, 2007: 156). The presence of this principle, it is suggested, 'internalizes—and even reinforces—social norms among the public and, thereby, from the expressivist perspective, proactively promotes law-abiding behavior' (Drumbl, 2007: 174). Furthermore in the view of some critics the presence of a framework of retributive justice has a twofold deterrent effect. The potential violator 'abstains because the condemnation of the crime by society and the state has brought its wickedness home to him; and abstains from moral motives and not merely from fear of unpleasant consequences to himself' (Ewing, 1929: 96).

Punishment, then, would appear as the main line of defence for the victims and would-be victims. While such regulatory principles may work as deterrents for a potential violator they have their limits. In the view of some critics 'law is not exercised upon inert beings, but only upon those whose cooperation can be claimed' (Land, 1992: 73). It is, therefore, worth asking how the legal remits are viewed and exercised upon those found guilty while wearing the badge of the UN.

The UN, of course, has strict guidelines on the conduct of its peacekeepers. On matters of sex, it clearly bans its personnel from having any physical contact of a sexual nature with prostitutes and anyone under the age of eighteen. Furthermore, it 'strongly discourages' sexual relations even with consenting adults in the host population (*The Economist*, 2008: 74). However over the past two decades with the rise in UN operations in several hotspots around the world has been an increased consequential level of sexual violation of boys as well as men (not to speak of women) across various continents (Higate, 2007: 99–119).

The hiatus of a civil war and the subsequent chaos often render vulnerable boys and men doubly susceptible to abuse by external actors. Often in the post-conflict stage those responsible for guarding order may actually perpetrate abuses which they themselves were appointed to prevent. In Somalia, when the UN was in charge of peacekeeping in 1993–94 the Belgian and Italian blue berets were reported to be freely engaged in seeking sexual favours from boys and even forcing them into sex (Amnesty International, 2004: 55). From then it became a familiar allegation against the UN troops.

In the Democratic Republic of Congo (Congo DRC) UN peacekeepers from Morocco, Nepal, Pakistan, Uruguay and South Africa are alleged to have committed rape, sexual exploitation, and abuse of minors (Lynch, 2004; Higate, 2007). In 2008 Brazilian troops were found to be sexually abusing Haitian boys as well as girls.

Retributive justice seems to have lost its relevance in the context of extra-territoriality. We find an enormous legal loophole when confronting cases where the UN personnel are the alleged violators. By and large, the bulk of sexual violence committed by the UN personnel belongs to its peacekeepers. But when it comes to prosecuting its blue helmets, the UN has appeared utterly powerless. The world body takes such allegations seriously. It investigates and often tries to ascertain the truth. However, it has no jurisdiction over those found guilty. For these peacekeeping troops belong to a third country, where these allegations are rarely pursued. So, all the UN is capable of doing is dismissing the violators. When we turn to the host society we find it has been doubly violated. The victims, in this context would appear to have been victimised twice over—first by their own society and later by those who came to protect them from the conflict.

This problem of 'guardians behaving badly' is not limited to the UN personnel alone. This has also affected many initiatives of country-led operations where officials under the strict command structure of a given army also have gone on to commit such violence. And on occasions we have incidents of aid agency workers entertaining such forms of violence in conflict zones. In the first place such occurrences are not new. Second, as suggested above this form of deviation among some of its personnel affects a multitude of organisations working in conflict settings. What is critical, however, is to work out why this offence continues to be repeated. Also, what makes some of these personnel behave in a way that is unbecoming while others continue to perform their task admirably? Is this simply a case of bad apples?

There are two possible explanations one can introduce here. In the first place, according to one critic male military masculinity and lack of appropriate training may have something to do with this lapse. 'There is no switch inside a blue helmet that automatically turns a soldier trained for war-fighting into an individual prepared to work non-violently and with cultural sensitivity in a highly militarized environment' (Fetherston, 1995: 21).

Second, the reason why protectors turn into predators and succeed in continuing with their activity has to do with the failure of 'successive chains of command to acknowledge the severity of the problem' (Shanker, 2004). That being the scenario, unsurprisingly the problem is exacerbated in those situations where these undertakings are carried out by 'out-of-control agents' (Butler, Gluch & Mitchell, 2007: 673). This would suggest that in every operation or within every platoon or battalion that is in charge of protecting the civilians in a war-torn society there are individuals who see an opportunity to indulge in sexual crimes.

Thus we have some cases of US army personnel engaging in sexual violence against a particular civilian population while others remain exemplary in their professionalism. As some critics put it, these forces or personnel will differ in the degree of control and discipline and the resultant behaviour (Butler, Gluch and Mitchell, 2007: 672). What is true of US army personnel is also valid in terms of creating a character sketch of those UN blue berets that have gone 'feral' and sexually abused boys and men in locations where they were posted to ensure peace.

In contexts such as the above even if there were clear guidelines in terms of 'personnel behaviour' for field operations and the command structure was aware of the happenings on the ground it would not be possible to completely root out such occurrences. For unbecoming conduct is reflected when the personnel are devoid of self-regulating capacities. It may also result from the knowledge that the violator can engage in such an act in a third country and escape the laws of his or her own country, or at best receive a short prison sentence (as in the case of Private Lynndie England of Abu Ghraib fame upon her return to the United States). In the end it is the variation in control or the degree of slack given agents, that influences the incidence of sexual violence (Butler, Gluch and Mitchell, 2007: 672).

Legal loopholes

In cases involving sexual violence against civilians in armed conflicts the preferred legal option of dealing with such crimes is employment of some form of retributive justice. This traditional legal framework was developed keeping in mind primarily the position of women. Since an overwhelming majority of cases pertaining to such violence was directed at women by their male aggressors, such a lackadaisical approach is understandable. However, we need to spare a thought for the other gender too.

Sexual violence against men is arguably one of the most serious human rights problems in our time. However, attempts to develop a more 'inclusive' framework to deal with such crimes have run aground owing to the complicity of silence on the part of two sets of actors. The first one involves the victims and the second one concerns the jurists and law enforcers.

Given that most of the jurists and law enforcers in the non-Western world (where there is a disproportionate level of such crimes compared to its Western counterpart) are males, dealing with these cases has meant delving into a taboo subject which makes them extremely uncomfortable. For the jurists and law enforcers these crimes are abominable acts, an affront against their own dignity and masculinity. Their views are often a mirror reflection of the general male populace of the society they belong to and represent. They often mimic the masses when it comes to dealing with such crimes.

Given this cultural inheritance they (the jurists and upholders of law) either ignore it or heap abuses on the victim by suggesting, 'he (the victim) was asking for it', homosexualising the victim's identity and condemning him for failing to defend his dignity. If one could stretch the argument then the unspoken verdict the jurists appear to pass is that the victim should have died in the confrontation rather than face such indignity and humiliation. When the experiences of the 'victim' are considered, they are often labelled as unworthy of living; human beings who cannot be sympathised with.

Turning to the wider world one comes across a certain disdain for the victims of such violence. That the international community maintains a certain ambivalence over male-male sexual violence is not an exaggeration. Although there have been several reports of these incidents in the international media there is a certain silence on the part of the larger international community on this issue. While trying to situate the reason for this ambivalence one critic argues that by and large 'society considers any such contact to be indicative of homosexuality, regardless of any element of coercion' (Sivakumaran, 2005: 1274).

The prejudice and discomfort of the law enforcers, the silence of the victims and the awareness on the part of the aggressor that he will never be brought to justice have all contributed to an orchestration of silence on the whole issue. Unsurprisingly, the rectification of injustice through proper legal procedures which features so prominently in the case of female victims, is largely absent when it comes to male victims of sexual violence not because there are no legal measures but because a whole host of actors are unable to confront it headlong.

Curiously this reckoning is entertained both by the victim and the law enforcement agents (who happen to be mostly male in such situations). My interaction with both sets of actors caught up in this existential, moral and legal ambiguity produced some startling revelations. The victim, although aware of the possibility of demanding justice for the violations he went through during the conflict, finds it impossible to make such demands following the end of the conflict when the judiciary is in place and the law enforcement agents are in charge. For, by admitting his own victimhood (our victim feared) he would publicly raise questions about his own identity: he might homosexualise his being. This fear is real owing to the dominant ideas of the larger society about such matters, as I highlighted earlier. Thus men who were caught up in such conflicts and had failed to rise up to defend their honour or had not killed themselves owing to subsequent shame resisted the thought of claiming justice for bringing upon themselves further shame.

Among the law enforcement agents (in non-western conflict zones) such as the police and the judiciary I found an overwhelming reluctance to take up the case of the victim. The majority of these agents felt these victims to be 'proto-homosexuals'. By defending these victims and claiming justice for them, the prosecutors felt they were somehow homosexualising their own identity. Needless to add, such private prejudice and public fears on the part of these agents have in many occasions stood in the way of their seeking justice for the victims. If anything the whole scenario would suggest that this was a double-bind situation for both the victim and the defenders of justice.

Moreover, in some instances, even when there are legal avenues available for victims to pursue their case the prevalent political atmosphere may not allow them to approach the courts. The Mau Mau revolutionary group whose members were systematically sexually abused by the British colonial administration during the Kenyan independence struggle in the late 1950s (as discussed in Chapter 2) could not take recourse in local law to redress their situation as the organisation itself was proscribed by the Kenyan government until the year 2003.

Having eliminated the possibility of any intervention from both these sets of actors—the victim and those in charge of upholding the law—we invariably end up inquiring: What about the general public? How do they react to such events? What possible remedies do they suggest? Again, as argued earlier, given the 'prevalence of homophobia in society, this amounts to a "taint" on the part of the victim of such violation' (Sivakumaran, 2005: 1274). Fears of such double victimisation often prevent the victim from coming out into the open to declare his misfortune. On closer scrutiny one could argue that the absence of any clearly defined legal framework and an overtly homophobic attitude in certain societies encourages a predatory instinct among a given sector. For the violators find these lapses to their advantage.

Stemming it

If anything, the previous chapters conclusively established the fact that from a perpetrator's perspective the use of sexual violence serves a fundamental strategic purpose of crushing the enemy's self-esteem and morale for good. There are important caveats, of course. As underscored in chapter one and two not all of these undertakings are based within the context of a military strategic objective. Some of these violations are carried out by opportunistic perpetrators to satisfy their specific individually mediated private goals. However, if one were to exclude this particular aspect then it would seem by and large that sexual violence against boys and men in armed conflicts and wars operate within a clearly defined policy framework. If it is a part of a clearly thought through enterprise then one could put a cap on this practice, and better still, terminate it by introducing a writ from those very actors who are organising it or likely to enforce it.

According to some scholars:

The effectiveness of an armed group's command and control structure is also important for … the effective prohibition of sexual violence by the group's leaders. Even if leaders were persuaded of the military effectiveness of sexual violence against particular groups, they might decide to prohibit it for normative, strategic, or practical considerations (Wood, 2006: 328).

For instance, if a rebel group or militia has the intention of ruling over a given civilian population in the post-conflict/post-war phase then it is imperative that it does not get a bad press relating to its wartime activities. Introduction of such argument is likely to put pressure on the leadership of that group to restrain its combatants from engaging in sexual violence against combatants as well as civilians for fear of undermining their future support base (Wood, 2006: 328–9). Put simply, a leadership that is conscious of its long-term post-conflict goals is likely to actively discourage any such violence for normative as well as practical purposes.

While this may work as a deterrent, it does not guarantee a complete abandoning of this practice. As Wood points out, 'whether an armed group or an occupying force effectively enforces particular sanctions and norms decided on by leaders generally depends on the group's military discipline' (Wood, 2006: 330). As a rule of thumb the leadership might find it difficult to declare open support for sexual violence against enemy combatants and civilians.[3] However, that does not mean to say the rank and file below that leadership would not engage in such practices. The foot soldiers and irregular troops are unlikely to follow the laws set by command leaders to the letter if they feel their actions will not become public knowledge, especially if they act in a group or away from the public gaze. They may also be encouraged to engage in such practices if there exists a degree of impunity as in situations of them being the occupying force.

Turning to Rwanda and Sierra Leone we realise that the rebel leadership was itself complicit in ordering the use of such violence against its opponents while throwing away any social norms or legal codes. Since the rules of war were completely abandoned and to some extent non-existent in these theatres of conflict, one could not even imagine the leadership pondering the question of self-image in the post-conflict phase. If anything, there was urgency on the part of the Hutu leadership and that of the RUF in Rwanda and Sierra Leone respectively to cause maximum damage to their enemy. Consequently it was guided by the belief that if sexual violence helped towards the achievement of the objective of the subjugation of the enemy, then it should be used.

There is yet another shortcoming to the leadership-sponsored self-restraint on the part of the rebels, militias and the army. As a framework of deterrence it has a gender-specific connotation. Although I have tried to stress the fact that sexual violence against both sexes during armed conflict and war leaves behind deep scars, from the violator's perspective men and women have two different statuses as victims of such violence. For a start, the violator primarily views such undertaking against women as a personal reward for his/her participation in the conflict. For the violator, the enemy women are a form of lootable resource that needs to be extracted from the conflict topography. The violator is aware of the fact that violating an enemy woman is as heinous as robbing an opponent's property. If stealing is immoral so is the violation of women in this particular setting. Therefore, when the leadership issues an edict or dictat forbidding such undertaking the violator feels morally obliged to follow it.

Turning to the employment of sexual violence against men in arenas of conflict we notice the absence of any such framework at work. As I stressed in chapter two, the violation of the body of the male prisoner is not an act of 'taking advantage' of your enemy opponent (as is the case with the female body) but very much a part of the narrative of justifiable punishment. The male body does not represent the same degree of 'helplessness' as its female and child counterparts in theatres of war. Consequently it does not automatically enjoy the degree of protection that is accorded to female gender and children. Put simply it is a legitimate target.

Given this understanding, the leadership does not feel it needs to issue a dictat banning any form of sexual violence against men since the overall objective of armed engagement is to unseat your enemy (through torture, humiliation, violence and so on): the leadership may feel that by issuing a certain framework of interaction with the male opponent it is in fact restricting the ability of its forces from operating fully. Moreover, the taboo surrounding the employment of sexual violence against the enemy male populace also restricts the leadership from entering into any such debate; and, finally, that very few male victims actually come forward to make public their wartime violation erects a further barrier against any kind of meaningful debate about such abuses among those at the top of the hierarchy on the violator's side.

Owing to the combination of the above factors, we end up with a framework where there is no possibility of leader-mediated opposition to such forms of violence.

If we were to return to the debate surrounding sexual violence against the prisoners in Abu Ghraib and the issue of individual/group responsibility as well as justice, the overall picture is both startling and revealing. On closer inspection, it would appear that the administration was denying as well as absolving itself from any official or institutional responsibility on the matter. The Bush administration's response to such offences, in the first instance, was to distance itself from such actions. It equated the sexual torture and violence against the inmates of Abu Ghraib as the work of a few 'bad apples' or, at best, criminals. These were individuals who were working on their own initiative, independent of any official policy (Mestrovic, 2007; Lazerg, 2007).

Linguistic lapse?

The preceding discussion conclusively established that sexual violence against boys and men is both widespread and endemic in various theatres of conflict. More importantly it has been systematic and persistent since the 1990s. The violators range from opportunists, ultranationalists, warlords and humanitarian peacekeepers to regular soldiers working under the aegis of some established powers that hold human rights in high regard. However, in spite of the pervasiveness of this phenomenon neither an international human rights framework nor individual state-based laws have adequately addressed this problem. This does not mean to suggest that both sets of laws ignore the issue of sexual violence or gloss over it. Far from it.

Most of the documents available in the international public domain that aim to address the problem either exclusively highlight the plight of the female sex or discuss sexual violence in a gender-neutral way. For example, the *Convention on the Rights of the Child* says, 'States and Parties shall take all appropriate legislative, administrative, social and educational measures to protect the child from all forms of physical or mental violence, injury or abuse, neglect or negligent treatment, maltreatment or exploitation, including sexual abuse…' (*Convention on the Rights of the Child*, art. 19, 20 November 1989, 1577 U.N.T.S. 3). In the absence of a specific reference to male victims, the assumption that all victims are female remains a possibility. Turning to global international bodies such as the UN we notice a similar omission. The explicit mention of boys as sexual victims in the UN documents is rare. And when they are named, they are included through the use of a term like 'the child' (Stemple, 2009: 623).

Moreover, whenever there is a reference to, or arguments for, gender-based equality or rights (given the overwhelming nature of male domination among the sexes) it automatically refers to the condition of women not men. Take for instance, UN Security Council Resolution 1325. It begins with member states highlighting concern 'that civilians, particularly women and children, account for the vast majority of those adversely affected by armed conflicts' (SC Resolution, 1325, preamble, U.N. Doc. S/RES/1325 [31 October 2000]).

This SC Resolution is problematic in the sense that while at the outset it refers to children (thereby one imagines it includes both boys and girls), at a later stage of this Resolution it becomes apparent that the reference is only to the female sex and males are excluded from this discussion. Note for example, the same Resolution 1325, which 'calls on all parties to armed conflict to take special measures to protect women and girls from gender-based violence, particularly rape and other forms of sexual abuse'. This lapse is not only grave but would appear to imply that boys do not matter when it comes to receiving sexual abuse and violence in armed conflicts.

The female-specific language in human rights law that is exclusionary and brushes aside the male condition is further evidenced if we take into account the UN Declaration on Elimination of Discrimination Against Women of 5 February 1999. It states, for example, 'countries should take full measures to eliminate all forms of exploitation, abuse, harassment, and violence against women, adolescents and children' (Art 12, 1,

U.N. Doc. A/54/38/Rev. I. Ch. I). Such a blanket declaration ignores the fact that boys and men may go through similar ordeals placed in such trying conditions.

Such arbitrary definitional understanding of gender-based violence as exclusively referring to women is widespread both in the legal canons as well as the documents of various UN conventions, resolutions and recommendations. Unsurprisingly, thanks to this confusion some critics have gone an extra mile to argue 'gender-based' violence is used only to describe female victimisation, thereby leaving no room for a much-needed analysis of male experience of sexual violence (Stemple, 2009: 619).

The nature of this partial and one-dimensional interpretation of sexual violence in armed conflict and war becomes ever more evident if we focus on various international commentaries, treaties and resolutions. For example, while there are well over one hundred uses of the term 'violence against women' defined to include sexual violence in the UN resolutions, treaties, general comments and consensus documents, there were no human rights instruments that explicitly addressed sexual violence against men in armed conflict and war until 2010 (Stemple, 2009: 619).

One of the key legal documents that provides protection of civilians during armed conflicts and war, the Geneva Convention IV of 1949, while explicitly prohibiting rape, enforced prostitution and indecent assault under Article 27, is gender-biased. Article 27 is expressly limited to women. It considers women as the sole victims and completely ignores the fact that the male gender could face or encounter similar violence.

The 1995 Fourth World Congress of Women in its Beijing Declaration and the Platform for Action, urged states to take 'special measures to eliminate violence against women, particularly those in vulnerable situations, such as young women, refugees, displaced and internally displaced women, women with disabilities and women migrant workers, including enforcing any existing legislation and developing, as appropriate, new legislations for women' (U.N. Doc A/CONF. 177/20 [17 October 1995: xxv]). However, not only has there been no such conference to highlight the male plight, what is glaring is that boys and men could find themselves in similar situations and require equal levels of protection as women, yet this is not even contemplated.

In the view of one critic, such an omission is patently unwarranted. For:

Men with characteristics that make them particularly vulnerable to violence are consistently excluded from human rights instruments. Subgroups of at-risk men, such as refugees, the internally displaced, migrant workers, disabled men, or men who are vulnerable to sexual violence because of their membership in a particular racial or ethnic group during armed conflict are excluded. The human rights instruments that do address the vulnerability of these groups to sexual violence address only the vulnerability of women (Stemple, 2009: 625).

In sum, the international instruments that contain the most comprehensive and meaningful definitions of sexual violence in armed conflict and war until recently excluded men, reflecting and embedding the assumption that sexual violence is a phenomenon relevant only to girls and women (Stemple, 2009: 619). What is more shocking, however, is that whenever boys and men are mentioned in the context of sexual violence they are included in their instrumentalist capacity—as actors who are important in exerting such violence as well as capable of contributing to its reduction—not as potential victims (Stemple, 2009: 624).

It is worth inquiring why there exists such a disproportionate response and treatment between the female and male condition in international fora and human rights legislations. Is there an institutional bias? Or is it a conspiracy of sorts that tries to muffle the male rights? On closer inspection one realises that the answer to this glaring lapse could be more to do with the lack of projection of the male plight than some form of prejudice, bias or, worse still, conspiracy. The point about lack of projection is understood fully if we examine the issue of the male plight alongside the female plight in the context of the dissemination of information and awareness.

Over the past few decades a host of NGOs, charities, legal bodies, individual states, visual and print media, and international institutions such as the UN have been very active in highlighting forms of violence suffered by women in armed conflicts and wars. By doing so these bodies not only helped consolidate a global awareness about the female condition but also forced the international community to take measures to protect and promote women's rights in the context of wars and violence.

While the female sex was fortunate in receiving this attention no such movement emerged that could frame the male plight and give it saliency. Again a combination of factors prevented any concerted effort to highlight the suffering of male victims. First, compared to their female counterparts the number of male victims of sexual violence in armed conflicts and war was minimal. Second, as we have seen, it is very difficult for male victims of sexual crimes to report them. Third, many media organisations,

NGOs and humanitarian bodies were reluctant to publicise the issue of male victims of sexual violence. Fourth, there was not a sufficient momentum in international fora to wrestle with this issue. It is the last point which is most disturbing. For while there were well publicised cases about male victims of sexual violence in the heart of Europe (such as in the Balkans) and later there was the highly publicised Abu Ghraib affair, the international community somehow did not feel sufficiently motivated to address the issue in legal and humanitarian contexts.

Had the plight of the sexually violated male victims in the Balkan civil war been addressed adequately, there may not have been sexual abuses of males in Abu Ghraib, Guantanamo or Afghanistan. Similarly, if various NGOs and humanitarian bodies had taken up the cause of these victims with full force then there would have been the establishment of some form of international legal regime providing adequate cover for the victims and preventing the recurrence of such violence.

Unfortunately, as I am going to stress below, there is neither the required regulatory framework nor the intent to address the issue. One of the most widely used documents to defend and protect the human and other forms of rights of civilians during armed conflicts is Security Council Resolution 1325 (which we have referred to elsewhere in this chapter). This resolution, while urging all states to end impunity for 'sexual and other violence against women and girls', is silent about the male gender. Thanks to this arbitrary and one-sided interpretation of 'plight' there is little or nothing to suggest what the boy victims such as those in Afghanistan or south Sudan can expect from the aegis of international legal regimes or from their own governments for that matter.

Furthermore, if this key resolution is any indication, male victims of sexual violence during such upheaval can expect little or no redress, legal or otherwise, in the post-conflict stage. For Resolution 1325 calls for all the concerned actors involved 'when negotiating and implementing peace agreements, to adopt a gender perspective, including, *inter alia*: (a) the special needs of women and girls during repatriation and resettlement and for rehabilitation, reintegration and post-conflict reconstruction...' (SC Resolution 1325, Paragraph 8).

Similarly in its Resolution No. 1820, the Security Council established that 'rape and other forms of sexual violence can constitute a war crime, a crime against humanity, or a constitutive act with respect to genocide' (UN Security Council 2008). However a detailed examination of this resolution brings us face to face with the fact that this particular under-taking was partial and was not all-inclusive. The gender-specificity of this resolution was evident from the very name of the resolution itself. Resolution No. 1820 was titled 'Women and Peace and Security'. While it explicitly denounced sexual violence during armed conflict, its explicit aim was to pass a resolution or legal ruling to protect women and girls in particular.

During the debate in the Security Council, the Secretary-General, Ban Ki-moon called it a 'silent war against women and girls' and there was no mention of men or boys in his speech.

One ought to remember that this resolution was introduced at a time when reports of sexual violence against men were pretty widespread; especially in the context of Abu Ghraib prison torture reports, there was evidence of similar incidents in various Afghan prison camps and occasional reports of the rape of men in DRC. If that were so why did the international community not take a sustained interest in the welfare of boys and men caught up in such maelstroms of brutality? Were those responsible for drafting SC Resolution 1820 as well as those implementing it partial to the interests of women and, as some critics would have us believe, gender-biased (Sivakumaran, 2007; Stemple 2009; Mouthaan, 2012)? Or, were there other larger issues involved which did not permit the said group of parties from introducing such measures?

Unfortunately the debates surrounding the issue prior to its introduction and subsequent passing of Resolution 1820 are not available for public consumption. Neither do we have a crystal ball to gaze into which could provide us with clues as to why this resolution was very gender-specific or whether there were actors who would have liked to make it more inclusive. In the absence of such hard facts, when we seek answers to the questions raised earlier we can only speculate and infer. If that is so, one could frame the answers to the questions in the following manner.

The inability or the reluctance on the part of the drafters as well as implementers of Resolution 1820 to specifically highlight the plight of boys and men might have been conditioned by: the fact that these events are not widespread and thus do not warrant a specific resolution; the belief that the said resolution is sufficiently inclusive because it outlaws sexual violence in theatres of conflict—and by its very nature can protect boys and men; and a general reluctance to face up to and confront such a taboo subject as male-male and female-male sexual violence.

Overall the official as well as general instrumentalist approach that paints the male sex in a particular way in relation to women sets a bad precedent, to say the least. The fallout of such an approach can be summed up in the following manner. First, it mistakenly suggests that the men are the only perpetrators of such violence. Second, that men could be victims in such undertakings is completely brushed aside while the legal and humanitarian literature dwells on the female plight. Third, this gender bias that favours females forecloses all options for male victims to seek out help (emotional, psychological, medical and institutional).

Criminalisation of victimhood

Law and the punishment it prescribes on transgression and criminality do provide some kind of index on a society's boundaries of tolerance and its sense of moral responsibility, justice, and fairness (Rousseau & Porter, 1987: 15). When we use this yardstick to assess the question of male victims' legal standing in the larger society we come up with some startling statistics. Legislation in many countries still does not adequately recognise sexual violence as a crime as it fails to recognise male rape (Bastick, Grimm, & Kunz, 2007: 155).

What does legislation have to do with our victims' rights one might ask. If, for instance, a male victim reported a case of sodomy or rape by a perpetrator then he was more likely to be persecuted and punished for inciting homosexuality. In countries from Uganda to Pakistan, victims of male-male sexual violence have received punishment from the law rather than protection. This is simply due to the fact that sexual violence against men is not recognised in the law of very many countries, particularly in cases where any male-male sexual event or incident is considered homosexual and thus liable to legal penalties under the laws of those states. Interestingly, as of 2010 some eighty-five countries around the world had enforceable laws that banned homosexual sex (Sivakumaran, 2007; Lewis, 2009). From the male victim's perspective this draconian legal framework is like putting salt on an open wound.

In the view of some critics, in addition to the manifest injustice of victimisation the legal prohibition against sodomy or homosexual sex also disadvantages many victims from reporting their abuse in the first place (Stemple, 2009: 632). For rather than seeing that justice is done the law marks victims down as culprits. This seriously undermines the victim's ability not only not seek justice in the first place but also forces him to hide from it after undergoing this personal misfortune or tragedy. Put simply, it is the failure of legal systems to accommodate and take into account the emotional, psychological and subjective dimensions of injustice which further consolidates victims' sense of victimhood.

In the long run it is not only the victim that suffers the indignity of being cast aside by the law and the legal system. The law itself loses its sanctity. Over time the victim loses his trust in the legal system and the perpetrator also feels that he cannot be punished for his actions. So the violation goes on. While the victim is certainly a casualty of this unfavourable system, one can say the same of the system of justice. Given that these two parties in the process of violation have little or no faith in the system of the law, that system itself becomes a mockery.

In addition, the immediate family and friends who are aware of the victim's plight and are conscious of the arbitrary nature of the system of justice, may also come to view the law as something that cannot be trusted, relied upon or, worse still, can be ignored. Thus in the ultimate analysis the criminalisation of male-male sex not only disadvantages the victim but also equally undermines the place of law and justice in the wider society. The group or actor that benefits most from this confusion is, of course, the violator. Aware that there exists a loophole that he can exploit with impunity, he is free to sexually violate his victims either for recreational or other purposes.

In some Islamic countries where there is strict prohibition against homosexuality and where there is currently civil unrest and continuing armed conflict, the problem associated with double victimisation of the victim is most acute. In Pakistan, for instance, where sodomy and rape of young boys and effeminate adult males is widespread, the victims often find it hard to report their abuse for the law condemns the victim for inciting homosexuality in the society.

Moreover even on those rare occasions when a victim does decide to approach the law, in many Muslim countries, following *shari'a*, two men must have witnessed the act of violence as part of evidentiary standards and procedural requirement (Bastick, Grimm, & Kunz, 2007: 162).[4] This conservative and selective approach to justice that commits the victim to double censure can hardly be called law. For some critics, by failing to grapple with such examples of sexual violence against men, both national and international human rights law helps consolidate ignorance and biases that perpetuate callousness towards the continued violation of vulnerable men and boys (Stemple, 2009: 633).

Given the catalogue of absences in acknowledging the sexual violence against the male gender it would not be an exaggeration to suggest that overall 'a human rights approach to sexual violence is beset by limitations when linked inextricably to one framework only: the women's rights framework' (Stemple, 2009: 641). Hence for these critics the ambiguities existing in the international human rights canon in coming to terms with sexual violence against boys and men is not only theoretically problematic but it has deep and disturbing practical implications. Thanks to the lack of clarity and determination at the international level to address the issue:

… the very states that failed to address any form of sexual violence for decades are likely to be unaware of or unconcerned with sexual violence against men and boys. The failure of the instruments to hold governments accountable for sexual violence against male victims, simply put, encourages states to continue to ignore the problem (Stemple, 2009: 637).

In addition, due to conventional hostility towards homosexuality in many states there exists very little legal recourse for males who have been sexually violated during both peacetime as well as during times of internal strife or conflict. While probing this aspect some critics have remarked, 'men residing in countries that prohibit (even consensual) male-male sexual behaviour provide little or no legal cover if a citizen complains of such an attack' (Lewis, 2009: 19). This is not surprising since many liberal Western societies have only recently recognised the fact that men can be sexually violated (raped). The United Kingdom, for instance, criminalised any form of sexual violence against men only as recently as 1994.

Even where legal recognition exists and the courts accept the fact that men can be sexually violated just like women during armed conflict, when it comes to delivering a verdict on these crimes those responsible for upholding the law often drag their feet or do not hesitate to be openly unsympathetic to the cause of the victim. Prosecutors and juries, for instance, are not always willing to accord such violence the seriousness it deserves. One need not go very far back into recent history to find evidence of this.

In the view of some critics, analyses of sentencing patterns at the International Criminal Tribunal for Yugoslavia (ICTY—that had to deal with a lot of cases of male-male sexual violence) show that the jurors were not entirely sympathetic to the victims' causes and that 'perpetrators of such violence against men often received lighter sentences than those who perpetrated sexual violence against women' (King & Greening, 2005). In fact ICTY's mandate focused primarily on women and their wartime sexual violation experience while omitting conceptually and de facto the Bosnian Muslim and Croatian male victims who had undergone severe sexual violence at the hands of Serb militia (De Zotto and Jones, 2002).

According to some other studies, at the time of the publication of its findings, ICTY had not charged any perpetrators of sexual violence against men with rape; the common charges appear to be 'torture' or 'degrading treatment' (Zawati, 2007; OCHA, 2008: 4). Moreover, when the investigators and prosecutors of ICTY pursued a case seriously they minimised the sexual nature of the attack on the victims and downgraded it to a systematic attack on the victims, and eventually the nature of abuse and violence was denied the seriousness it deserved (Stener, 2006). This cavalier judicial attitude was so prevalent and so entrenched in the workings of the ICTY that some exasperated critics ended up arguing that these international legal institutions 'never acknowledged the male victims of sexual violence' (Zarkov, 1997: 146).

Reinstating justice

If anything, our assessment of the issue of justice with regard to the victims, their perpetrators and the wider society suggested that highly state-centred formal judicial mechanisms to address these issues are not particularly helpful. This is especially problematic in underdeveloped post-civil war societies.

While reflecting on the horrors of Bosnia, David Rieff, an American commentator, argued, 'freedom cannot be asserted; it must be defended. It cannot hope to live on only in a few gilded corners of the world, any more than species can remain viable if the only places that their safety can be assured are zoos' (Rieff, 1995: 10). In contemporary international society, freedom of the violated and the oppressed assumes urgency only if the suffering of the victims is well known, or they are far too numerous to ignore.

While plenty of abusers escape the cold hand of justice, at times the law does catch up with some of them. This is made possible when the veil of silence is lifted or the stories of victims' trauma seep into the public domain. A case in point is that of the summary dismissal of the commander of the Uruguayan Navy's UN mission in Haiti. This occurred following a widely circulated video that allegedly shows Uruguayan peacekeepers sexually assaulting an eighteen-year-old Haitian man. The event prompted the country's president Michel Martelly to condemn the alleged abuse and describe the alleged crime as 'collective rape' by outsiders.

The judicial conviction of the aggressor surrounding this particular case was made possible owing to two interrelated factors. First, there was the weight of the entire Haitian society behind the demand for justice. Second, the UN and the Uruguayan government's credibility and international standing was at stake, which prompted both parties to oversee the handing out of punishment against the violator(s).

With the wisdom of hindsight, one could argue that had there been no such high-profile media attention the case would have simply been brushed under the carpet (like so many instances of abuse by UN peacekeepers in their missions in many other conflict locations as I stressed earlier). Equally importantly when it comes to the issue of due process and handing out of punitive measures against the violator(s) is the widespread cynicism surrounding the nature of these punishments. Questions such as whether the aggressor(s)' punishment was sufficient dominate the politico-legal debate.

In March 2012 the UN revealed that three of its Pakistani peacekeepers serving in Haiti were found guilty of sexually assaulting a fourteen-year old Haitian boy. The Pakistani military hearing that found the three personnel guilty of the charge sent them back to their country of origin in order to serve a one year jail sentence. For organisations like Amnesty International (AI), such lenient sentences amount to nothing but a travesty of justice.[5]

While mindful of the fact that something is being done in a legal framework, AI—the organisation known to defend the rights of victims around the world—also succeeded in underscoring the existing grey areas surrounding such trials. According to Javier Zúñiga, a special advisor at AI, at this particular trial there were three glaring mistakes. First, very little information was available on this case and the nature of the sexual assault. Second, the military trial was conducted in virtual secrecy. Third, the handing down of a one year sentence to the guilty parties was utterly unacceptable.

For Zúñiga, in order for a transparent legal mechanism to have functioned adequately in this case (and by extension in similar cases), there should have been an altogether different juridical course. For instance: the UN should have informed the public about the exact circumstances of this crime, the extent to which these peacekeepers and possibly others were involved; such cases of sexual abuse should never have been dealt with by military courts (this should have been dealt with by civilian courts prepared to deal with human rights issues); and the right of the public to know if there were any rehabilitation measures undertaken for the victim and his family should have been respected.

What is abundantly evident from the above is that in order for justice to be seen (in terms of its effectiveness) and appreciated (providing compensation or reparation to the victim and his family) the relevant authorities or judicial bodies in charge of reinstating it should be mindful of a whole host of issues. From a human rights perspective, it would appear, the understanding is that the judicial mechanism should not only be transparent but also appear to have teeth. And, in addition, it should be capable of making provisions for the victim in the immediate and the long-term.

While all this is very good, it is also worth asking if the victim and his immediate family should be forced to undergo this public spectacle of justice in order to uphold due process and transparency. What if they do not want an open trial, as it is likely to embarrass the victim and his family further?[6] Another and a larger challenge, of course, is that there may exist one set of justice measures for the victim in his country of origin, and another for the aggressor in his or her country of origin. Such inequity can undermine the full remit of justice according to some observers (Vezina, 2012: 445).

A silver lining

In spite of the overwhelming humanitarian legal black hole that exists in addressing the issue of sexual violence against boys and men in armed conflicts and war there has been some progress made in the past few years. The organisation that has been at the forefront of addressing the issue and whose legal strictures can be regarded as pioneering is the International Criminal Court (ICC). The Rome Statute acknowledges the seriousness of sexual violence, as capable of being an international crime and as crimes against humanity (Bastick, Grimm, & Kunz, 2007:

157). While responding to the issue of war crimes and crimes against humanity, the Rome Statute of the ICC laid down specific rules with regard to all manner of sexual violence in armed conflict and war (including sexual slavery). The ICC's vision was wider and farther reaching in the sense that it was the first such organisation to provide a gender-neutral definition of sexual violence that gave equality to both sexes when it came to their victimhood. In addition it also took a broad view of sexual violence when it laid down the rule that a war crime may constitute a context where:

The perpetrator invaded the body of a person by conduct resulting in penetration, however slight, of any part of the body of the victim or of the perpetrator with a sexual organ, or of the anal or genital opening of the victim with any object or any other part of the body (ICC, Art. 7 (1) (g)-1).

Furthermore, it explicitly expanded its definition of sexual violence by including cultural practices like 'sexual slavery and sterilization' as crimes against humanity and thus war crimes. Interestingly, although adopted at a diplomatic conference on 17 July 1998 and entered into force on 1 July 2002, not all countries of the international community have signed up to its membership. As of 1 May 2013 only 122 states were party to the statute. And those who are its signatories have not always succeeded in preventing such crimes from taking place.

In the view of Dustin A. Lewis to reduce or prevent sexual abuse and violence against boys and men in conflict settings, international law should be interpreted, applied and enforced in ways that not only delegitimise the prejudicial and discriminatory conceptions of gender, sex and homophobia, but the law will also have to use a definition of sexual violence that includes all manner of such abuse within that framework which targets a male's imputed, perceived or actual sexuality (Lewis, 2009: 2).

Although a visionary institution with a robust framework, the jurisdiction of the ICC is ultimately hamstrung by three key hurdles regarding its overall remit. In the first place, its jurisdiction is limited. The ICC can only prosecute accused individuals if they belong to a country that has accepted the Court's jurisdiction, the said crime has taken place within the borders of a country that accepts the Court's jurisdiction, or in the extreme event, the UN Security Council has referred the specific individual, group or situation to the ICC's prosecutor. Second, in order for the court to take up a given case the purported crime must have taken place after the date by which the Rome Statute of the ICC came into force. Third, and most important of all, the ICC can only prosecute a given violator provided there is sufficient evidence to suggest that the national court system did not entertain the case against him.

In other words, the ICC's jurisdiction is all about the principle of complementarity. The Court is designed to complement—not replace—individual state-based judicial systems. As such, the ICC is not in a position to assume full accountability for enforcing international norms against sexual violence. And, ultimately, it is down to the individual nations to do their part to complement the Court's work (Koenig, Lincoln & Groth, 2011: 2).

Theoretically in situations of inter-state conflict where the aggressor and victim belong to two separate political entities an overarching legal framework such as that of the ICC's jurisdiction could perhaps provide appropriate punitive measures. To the defenders of the ICC such a mechanism is capable of alleviating the legal and humanitarian loophole that is so endemic in many conflict-ridden and post-conflict states. However, as we have seen the ICC has only a limited amount of power. If it tries to flex its muscles and appear gung-ho in its juridical demands upon states who are not its members or those who refuse to recognise its sovereignty over the national courts there is very little in the way of justice that the victims can expect.

Thanks to the inviolability of state sovereignty and the impunity of soldiers fighting under certain flags, the ICC can only watch the events like Abu Ghraib from the sidelines and do nothing. Put simply, although it has robust sentiments, in the end, given the enormity of these three 'controlling' clauses casting shadows on the ICC, more often than not it is not in a position to demand or prosecute alleged perpetrators of such crimes.

Then, of course, we have events such as Liberia and Sierra Leone where a decade-long civil war facilitated an atmosphere where child soldiers committed most heinous sexual violence against their victims. In some other ongoing conflicts such as the civil war in DR Congo this remains a continuous affair. From a purely legal perspective how do we address this question? According to the *International Protocol on the Documentation and Investigation of Sexual Violence in Conflict* (a product of London Global Summit to End Sexual Violence in Conflict, 2014):

In cases of sexual violence committed by children associated with armed groups and forces, [we] must remember that children who commit acts of sexual violence have often been manipulated or coerced into such acts and are victims themselves. Children should be treated as survivors/witnesses and not as perpetrators, in accordance with UN Guidelines on Justice Matters Involving Child Victims and Child Witnesses of Crime 36 and the UN Convention on the Rights of the Child (2014: 42). https://www.gov.uk/government/uploads/system/uploads/attachment_data/file/319054/PSVI_protocol_web.pdf last accessed 21 October 2014.

In these situations do we want bodies such as ICC to bring to book the faraway rebel leaders previously in charge of some marauding child soldiers that committed these crimes? What if this leadership (if ever brought to book) claims never to have recruited these child soldiers?

Assessment

The validity of 'law as a system of rules' depends not on content but on the procedures by which they are represented (Dworkin, 1977). Similarly, as we have often been reminded, 'our practice of punishment is taken to be governed by certain rules, such as the rule that the guilty but not the innocent are to be penalised' (Honderich, 1984: 66). While most modern societies have copious amounts of legal frameworks to protect their civilians in times of war and peace it is their ability to enforce and follow through the procedures during these contrasting periods which marks them out as stable or unstable societies.

This is most noticeable in the context of sexual violence against boys and men during periods of conflict and war, and the absence of a clear and responsive mechanism to impart justice in one form or another to the aggrieved parties afterwards.

Despite several high-profile international trials (as was with ICTY) and advances in international law (ICC's *Elements of Crimes* framework) there is currently no adequate mechanism available to deter, prosecute and punish individuals who have committed various degrees of sexual violence against boys and men in armed conflicts and wars. This state of affairs has led some legal scholars to argue that 'an overwhelming majority of perpetrators or facilitators of sexual violence are not held accountable for their crimes and few survivors ever receive justice or any other form of accountability or reparation, much less psychological or financial redress' (Askin, 2003: 509).

While the lack of interest in prosecuting the violators may stem from a general discomfort with dealing with the 'male condition', a part of the problem rests with the reluctance of several international actors to confront the challenge head on. For instance, while the United States was at the forefront in pushing forward the agenda of ICTY and ICTR to prosecute the Serbs who had committed those heinous crimes against their Bosnian Muslim captives, the former developed cold feet when it came to addressing the crimes committed in Abu Ghraib, Iraq, Guantanamo Bay and Afghanistan.

As some studies have stressed, 'states have a duty, set out in numerous international instruments, to effectively prosecute and punish acts of sexual and gender-based violence where such acts are perpetrated by the state or by private persons' (Bastick, Grimm, & Kunz, 2007: 163). Yet, some states have gone to extra lengths to make sure that when it comes to criminal prosecution they stay clear of it. The UN Security Council Resolution 1487 (2003) adopted on 12 June 2003 introduced at the behest of the United States, explicitly exempted US troops and personnel serving in any UN force in Iraq from prosecution for international war crimes under the Rome Statute of the ICC (Zawati, 2007: 37).

As if the prevention of the universal jurisdiction of the ICC and other bodies was not enough, the US went an extra mile in making sure (following the Abu Ghraib incident) that some aggrieved parties do not have the recourse to hold either its government or its troops accountable in the domestic court of law. Note, for instance, the US Military Commissions Act (MCA) of 2006. This bill, which was passed by the Congress and signed by the American president before it became law, is a gross assault on the international humanitarian standards and law. Section 5 of the bill, for example, rendered the Geneva Conventions and related treaties as unenforceable in court in civil cases involving the US government and its agents. If that were not enough the law also bars 'aliens' and 'unlawful enemy combatants' held in US custody from filing cases to challenge the legality of their detention or raise claims of torture or other abuses (Zawati, 2007: 35).

This deliberate lapse by the United States has not been lost on some other members of the international community. As mentioned earlier, not all the states have signed up to the ICC's jurisdiction, fearing it may compromise their service personnel serving abroad or endanger their national security agenda.

Reflecting on these double standards, a self-established culture of immunity and the lack of progress in prosecuting the violators, some commentators have noted that, 'guided by normative values that promote individual criminal responsibility, international criminal law operates in a highly politicized environment in which policy-makers may choose to implement international criminal law enforcement mechanisms in some situations but not in other, seemingly analogous situations' (Lewis, 2009: 47).

Conclusion

The task of a critique of violence can be summarized as that of expounding its relation to law and justice (Benjamin, 1986: 277). The foregoing discussion amplified the prevailing disquiet between violation and justice. While there exists a great deal of ambiguity in terms of the presence and prevalence of legal measures for the protection of victims and reconstitution of their rights in a post-conflict phase, in the domestic context such discourses either do not exist or are few and far between. In the end, the whole issue boils down to a weak legal framework that either fails to protect the victims effectively or does not protect at all.

'Codes of law,' wrote Rabelais, 'are founded upon necessity and not upon justice.' For the law to be effective it must be conscious of the judicial needs of the victim. To be seen as effective it must be responsive to the sufferings and post-conflict aspirations of the victims as well as the community to which they belong. Only when these twin objectives are fully introduced and implemented, can the judiciary be seen as an effective means of grievance redressal.

Regrettably, owing to a multitude of factors that range from the feminist monopolisation of female plight, to the reluctance of judges and the judiciary at the international level to fully engage with the issue of male victimhood, and discriminatory domestic laws against men who have experienced sexual violence, there is a lopsided legal framework that disadvantages the male victim.

Needless to say, male victims of sexual violence in armed conflicts and war need to be fully represented without prejudice in international justice initiatives. Similarly, national laws should be broadened to protect their interests and they should not be discriminated against when it comes to delivering justice for their victimhood.[7] Individual states should criminalise the wartime sexual abuse of men as they do with regard to women.

True, the bottom line for sexuality and sexual violence remains the law (Rousseau & Porter, 1987: 15). Yet this very law may at times seem to be wanting in terms of victim protection. On balance, one could argue, the legal system we currently have is not the result of peaceful teleological growth; the evolution and establishment of laws that seek to protect other such victims (women in particular) emerged owing to the constant violence. Gross egregious violence of this kind, in other words, has been a principal determinant in shaping universal values and laws surrounding what is permissible and what is punishable. If violence is indeed the progenitor or midwife to the emergence of laws prohibiting such crimes and responsible for initiating moves towards protecting victims' rights, one can only hope the collective experience of male victims of this form of aggression leads to the unveiling of far-reaching protective legal measures.

6

MAPPING MEMORY

Each person's life is dominated by a central event, which shapes and distorts everything that comes after it and, in retrospect, everything that came before.

Suketu Mehta, *Maximum City*, 2005: 6.

It is hard to comprehend the singularity of a victim's experience either in part or in its totality. To quote Emmanuel Lévinas, the barbarity of violence in war 'does not consist so much in injuring and annihilating persons as in interrupting their continuity, making them play roles in which they no longer recognise themselves' (Lévinas, 1969: 21). The victims' experience imposes a condition which implies that because an injury has been inflicted, pain must subsequently be suffered (Deleuze and Guattari, 1984: 191). Thanks to the 'voice of memory' our subject finds himself cast deep into an objective order from which there is no chance of escape. He cannot return to a space punctuated by ordinary reality. Or, as Cavarero puts it, the other, the torturer, through that specific action, 'wounds him and is there to wound him'. There is an invisible eye that casts a long shadow on his present and is there to extract pleasure from his dehumanisation. There is no way out, only the infinite and prolonged repetition of unilateral suffering (Cavarero, 2010: 114). He truly experiences an annihilating negation of the self.

Is there is an alternative or option for reciprocity? Is there scope for getting even? How can one 'pay back' (Deleuze and Guattari, 1984: 191) the violator?

In conventional warfare and armed conflicts where the captured victim undergoes intense physical punishment at the hands of his enemy captors, a large majority of the victims are often able to ease their future suffering by thinking of it as part of a collective experience (the Japanese PoW survivors, Second World War returnees, Vietnam veterans, and so on). To some war veterans, undergoing conventional violence while being held by the enemy is very much 'a part of the job'. It is often a collective experience. It helps establish bonds (Herr, 2004; Bourke, 2007). It facilitates in the consolidation of a common identity. And at a later date this whole experience is put in the context of camaraderie.

On some rare occasions the torturer and the tortured come face-to-face with each other in a spirit of reconciliation. On Remembrance Day, in the United Kingdom, for instance, such public acknowledgement of the reconciliation is very much a part of the prime time evening broadcast. In this very public spectacle you might have a German ex-Nazi corporal facing up to his own atrocities and an ageing British soldier repeating the sentiment of his former perpetrator that it was all part of the discourse of war. Or, as Clint Eastwood's character, facing his former enemy and recounting the banality of the US Civil War and the uselessness of holding grudges against former enemies, puts it in the final scenes of *The Outlaw Josey Wales*, 'I guess we all died a little in that damn war.'

Such public acknowledgements of reconciliation either in a real life context or in cinema are in no way an orchestrated bonhomie between the victim and the violator as some sceptics think, but a clear recognition of the need for moving forward and acknowledging the banality of such violence. Therefore, for everyone watching such spectacles, it is both a collective moment of mourning and forgiving.

Turning to our victims of sexual crimes in conflict zones, we find no such enactment of mutual orchestration. This is because of a variety of interrelated factors.

First, while the violator has now found ways of looking away from the full nature of his/her acts, the victim finds it hard to believe what has happened to him (Morton, 2004: 14). Through a given action the violator permanently interrupted the subjective continuity of that particular individual—now victim. The specificity of that action alienates the victim from the structures of meaning, which defined him in the first place. Hence it is the impossibility of reconciling oneself to that action which forever imprisons our victim to that experience. As the literature on moral philosophy suggests, 'one is reconciled with a person, not with his action, and one does not act as if the actions had not been performed' (Morton, 2004: 125).

Second, the possibility of any gesture of reconciliation in future between the victim and the violator is hard to establish, as the victim shudders at the thought of meeting his violator. Just as a society would not force a rape victim to go face-to-face with their rapist, even in a court of law, so should be the case of a sexually violated man in armed conflict.

Third, while the victims of conventional wartime violence can enter into a public solidarity of suffering with his co-sufferers in the post-conflict phase this option is closed to our victim. For every victim touched by this particular horror the trauma is both irrevocable and forever private.[1]

And, if he were to project his unfortunate experience upon the society to which he belongs he can only expect to bring shame to his own being and consign the collective to even a greater degree of indignity and humiliation.

Fourth, the wound of our victim is so extraordinary that even if he wanted he could not bring himself to an *Outlaw Josey Wales*-style change of heart either in abstraction or in reality. There is no such vocabulary available for our victim. As a heterosexual male victim his physiognomy as well his psychology conspire against coming to terms of this oddity. Both psychologically as well as physically he finds it impossible to entertain the degree of flexibility required to relate to this experience.

Fifth and finally, if reconciliation over that action and the act of the perpetrator is ruled out either in private or in public, does the victim nurse a private grudge for revenge against his violator in future? One of my interviewees produced a rather inimitable response. What sort of retribution—if there is such a thing? Retribution in this context would imply taking away from the offender(s) what they value. Could the victim impose upon his violator the punishment that he was accorded? The uniqueness of this violence, in the view of my interviewee, did not even allow the victim to reciprocate in a similar manner. Given a choice our victim might succeed in killing his past perpetrator but can hardly bring himself to sexually violate his past tormentor.

Or, as Paulo Nzili our Mau Mau victim (referred to in Chapter 2) reflected: "You cannot repay a sin with a sin. That will not give [you] back what was taken away from [you].... (Nzili, quoted in, Taylor, 2012: 9).

Owing to the enormity of this mode of violence upon the subject, what we end up with in our assessment of effects is a narrative of pain and suffering that the victim is forced to undergo throughout the remainder of his life. While there exists a cluster of feelings that are ever present affecting victims' physical and emotional being, the defining aspect of this affliction is one of pain in its various forms. It is apt, therefore, that we spend some time exploring the subject of pain.

Pain

Is it possible to identify the specific pain carried by the victims? If yes, how does such pain manifest itself? What sort of pains are they? Do they exhibit physical pain? Are there outward representations or tell-tale signs of the pain caused by violation? Or does it belong to the domain of psychological suffering? There are two ways of experiencing such pain—visible external pain and invisible internal pain. In the first place the physical materiality of human existence reveals an outward representation of that pain. 'A body will bleed when it is cut and can be seen to bleed, and an embodied individual feels the pain of the wound and experiences that pain as his own' (Jackson & Scott, 2007: 99). Second, as we are reminded, embodiment is not simply an external physical given, it is also well grounded in the invisible recesses of that body. The second kind of pain, while not visible to the external observer to quantify or examine, nonetheless has an affective capacity over the victim.

Sima Qian or Ssu-ma Ch'ien (ca. 145 or 135 BC–86 BC), the greatest of Chinese historians and a victim of such violence owing to his opposition to the regime, quips on the enormity of his private pain following his castration: 'I look at myself now, mutilated in body and living in vile disgrace. Every time I think of this shame I find myself drenched in sweat' (quoted in, Watson, 1958: 77).[2] What we are confronted with here is the profound nature of psychological pain that lingers even after the externally visible physical wound has healed.

Typically a male victim of wartime sexual abuse and violence displays two sets of scars. The first one is physical and the second one is psychological. Given the complex nature of such violence these two sets of conditions often manifest in a set of pains where the two are conflated. Put simply, someone who has been sodomised and raped will likely suffer psychological as well as physical pain. These events have the capacity to have a pathological effect on the sufferer's psyche. It would not be wrong to suggest that this experience is an attack upon the man's very sexual identity leading to a non-healing 'psychic wound'.

Examined within trauma theory, the constant psychological suffering affecting the victim's inner being or the violated self is often far too profound to heal. It is a misery that lingers for months and years, and sometimes the whole lifetime of the victim. In the words of Paulo Nzili the Mau Mau victim referred to earlier, "… after I was castrated I thought that I had been cut off from any sexual life and that I would never be able to marry and have children, which is a man's pride. I felt completely destroyed and without hope (Paulo Nzili quoted in, Taylor, 2012: 9)."

According to psychoanalytically informed trauma theories, where the damage is psychological, pain might issue from numerous different hiding places. One critic interrogating such chronic ailments describes the perpetual nature of such pain as like the smoke from a smoldering ruin. Pain here arises from multiple sources, layer upon layer of pain. Unmask one pain and the next simply replaces it (Morris, 1993: 68–9).

It is the chronic nature of such psychological affliction that makes such pain singularly unique. In the view of Morris, while '[a]cute pain … serves a recognizable function in protecting us from further harm', for example warning 'us to remove a hand from a hot stove', 'chronic pain … possesses no biological purpose' (Morris, 1993: 70). The problem with such chronic pain is that while the cause is clear the cure is not.

In addition, some of the victims the author interviewed said that they were living nightmares following their violation. What does 'living nightmares' imply? In the view of some specialists dealing with the issue of nightmares the former is often symptomatic of a patient suffering from chronic pain. In such cases, the universe perceived by the victim or patient is structurally identical with the universe of the nightmare.[3] Nightmares, according to Lawrence LeShan, comprise three homogeneous features: terrible things are being done and worse are threatened; the person experiencing it is helplessly under the control of outside forces; and for the individual perceiving such nightmares there is no proof when such visitations will actually come to an end (quoted in Morris, 1993: 71; also see LeShan, 1964: 119).

Furthermore, in LeShan's interpretation the person in such pain is in 'the same formal situation: terrible things are being done to him and he does not know if worse will happen; he has no control and is helpless to take effective action; no time limit is given' (LeShan, 1964: 119). While not every victim expressed similar experiences an overwhelming portion of them did allude to forms of living nightmares. Although they were aware that they no longer inhabited conflict conditions, that they lived in protected environments and the overall situation was that of peace and not war, they still could not escape from the chronic nature of such nightmares.

Felix (the assumed name of our victim), who escaped the killing fields of the Democratic Republic of the Congo (DRC) and lives as a refugee in a Western European city, now describes the chronic nature of his pain in this manner: he always feels breathless, as though he is constantly running even when sitting in his council flat in front of the television. In fact, his voice betrayed hints of breathlessness while describing his condition. Felix along with several fellow Congolese was chased a good distance in fields of corn. Caught, he was tied to a nearby tree, sodomised and then raped by a group of male militia. Once they were done he was viciously stabbed on his genitals. It was a miracle he survived given how much blood he lost. The chronic nature of Felix's nightmarish daydreams consisted of going numb in his legs and the intense feeling of breathlessness that one associates with running from a scene of potential life and death.

Hashim (not his real name), a Bosnian Muslim/Bosniak in his late thirties, still could not reconcile himself to the fact that he was violated nearly fifteen years ago. 'Whenever I see a soldier in uniform my legs go numb, a sweat builds up all over my body even in deepest winter, I feel lifeless.' From a biopolitical approach, such a reaction is the manifestation and production of a given fear and terror implanted in Hashim by the regime which violated him in the first place. In this recurring production of fear, there is no shift to a new altered condition, there is no escape route from this nightmare and there is no antidote to dispose of this state of affairs.

Meditating on the effect of pain on individual bodies some two millennia ago, Aristotle wrote, 'pain upsets and destroys the nature of the person who feels it' (Aristotle, *Nicomachean Ethics*, 1984: 1767). Jeychandran (not his real name), two decades removed from Sri Lanka and now a British citizen, still wakes up several nights a week sweating. His nightmares are always the same: being dragged out of his house by Sri Lankan soldiers and gagged and raped by soldiers in uniform in the barracks; someone binding his hands and legs before fixing two metal clips to his scrotum and penis and then putting the wires in the plug. He twitches as he speaks about his experience (although we are sitting in an outside café in London in broad daylight). He disappears into his thoughts in the middle of the conversation. Small beads of sweat build up on his temple and neck. When he wakes up from this nightmare and returns to the conversation his throat is dry and his voice affected. Here I was witnessing the chronic pain of a patient second-hand.

Felix, Hashim and Jeychandran had no known way of escaping their perpetual nightmares. Both Hashim and Jeychandran had sought psychological counselling. Several sessions in the psychiatrists' chair, however, were unsuccessful, leading to their GP's suggestion that their condition was chronic and that they had to learn to live with it. For all practical purposes, this enforced condition is inescapable for 'if the experience was synonymous with horror it is beyond survival and life' (Cavarero, 2007; Debrix & Barder, 2012). It is a human condition that disintegrates into multiple shreds leading almost to the devastation of the body and the soul that resides within it.

Furthermore the victims' experience often boils down to their past eating up their present and future. According to some critics, 'silence is often the most frequent response to [chronic] pain' (Morris, 1993: 72). Morris goes on to suggest that:

… patients with chronic pain soon discover that their complaints (potentially endless, like their pain) often exhaust, frustrate, and finally alienate family and friends and physicians. Many patients thus learn to retreat into a defensive isolation. They keep to themselves. They experience firsthand the failure of words in the face of suffering' (Morris, 1993: 72).

While this form of assessment is correct and in some ways applicable to most victims of chronic pain, the reason our kind of victim keeps silent is often different from other sufferers of chronic pain.

For Felix his relationship with his girlfriend (following his trauma) was always fraught. They could not communicate very well. She could not come to terms with his brooding silence and recurring nightmares. Eventually the relationship broke down. 'How could I tell my girlfriend that I was chased down a field of corn, brutally raped by a gang of militias and then had my genital flayed?' It was this unspeakable act that forced Felix to commit to a perpetual state of silence about his suffering and pain. The experience was so brutal that he could not even share it with his partner. 'It is a pain that cannot be allocated. Hence I remain silent,' were Felix's last words about his pain as I made my way out of his council flat.

The silence that the likes of Felix and similar victims maintained about their pain was different from other chronic pain sufferers; their silence was largely a result of the inability to share the enormity of such pain, its uniqueness and the overall shame associated with it (that I have high-lighted on several other occasions during the course of this discussion). In the end it is the inarticulate silence of the victims, which serves as 'the expression of otherness so alien that we (as non victims) have no words or language with which to comprehend this chronic suffering' (Morris, 1993: 74).

While the chronic pain of the kind that our victim suffers from is an 'unrelieved disaster' (Morris, 1993: 74) for him personally, it can also spell disaster for the people around him, especially his family and close friends. Given that pain is a subjective experience, even if the near and dear ones wish to share the pain of the victim there is very little avenue for such recourse. It is the kind of pain that is felt only within the invisible soli-tude of the victim's mind. How is it possible for outsiders to step into that invisible domain of suffering? 'He was not the same man, I knew. He would brood for hours on end while sitting in his dark room,' con-fided Farida (not her real name), the now conscience-stricken wife of Shahnawaz (not his real name), a victim of such violence in Indian-held Kashmir. Farida was speaking out about her violated husband's agony with the promise that Shahnawaz should not know that others were aware of his violation.

Self-censorship

The nagging question, of course, is why do violated men not talk about their experiences? Female victims of sexual crimes are now often encour-aged to report them, but male victims tend not to be. Why is this? The answer could be located in our broad cultural inheritance. Dennis Altman, the author of a seminal study entitled *Homosexual Oppression and Liberation* (1993), argued that thanks to a given religio-cultural and com-plex civilisational inheritance that both prescribes as well as proscribes a set of 'dos' and 'don'ts' which go back centuries, individuals have been pre-programmed as to what can be admitted and what cannot. An individ-ual violation of the self, in other words, if proclaimed in public, becomes a collective social insult.

Given the dominance of this mode of discourse, societal non-condem-nation of all forms of sexual experience that is not heterosexual (Altman, 1993) has become a norm. Unsurprisingly it is because of this specific burden of civilisation's expectation that the heterosexual man, having been forced into a homosexual experience, simply finds it impossible to break free of the overarching norms and remains imprisoned by this taboo. More importantly, admitting to this experience puts him in danger of being associated with homosexuality, which the society has so long and hard tried to inch away from.

Such being the overarching narrative, in most cases of sexual assault during armed conflict and war there is some recalcitrance on the part of the victim to admit such abuse (Carlson, 2005: 22). While reticence is common to both female as well as male victims, it may be more widespread in cases of male sufferers of such violence. As I detailed in chapter four, the aggressor or violator is in possession of the knowledge surrounding the societal taboo on such experience and the burden of silence that the victim is expected to carry. Consequently, it is these twin forces—society-imposed censorship and individually mediated self-censorship on the part of the victim—that gives the upper hand to his violator.

In addition, even if the victim wishes to break free from the societal taboo and proclaim his victimhood he may be forced to maintain silence about his experience owing to a whole host of attendant issues. For instance, victims very often have the disadvantage of providing supporting evidence about their violation. As one critic put it:

For a man's degradation and pain to be certified as valid only if his penis or testicles are cut off has a parallel in the rationale historically applied to female rape and which, unfortunately, continues to exist. That rationale requires that a woman show bruises, torn clothing and a pulverised face before an investigator believes she has not been a willing participant in her own brutalisation (Carlson, 2005: 21).

When faced with this task of medically proving his abuse in a post-aggression/post-violation context (when there is a considerable time lapse, for the violated may have been in prison and released later) our victim is faced with an uphill battle to prove his victimhood before an investigator, adjudicator or jury.

In addition, many victims are unaware as to what constitutes sexual violence when caught up in the melee of an armed conflict or war. Is forcible nudity an act of sexual violence? If the victim has been hit on his testicles does that constitute a form of sexual assault? In fact some men 'who are beaten up on the testicles do not report the crime not because they are afraid of revealing sexual assault, but because what happened to them does not fit their own conception of sexual assault' (Carlson, 2005: 22).

Hence, '[i]t is ... not surprising that the use of sexual torture methods is so widespread' (Agger & Jensen, 1994: 42), for perpetrators know that their actions will likely go unreported and thus unpunished.

In their assessment of Croat male victims of Serbian sexual abuse and rape Loncar et al. highlight how a traditional understanding of honour and humiliation has led to many of these victims actively refusing to come to terms with their trauma either in terms of admitting to their violation or seeking psychological counselling and help provided by local NGOs. The pronounced feelings of 'shame, dishonour, and humiliation in a tradition-bound male-dominated society', argue the authors, has created a wall of silence around their experience (Loncar et al., 2010: 199). Therefore, while there are mechanisms available to address these particular traumas (post-traumatic stress disorder [PTSD] combat facilities, medical and psychological facilities), victims are often unwilling to accept this professional help.

In Croatia the victim's ability to come forward and make a clean breast of his wartime experience and seek psychophysical treatment is encumbered by an additional factor. Croatian society does not acknowledge male sexual abuse. It holds that this is an experience or tragedy that can befall only women, not men. Since common public opinion reinforces the fact that 'only women can be victims of sexual violence' (Loncar et al., 2010: 199) this gender-specific understanding also deters the male victims from finding a suitable outlet to redress their trauma and attendant grievance.

What was true of the Bosnian and Croat experience is amply manifested in other theatres of conflict. For instance, 'the majority of Tamil males in Sri Lanka who were sexually assaulted during the country's quarter-of-a-century long civil war did not report it to the authorities at the time' (Stemple, 2011: 25). What was the reason behind such self-censorship?

Sin and shame

In instances where such transgressive sexual violence has taken place the violated often feels that he has fallen below his own moral standards. The value he attaches to the purity of his own being before and after the violation takes a drastic turn.

Condemned to a value-less physical self he develops a set of interconnected responses, which involve denial of the trauma and strategies to fight off any potential threats that might arise if stories of the transgression become public. Put simply, our victim is a prisoner of moral as well as practical challenges.

Owing to the violation he is at once physically as well as morally flawed. From the gaze of an external eye or societal perspective the sacredness he held about his own being and identity is both destroyed and rendered morally inaccessible following the violation. Thanks to this private tragedy he has become an outsider and an outcast to the value system that surrounds him. Similarly, the existence of his physical and spiritual self becomes objectionable to himself. The experience pushes our victim into an inescapable concentric circle of sin and shame. It is a suspended state where while the victim is too weak to kill himself, neither does he possess the required strength to go on living.

For Agamben, shame is produced through an act in which the subject (here our male victim) works as the agent of his own desubjectivation, its own oblivion as a subject. It is an auto-affectation. The subject, having been violated, feels that he was somehow responsible for bringing this humiliating condition upon himself.

The forced sexualised violence between the inmates of the camp or between members of the same family or ethno-religious group is often aimed at condemning them to a grey zone. Or, as Diken and Laustsen put it, 'victims in this context are forced to transgress constitutive prohibitions marking their identity as human beings' (Diken and Laustsen, 2005: 121–2). Forcing them to execute perverse rituals against one another is very much aimed at destroying the captive victims' dignity and feeling of moral worth.

As a victim tainted by this violation, his life becomes a repository of guilt, shame and sin all together. And on some occasions even if he wishes to steer himself out of these feelings, they are reinforced by the immediate family and the society to which he belongs. The case of Jean-Baptiste, a twenty-two-year-old Congolese man who was raped by a female *mayi-mayi* fighter on the shores of Lake Edward in Lubero Territory, is a typical one. Following this nightmarish experience he was forced to 'stay quiet' about the rape by his mother and not seek any medical or legal aid. His mother feared the community would declare the family outcasts if they came to know about Jean-Baptiste's sexual violation by a rebel female (Amnesty International, Country Report, DR Congo, 2009: 12–3).

Polidor, a forty-year-old victim from the Kazima in the South-Kivu region of the DRC was raped in front of his wife and children in January 2003 by members of a Burundian insurgent group. While gang-raping Polidor his violator kept telling him, 'You're no longer a man, you are going to become one of our women' (Amnesty International USA, *Democratic Republic of Congo: Mass Rape–Time for Remedies*, 25 October 2004, p. 9).

For Joachim, raped and robbed by Burundian soldiers while on his way to the market to sell fish, life following his violation was one of complete ostracism by his fellow community members. After his rape and the public knowledge of his violation 'the community looked down upon him. When he talked to other men of the village, they looked at him as if he was worthless as a man' (Amnesty International USA, *Democratic Republic of Congo: Mass Rape–Time for Remedies*, p. 9).

This is not surprising, given African society's traditional understanding of the role of the masculine sex. In the words of one such victim, Owiny, in Uganda, the immediate family, the neighbourhood and the society unhesitatingly despises the man who has been sexually violated by other men. For there are certain cultural mores to be observed if you are a man.

In Africa no man is allowed to be vulnerable. You have to be masculine, strong. You should never break down or cry. A man must be a leader and provide for the whole family. When he fails to reach that set standard, society perceives that there is something wrong (Storr, 2011: 7).

What we encounter here is not prejudice but the prevalence of a particularised mainstream ideal. A shared mainstream ideal often leads to a shared sense of grievance. Some societies feel these specific occurrences have a contagion effect capable of debilitating its sense of self-worth, leading to communal, societal and ultimately national decay.

Thanks to this skewed understanding, for the male victims in Africa their victimhood is a double curse. First, because they got violated. Second, the family, the friends and the society curse them for their particular victimhood. Once their story is discovered the victims simply lose the support and comfort of those around them (Storr, 2011: 7). When wives discover their husbands have been raped by other men in the bush they leave their husbands. For upon the discovery of the victim status of a given male the neighbourhood asks his wife—how is she going to live with him? As what? Is the violated victim still a husband? Or, has his violation given him the status of a female? But most important of all 'if he can be raped, who will protect her?' (Storr, 2011: 7)

Although it might appear as simple prejudice, such reactions are based on a complex set of explanations. To an onlooker or external person, a violated body can never be just a body abstracted from mind, self and social context. The masculine meanings associated with the male body are changed its violation. With violation comes the title of perpetually 'diminished manhood'.

Such a value-laden reaction also receives its sustenance from the traditional understanding of the role of men. Here 'gender essentialism involves asserting that men and women have specific roles assigned to them by nature and biology' (Franks, 2014: 574) which they ought to uphold at any cost. As Cynthia Enloe argues, every society entertains a fixed idea surrounding the role of men in conflict: 'men are called to fight or be killed' (Enloe, 1983: 46). Consequently, in many societies the assumption is that in armed conflicts and war sexual violation and victimhood is suffered exclusively by women. In warfare, then, men are not only set to be men but to be 'militaristic men', by undertaking the role of an active fighter and defender of their physical self and those needing protection (Enloe, 1993: 52). It is when men fall outside this image that they receive a battering.

If the victim failed to live up to the age-old standards of manliness set by the society he is no good. It does not matter if he were caught up in a civil war. It is immaterial if there were ten AK47-wielding rebels who forced their way into his body. The man simply was not supposed to give in to this violation. His victimhood is his own responsibility—the wife, the family, the friends, the village, the township cannot and are not expected to express sympathy. Put simply, in such contexts, 'real men' are above and beyond such subjection. Consequently, the experience of rape both by the victim and those surrounding him gives rise to two other deeply problematic perceptions. First, for the victim, this experience dissipates once and for all his own hegemonic views about male masculinity. Second, for the society, the man is a failed 'masculine project'—a stigma.[4] Hence he forfeits any sympathy, protection or call for justice.

Here patriarchy and homophobia both contribute to silence the victim. As if that were not enough, survivors of such violence in Africa are often assumed to be gay, which is a crime in thirty-eight of fifty-three African nations and carries extreme penalties including death. Given this cocktail of societal and regime-sponsored callousness, in the view of some NGOs working towards victim support and rehabilitation, 'it is never possible to ascertain whether the victims will ever receive any justice from the system and the government at large' (MSF, 2004: 16). And on top of this there is the problem of social isolation for victims whose communities in some way blame them for what happened to them.

Hierarchy of sympathy (or the lack of it)

The way a society reacts to victims of sexual crimes can differ depending on the nature of the victim. For example, when notable political prisoners or civil rights activists have been raped in custody in conflict locations like Kashmir, Chechnya and parts of Latin America, they have often been treated as heroes when released. By contrast, victims who were already perceived to be effeminate or homosexual prior to being sexually violated tend not to receive much sympathy. According to some critics they sit at the bottom of sexual victim hierarchy and following their victimisation are treated as the lowliest members of the society (Wakelin & Long, 2003: 483).

Does this prejudice have any basis? In his seminal study, *The Psychology of Crime* (1960), David Abrahmsen argued that in situations of sexual violation there might be an element of 'unconscious complicity' on the part of the victim with his violator. In other words, 'a shared psychological and biological drive' between the victim and violator may on occasion put them in the context of violation. If this is so, the argument goes, the victim, owing to his own peculiar inner personality traits, has somehow unknowingly appealed to a force within the violator to instigate violation.

A Sri Lankan Tamil prisoner of war who was repeatedly sexually abused and raped while in government custody would later reveal (during the course of an interview in London) that he was not only singled out by his captors for his supposed femininity and homosexuality but was consciously castigated by his fellow Tamil prisoners. Asked as to why they did so, the group, which had escaped from custody at a later stage of the conflict, was very explicit in its remarks. According to one of the former captives, the presence of the feminine male prisoner among them promoted a direct inclination towards sexual violence among their captors. The homosexual prisoner's presence encouraged the tendency to orchestrate forms of sexual violence against the prisoners. Consequently, the soldiers would force the heterosexual prisoners to rape their effeminate fellow Tamil prisoner.

Looking back, the group that underwent this violation was of the opinion that had there been no homosexual prisoner of war in their midst then the violation may not have occurred in the first place.

From the perspective of other male Tamil victims and from the Tamil society's point of view there was little sympathy for our victim. For them it was the 'twisted' sexuality of the Tamil homosexual that was responsible for all the violence. In fact, one heterosexual prisoner of war suggested that perhaps the victim actually 'enjoyed' such violation being done to him. In other words, the collective humiliation, violation and shame that they underwent and were still suffering from was primarily due to the presence of this homosexual prisoner in their midst.

That this prisoner had suffered equally or even more did not register in the minds of his fellow victims. While other straight male victims of this violence were treated with some respect and accorded sympathy by the Sri Lankan Tamil refugee/expat community in Middlesex, England the effeminate homosexual victim received no such consideration. For the Sri Lankan Tamil community he was seen as an outsider, someone that should be avoided.

If the root meaning of compassion is 'suffering with', what we witness here is the refusal to share the grief and suffering of this particular victim. In the view of Wakelin and Long, the absence of compassion and the justification of the communal condemnation of our victim is a function of prejudice against gay men and the mistaken idea that victims must somehow have been responsible foe what happened to them (Wakelin & Long, 2003: 484–5). From a homosexual male victim's perspective such communal bias has to do with society's innate disgust with the traditional view of male-on-male rape. This biased attitude is not only shared by the wider society but also equally held by the law enforcement agents. In some countries, police simply do not regard sexual violence as a priority compared to other crimes (Bastic, Grimm, & Kunz, 2007: 147). Understandably, when reporting their victimisation homosexual victims sometimes claim to be heterosexual in order to improve their chances of being believed (Wakelin & Long, 2003: 486). Again, if the reaction of the law enforcement agents towards our effeminate/homosexual victim is anything to go by then it would appear that the latter was also placing our particular injured party at the bottom of a hierarchy of victimhood.

Complicity of silence

Part of the reason why male experience of sexual violence in armed conflicts is not very successful in attracting the attention it deserves is that those who are responsible for making rulings on such matters themselves often entertain prejudices about the issue. As I stressed in the previous chapter my interrogation of this subject with many police officials, public prosecutors and judges in several conflict-ridden non-Western settings has elicited the following response: by publicly delving into these crimes the police, public prosecutor or the judge feel they will bring shame on themselves. Consequently the refusal to delve into this issue becomes an effective tool to counter any potential shame.

The situation is compounded by the reluctance of victims to report crimes. On top of the shame, humiliation and prejudice that prevent the victim from coming forward, cultural norms surrounding masculinity and manliness condition many victims to feel it is below their dignity to acknowledge such violence. A direct consequence of this state of affairs is the victim's slow slide into a state of denial that draws a curtain on such experience.

For instance, in Croatia, where many men were sexually violated by Serb militias, many were silent about their wartime experience for fear of undermining their own position in society, as a report produced by the health workers of the Medical Centre for Human Rights in Zagreb highlighted (MCHR, 1995a: 5). Whether those boys and men who have suffered some form of sexual violence 'are willing to report it, to health workers, to police, to ethnographers, or in surveys, also varies substantially across societies' (Wood, 2006: 318). Once touched by this form of violence the victims feel their condition can never be altered. It is almost similar to the fear that HIV-affected patients have in many societies. Even in societies with liberal sexual norms, victims may feel reluctant to come forward to admit to their violation and trauma owing to the associated stigma, shame and fear.

These challenges are compounded during armed conflicts and war when there exist few opportunities to report such violence as there is a near absence of law and order services (either in the form of the police or health personnel). Furthermore, the victim's chances of declaring his condition becomes restricted in those situations where his immediate family and the social group he belongs to is displaced and dispersed owing to the ravages of the conflict (Wood, 2006: 318). Hence, even on those rare occasions when a brave victim seeks out help and demands the society to acknowledge his pain and tragedy there are plenty of obstacles blocking his way to recovery.

Society and its double

When it comes to acknowledging the suffering of victims of sexual violation wider society surrounding the victim can be very slow to recognise its effects. Post-Traumatic Stress Disorder (PTSD) has only become well-known relatively recently. In some countries it is hardly acknowledged at all. And there remains a lot of ambiguity in terms of its effects and ways of countering it.

It is also difficult to diagnose PTSD. A victim who has undergone such traumatic experiences through sexual aggression and violation may not demonstrate outward physical manifestation of this condition. But the victim continues to live a shattered life like anyone with a physical wound.

There are a multitude of psycho-physical conditions that a victim can suffer from following his violation and male victims may experience similar psychological effects to those suffered by female victims. This is mostly found in the context of PTSD, which is often poorly understood in countries with underdeveloped health-care systems.

To many observers, T. E. Lawrence suffered from psychological effects after his sexual violation in the context of conflict. His personality following his violation at the hands of the Ottoman Turks underwent a severe change. He displayed all the classic symptoms of PTSD, including workaholism, depression, anger, an increased sense of vulnerability, destructive self-image, emotional distancing, and so on (Brochman, 1991). If one were to believe various theories surrounding his rape and the negative impact of it on his personality, Lawrence tried to change his identity twice by adopting a new *nom de guerre*. This attempt to embrace a new identity, to some, was due to the fact that Lawrence 'felt emasculated by his violation' at the hands of his captors and wanted to escape the wounded violated victim persona.

And PTSD is likely made worse by prevailing attitudes towards victims of sexual violation. There is a tendency in some societies to think that the victim is somehow 'responsible' for whatever happened to them. Amnesty reports that female victims are often 'accused of not having resisted enough, of having somehow consented to sex or of having cooperated with their attackers (Amnesty International, 2008: 16); the same is true of male victims. There is also another side to this mode of behaviour.

It is often suggested that during times of crisis or deep socio-political upheaval, 'our conduct towards our fellow-men is determined by the principle of self-preservation. The individual acts towards his fellows in such a manner so as to obtain advantages which otherwise he could not get or to avoid evils which they might inflict upon him' (Maugham, 1967: 33).

According to an overwhelming proportion of members of many of these underdeveloped societies, a victim who is a survivor is less in need of sympathy and concern than someone who has died. It is felt the victim should consider himself fortunate and not expect the society to feel sorry for him as his life was spared when many of his compatriots were not so lucky. It would appear the society is resentful of the fact that the victim survived through some strange physiognomy. He is less of an individual because he did not sacrifice his life like his compatriots. And also, it can be implied, his life was spared because he was less of a virile, brave and courageous human being than others who laid down their lives. Therefore, on a comparative qualitative scale, his life is less valuable and important compared to those who have fallen. This common peddling of the notion of a survivor's life being less important than a dead person's life creates further alienation for the victim.

Conflict-related sexual violence can have serious physical, social and psychological consequences on the well-being of not only the victim but also the survivor's immediate and extended family and the larger community (Johnson 2010: 561). As we discussed in chapter three, through the victim's experience, the society in the midst of a nationalistic uprising also felt violated. Communities can harbor fear that its image might be contaminated by association with the victim. No group, community or nation likes to be seen as an emasculated one, if it can avoid it. The greatest fear it harbours is the fear of being branded as effeminate and incapable of protecting its honour. Ultimately, more than the violator's violence, it is the society's reluctance to acknowledge and tolerate such violation that eventually compounds the victims' sense of victimhood.

Clinical findings

Male survivors of sexual violence experienced during armed conflict and war may face severe and multidimensional short- and long-term conse-quences (Zawati, 2007; Lewis, 2009). So far as the effect of the violence in their post-conflict state is concerned it can be divided into three sep-arate categories. In the first category one can include the immediate and recurring physical affliction. In the second category one may put the emo-tional or psychosomatic effects or pains. A third kind of affliction is the psycho-social damages experienced by the victim in the post-conflict stage. This last category of damage may not be shared by all victims and is mostly culturally specific.

Now let us return to these individual afflictions and assess their impact and effect on the victim. So far as the immediate and long-term physi-cal affliction is concerned the survivor/victim may suffer from a range of maladies which may include sexual dysfunction, complete or partial dam-age to his reproductive capacity, severe abdominal pain, rupture of the rectum leading to continual and sporadic abscesses and passing of blood. And in some cases the most damaging physical affliction may be the development of various sexually transmitted diseases including HIV/ AIDS. Although very few in number, studies nonetheless confirm the post-conflict physical afflictions in the survivor-victim (Lancet, 2000; Oosterhoff, 2004; Lewis, 2009).

Linos suggests that, 'because of their anatomy men may be more at risk of permanent damage to their reproductive sex through different forms of trauma inflicted to their genitals' (Linos, 2009: 1550). Emasculation and inability to come to terms with this new condition may manifest in serious negative health outcomes for many of the vic-tims. The problem is exacerbated by the fact, just as male victims rarely report crimes to legal authorities, they also rarely seek help from medi-cal professionals.

The second category of affliction, that of psychosomatic disorders, may not be externally visible but is likely to affect the survivor/victim on a long-term basis. The victim may suffer from anxiety, depression, persis-tent unguarded anger, loss of self-confidence and self-respect, self-blame, emotional distancing or desensitisation, and various forms of self-harm-ing behaviour ranging from laceration of veins to physical abuse and, ultimately, suicidal tendencies (Walker, Archer & Davies, 2005: 69). These conditions may be persistent along with other psychosomatic afflictions such as perpetual exhaustion, dizziness, palpitations of the heart, consistent headaches, insomnia and sleeplessness, anxiety attacks, a fall in body weight triggered by loss of appetite and so on.

A 2010 medical study on the physical and mental health conditions of sixty Bosnian and Croat men who had undergone various forms of sexual violence by their Serb tormentors produced for the first time a detailed scientific picture of the victims' physical, emotional and psychosomatic condition in a post-conflict setting. The overwhelming majority of those interviewed and examined reported having:

Symptoms of traumatic reactions including sleep disturbances, concentration difficulties, nightmares and flashbacks, feelings of hopelessness, and different physical stress symptoms such as constant headaches, profuse sweating, and tachycardia (Loncar et al., 2010: 191–203).

The third damaging aspect of the violence often manifests itself in victims' social settings. As we have already seen, different societies and cultures perceive the victims in different ways. Therefore, the treatment or reaction he receives from the larger society on account of his victim status varies significantly. According to some critics, depending on prevailing cultural norms, male victims of sexual violence may face isolation or abandonment by family members (including their girlfriend, partner or wife and also children) (Lewis, 2009: 16). These outcomes are often linked to the society's (in)ability to sympathise and empathise with the victim. If the family as well as the society at large harbours feelings of shame and stigma on account of the victim's particular abuse, then it may push him outside its comfort zones.

Even in those cultural contexts or settings where the family and society is liberal and professes a tolerant attitude to the victim's condition, that may not be enough for the latter to fully come to terms with his pain. In such scenarios the victim may enter into conditions of auto-isolation resulting in social withdrawal, intolerance, persistent and/or violent outbursts, loss of interest at work, and forms of substance abuse (Oosterhoff et al., 2004; Lewis, 2009). Put simply, no matter what are the surrounding conditions or availability of professional care and advice, the victim following his abusive experience in the conflict is unlikely to return to his pre-conflict or pre-violated state and will likely suffer from problems in one, two or all three of the categories described above.

Now let us probe the long-term damage to the victims of such violence. According to some medical practitioners, victims often complain and demonstrate visible signs of external pain and damage to their body such as physical sequelae of genital pain, including pain during urination, anal pain and testicular pain, and the most common of all ailments—the loss of potency as evinced in erection problems, sexual dysfunction and impotency (van Tienhoven, 1993). However, overall it is the trauma in the aftermath of his violation that dominates the victims' everyday existence.

A victim of such violence typically exhibits three sets of trauma. The first one relates to the question of his sexual identity. The victim perpetually nurtures the inquiry as to whether he is indeed a man or a woman. If the society to which he belongs or originally came from holds the view that such violence is meted out by the enemy only to effeminate bodies, the victim's concerns about his gender identity will likely be intensified. Second, on those occasions where prisoners are forced to engage in sexual acts with one another, both victims may end up nurturing a deep feeling of homophobia. Third, in instances where the victim has undergone any of the above mentioned tortures or has witnessed his fellow prisoners being partially or fully castrated by the enemy or by his own fellow inmates then he may develop a 'castration anxiety'. Even though the victim may be living in peacetime in a relatively safe and protected environment this fear of losing his male sexual organ remains pervasive. Loncar et al., identify these three to be the primary psychiatric or mental health problems affecting the Bosnian and Croat victims of the Yugoslav civil war (Loncar et. al., 2010: 200).

Thus the argument goes that from a 'psychiatric viewpoint, mental health problems in the male victim following his ordeal are not the consequence of mental illness but a product of his violation' (Loncar et. al., 2010: 200). This situation often leads to self-harm. The sacredness of the body, which is part of every normal human being's attitude towards his own physicality, is often the first victim in this process of violation. For the victim his own body following its violation carries very little self-worth. An individual loses the intimate respect he usually has for his own body prior to its violation. Some victims confessed to the fact that they considered committing suicide several times following their violation.

In some African societies where male-male rape is often considered worse than death some victims may lapse into deep depression, leading to suicidal tendencies or actual suicide. Reports emerging from South Africa where a lot of rape victims of the Zimbabwean civil war took refuge, showed that to be the case (Hill, 2007). Similarly, anecdotal evidence from the DRC suggests that male rape victims are more likely to commit suicide as a result of their sexual violation at the hands of the enemy than female victims. This rate is significantly higher if the victim has undergone some form of mutilation of his sexual organs including castration (Sivakumaran, 2010: 266).

The lack of self-worth that the victim was harbouring following his ordeal is further reinforced by society's mute response to his suffering. Lacking a suitable outlet to talk about his experiences, and lacking the attention of medical professionals, his frustration might manifest itself in forms of violence in interpersonal relationships where the victim's children, wife and the family become targets for his own psychosis.

For both the practitioner and researcher studying the mental and physical health of the victim there needs be a clear distinction between male and female victims of sexual violence. Currently there is no separate approach to treat male victims. Their needs are either ignored or they are clumsily put in the category of general victims of sexual violence in armed conflicts (who happen to be overwhelmingly female).

Some critics have argued that current public health research on the experience of sexual violence in armed conflicts and war is primarily interested in looking at the welfare of female survivors (Linos, 2009: 1549). We need to appreciate and recognise the fact that the 'victims and survivors of such atrocities may have different mental and physical health needs depending on both their sex and gender' (Linos, 2009: 1550).

Even in those situations where health professionals are available to address the pain of the victims the former often fail to treat them efficiently. According to Stemple, physicians and aid workers are often 'not trained to recognise the physical sequelae' of rape in men or to provide the necessary and adequate psychological counselling that is required in such contexts. In some ways many are even unaware of the forms of sexual abuse boys and men may experience in such conflicts (Stemple, 2009: 612).

While some deductions have been made as to the impact of such violence on adult males there is no sustained exploration into its effects on boys. Several researchers that looked into the sexual abuse of boys from a sample of countries during peacetime suggested that the impact of childhood sexual abuse 'substantially increases the risk of problems such as post-traumatic stress disorder (PTSD), depression, suicidality, sexual perpetration, and poor academic performances' (Paolucci et al., 2001: 135; Stemple, 2009: 616).

A comprehensive exploration

Speaking to victims about their experiences was the hardest undertaking of all in this study. Although aware of the extreme sensitivity of the topic, one could not avoid asking each of these individuals who had gone through their own private ordeal about their subsequent life. In such contexts one feels the inescapable burden of evaluating the aftereffects. It was vital to inquire about the kind of psychological effect it left behind on them and the ways in which their lives had been changed.

Teasing out details from these private disasters always led one in a single direction. One emerged with a singular narrative of overwhelming trauma. None of the victims were the same again. They all felt ruined. Yet, while they did not ever recover from the shock they nonetheless took up their lives as best they could while making the most of the opportunities available. But for the most part our understanding of their suffering is limited.

Examining the victims' condition up close one could not escape the fact that what the violated sought in his silent moments was a comprehensive answer to the question: Why? Why was he singled out to undergo such physical and mental torture? Did the torturer not have an identity as a brother or father or a husband? If so, how could he lower himself to committing such inhuman acts?

Although we have some medical studies that have looked at the physical effects of such violence there is as yet no detailed analysis on the psychosocial consequences for male survivors. For instance, there have been several detailed and exhaustive studies on the effects of sexual violence in the eastern DRC by various NGOs including Human Rights Watch (2002) and Médécins Sans Frontiéres (2004). These are only regional and country studies on the condition of female victims. If one were to compile a list of such studies published covering the trials and tribulations of female victims across the world then they will fill an entire bookshelf.

Put simply, while tomes have been written about the scope and nature of such violence on female victims there is no comprehensive study in relation to male victims. This definitely undermines our understanding of the armed conflict and war in general and the place of sexual violence against boys and men in this context in particular. As one critic put it, 'we remain ignorant of the place that such violence occupies in the per-petuation of conflicts or in the choice of particular forms of retaliatory violence' (Russell, 2007: 22).

For instance, what happens to the violators (who are at times under-age conscripts in many civil wars in Africa) following their return to their families and societies? Do they behave as normal human beings adher-ing to the rules and requirements of post-conflict reintegration? Or what kind of life does a victim of such violence lead following the cessation of conflict? Equally importantly, what happens in those contexts when civil-ian men (as in India, Bosnia and several African cases) are forced to per-form acts of incest by their enemy aggressors? Do they continue living in their respective families and communities?

How do the reluctant violator and the violated interact in the post-conflict setting? Does the violator run away as an act of self-banishment? Does the civilian forced violator commit suicide as the knowledge of vio-lating his son or father is too hard to bear? The truth is we simply do not know. There is definitely a knowledge gap. What we have, instead, is some ad hoc understanding, some supposition and that is it.

Similarly, while we have some credible studies available that provide snapshots into the victim's physical, emotional and psycho-social condi-tion there exists, as yet, no formal or sustained analysis of the impact of such violence on a given group or society known for its distinct identity for which it was targeted by the enemy aggressor. The question as to how a community like that of the Bosnian Muslims, the Tutsis of Rwanda or the Tamils of Sri Lanka feels having witnessed a great many male mem-bers of their society being carefully selected and sexually violated by the enemy aggressor is a very profound one.

At the moment none of these complicated and complex questions are thought about or addressed in the conflict literature. Our understanding of the victim psychology and the overall nature of post-conflict peace and stability in a given society affected by this sense of victimhood will remain poorer unless we attempt to answer the questions highlighted.

Conclusion

At a metaphorical level the violated body and the silence that accompa-nies the experience of the victim often become the unspoken narrative of the conflict, which can only exist within the framework of disruption or a gap, simultaneously unbridgeable and yet bridged by that particular event. It is consigned to that domain where the victims' living body is understood as having been 'displaced, othered, and made precarious' (Butler, 1993). Consigning the victim to this experience, then, is a form of victory for the violator.

Yet, these specific undertakings of violence would not be such an effective weapon of war if it were not for concepts like honour, shame, guilt and self-abnegation that surround the discourse on male identity.

There is no denying the fact that when we talk about the victims' experience we are only scratching the surface of this enormous topic. It is not only that we have gaps in our knowledge surrounding this violence but more importantly that our attempt to explore this subject is undermined by a certain kind of silence. Victims of such violence seldom wish to discuss their ordeal, much less embellish and magnify it (Kressel, 2002: 3). What they do is engage in memorisation of the event. The memory they recall and engage with is an involuntary memory. And, by their very nature, involuntary memories are abrupt. They surge up. They 'break into the present in sudden, unexpected ways that could not be prepared for or anticipated' (Couzens Hoy, 2012: 192).

At another level the persistence of this involuntary memory and the attendant 'memorisation' reinforce a sense of guilt. It is a special kind of guilt, which forever imprisons the survivor in a conception of moral failing. It forces him to think that he survived while others in his situation did not because he traded his own bodily violation for freedom. It is a moral self-abnegation from which the survivor never succeeds in freeing himself. When coupled with the question as to why he was violated and allowed to live while his friend and co-prisoner remained untainted but killed, the survivor's guilt becomes manifold indeed.

The male victims' condition also poses questions about individual subjectivity and social expectation. In Erich Fromm's interpretation, 'the necessity to unite with other living beings, to be related to them, is an imperative need on the fulfillment of which man's sanity depends' (Fromm, 2002: 29). Survival of the body after having undergone forms of violation presents various metaphors. It straddles two distinct worlds. While it is a part of the public domain it is also external to it. Very often societies 'hide from themselves the pain, which is inflicted upon individuals as prices of belonging' (Das, 2006). The absence of that ontological security, 'the confidence that most human beings have in the continuity of their self-identity and in the surrounding social and material environments of action' (Giddens, 1990: 92), can do more harm to the victim than his original violation. In the absence of an audience to grieve for him our victim remains forever trapped in this private tragedy.

7

COMING TO TERMS

I saw Negroes being hung, a boy named Emmett Till, castrated and burned up.
I said I'm gonna be a boxer and I'm gonna get famous so I can help my people.

Cassius Marcellus Clay Jr., in Morris, 1993: 266.

One need not think of violation and rape of boys and men in conflict zones in legal, political or sociological terms in order to be angry about it. It is a basic human rights issue. To its survivors, sexual violence experienced during these maelstroms is often physically and psychologically devastating. It affects the families and communities to which they return. If one were to try to calculate the compound effects of these occurrences then one would find a long trail of devastation.

Yet, addressing this particular form of violence during and after the armed conflict is a task steeped with insurmountable hurdles. Given the nature of this violence, it is harder still to prescribe and impose any clear measures, legal or otherwise, that effectively confront this problem. In addition, it is a tragedy that is not only personal but affects a whole host of people and can cast a long shadow over the community or society to which the victim belongs. Hence any strategy aimed at stemming the violence and addressing the victim and his society's sense of shame, humiliation and loss should be holistic and multi-dimensional in nature.

Overall this chapter is a meditation on new ways of looking at the problem. It dwells on the issues of taboo, gender inequality, ignorance and, above all, apathy which contribute to the lack of understanding surrounding the violence and refusal to come to terms with them. What I do in the following pages is highlight specific issues that act as stumbling blocks in the move towards successful rehabilitation of the victim. While framing that narrative I also suggest possible ways forward that transcend these challenges and obstacles.

Bridging the gender divide

Perceiving men only as offenders and never as victims of rape and other forms of sexual violence causes grave problems (Zarkov, 2001). Therefore, as Linos suggests, 'Discourse on gender-based violence during conflict, should step away from the stereotype of women as victims and men as aggressors' (Linos, 2009: 1550). Moreover, legal systems should clearly recognise the existence of sexual crimes against men. As a first step in this new thinking we not only need to identify violence against men as gender-based violence and therefore recognise it under a separate category (or sub-category) but we also need to devise the necessary legal and health-related undertakings to confront the problem.

While there is very little concerted effort at the institutional and societal level in identifying the victims there is even less concern about what happens to them in the post-conflict setting. According to Russell, there is as yet no clear understanding of the role that such violence plays in conflict perpetuation (Russell, 2007). For instance, does the victim engage in retaliatory violence? Or, given that the enemy that had violated him in the first place is no longer around, might the victim seek out civilians and subject them to similar kinds of abuse in a domestic setting? Similarly, how does the victim react to post-conflict reintegration into the family and society at large? Most critical of all, if the victim happened to belong to the police, military or rebel forces, how is he going to behave if he is placed in a position of strength that requires him to maintain law and order? Does he try to enforce his own humiliation on the people who he now controls or does he follow a pro-victim policy?

That there needs to be some form of regulation when it comes to sex and sexual violation is accepted by most modern societies. This regulatory principle has its basis in various sociological theories. Malinowski, for example, argued that of all human emotions sex is the most powerful instinct, which makes it necessary that there should exist powerful means of regulating, suppressing and directing this instinct (Malinowski, 1963: 120). If one could put forward such a strong framework of interaction in matters of simple sex there is no denying the fact that there is scope for organising something equally strong if not stronger in matters of sexual violence and violation.

What is the thinking person's reaction to such acts? How do they view such violence? What is their overall take on the victims and the violators? There are no commonly agreed answers to these questions, and people tend to answer them emotionally rather than rationally. Take, for instance, former US President George W. Bush's response to the issue.

Bush's presidency saw the revelation of sexual crimes committed by US military personnel in Abu Ghraib prison in Iraq (discussed in earlier chapters). As part of the debriefing Bush saw the photographs of such violence in the Senate chambers. Due to the general public's desire to hear what the commander-in-chief of the US armed forces had to say about the incident, there was a melee of journalists outside the chamber waiting for Bush. When he finally emerged from the debriefing and was asked by the waiting journalists about his response he uttered these three words, 'It is disgusting.' For critics such a response was ambiguous at best and cavalier at worst.

By calling it 'disgusting' was he expressing his disgust towards the acts of sodomy, fellatio, homosexual sex and so on? Or, as the commander-in-chief was he condemning the debased crimes of the US soldiers? In the view of Judith Butler, an American post-structuralist philosopher, such a lack of linguistic clarity may have been a one-sided reaction that portrays the victims rather than their perpetrators in a poor light. She writes:

If it was the homosexual acts that he found 'disgusting' then he (Mr Bush) had clearly missed the point about torture, having allowed his sexual revulsion and moralism to take the place of an ethical objection. But if it was the torture that was disgusting, then why did he use that word, rather than *wrong* or *objectionable* or *criminal*? The word 'disgusting' keeps the equivocation intact, leaving two issues questionably intertwined: homosexual acts on the one hand, and physical and sexual torture on the other (Butler, 2009: 87).

Finally, we are confronted with the question of what policy guidelines we can suggest following deeper analysis and reflection on this issue. In the context of armed conflict and war, sexual violence 'remains hidden behind other offences that are considered to be more important, such as homicide and displacement' (Carlson, 2006; Sivakumaran, 2007). And even if such violations are brought to the fore, the focus is on the sexual violence experienced by women rather than men. For instance, in 1998, under the auspices of the UN, the International Criminal Tribunal for Rwanda made a landmark intervention, stating that 'rape is a crime of genocide' and therefore a war crime under public international law. One of the sitting judges stated that 'rape is no longer a trophy of war'. This statement, while seeking to protect the rights of women, had very little to say about the rights of male victims.

Similarly, in 2001, UN Secretary-General Kofi Annan targeted gender justice and the need to address sexual violence in establishing a culture of conflict prevention, arguing: 'In the twenty-first century, collective security should imply an obligation for all of us to strive to address tensions, grievances, inequality, injustice, intolerance and hostilities at the earliest stage possible, before peace and security are endangered. This, in my view, is the true core of a culture of prevention.' (United Nations, 2001: 9.) While many of the issues highlighted in his report have received close attention, the plight of male sexual victims has not received the attention that is due. With the broadening of the concepts of 'peace' and 'security', there is an unprecedented opportunity for male 'gender' issues to shape the peace agenda.

Owing to the rising levels of reporting of sexual violence against civilians and armed personnel in the frontline of war, especially over the past decade, there has been some soul searching on part of the international bodies such as the UN. Guided by stories of atrocities in African civil wars the UN Security Council passed Resolution 1325 specifically geared towards curbing such violence. The provisions made in this resolution called for gender-sensitive training in peacekeeping, greater recruitment of women in peacekeeping roles, and clearly defined efforts at promoting girls and women in conflict zones.

Following on from Resolution 1325, there were two other seminal interventions by the Security Council. In 2008 it passed Resolution 1820 'prohibiting acts of sexual violence against civilians in armed conflicts'. The following year the UN Security Council adopted 'Text Mandating Peacekeeping Missions to Protect Women, Girls from Violence in Armed Conflict' under Resolution 1888.

All these efforts, while noble, are nonetheless partial. All three resolutions highlighted above primarily focus on the female experience. All these agreements, efforts and undertakings to protect the would-be victims clearly neglect to address sexual violence against boys and men.

Similarly, celebrating the tenth anniversary of Resolution 1325 in the year 2010, United States Secretary of State Hillary Clinton announced that Washington would accelerate its implementation. As part of this initiative the United States launched a $44 million fund for addressing the plight of women around the world. But hardly anything in that new initiative spoke of improving the condition of men whose lives were blighted by such violence.

That there is a need to recognise the exclusivity of Security Council Resolutions 1325, 1820 and 1888 and therefore move beyond their short-comings is not hard to follow. In light of this one could hardly exagger-ate the narrowness of the policy framework that still dominates the think-ing surrounding sexual violence in armed conflict and war. Therefore the importance of including the atrocities suffered by male subjects in future peace processes and conflict resolution situations cannot be overstated.

Understanding male experiences of wartime sexual violence, in order to advance an inclusive vision of gender justice and reconciliation in post-conflict settings, is an element of the objective of this study. If we are to redefine the scope of redressing victims' grievances and move beyond the initial roadblocks—shame on the part of the victims and apathy on the part of the law makers—we need first of all to create aware-ness in both academic and policy circles about these experiences and their consequences.

Ultimately, a gender-neutral resolution that would commit the inter-national community to end wartime sexual violence against everyone irrespective of their gender, race, region and religion is needed. So too are policy initiatives that can address the sufferings of all in the post-conflict phase.

A gender-neutral approach

It has not been the intention of this study to consider the female experi-ence of sexual violence in theatres of conflict and war. As I highlighted in the introduction, this is due to two interrelated factors. First, there exists plenty of literature on this topic. Second, this study by its very nature focuses on the male experience. While the male experience can be stud-ied as a completely separate category, there are times when our analysis can benefit when there is a comparative assessment of the two. Such forms of engagement allow us to see the issues, contexts and overall discourse from another vantage point with obvious scope for new insights.

When one makes such a comparative assessment it becomes amply clear that there is greater engagement from jurists, politicians, policy makers, social workers and, above all, law enforcement agents on the female experience of sexual violence in conflicts. Very often these actors treat the experience as if it is only females and children who are the victims of such atrocities. This emphasis on the female experience has led to a discourse which growing numbers of critics have argued neglects male victims.

Similarly, one could argue there is a 'gender bias' when one approaches the topic of sexual violence in armed conflicts and wars. There are several key factors that contribute to this. First, from time immemorial women have been the favoured targets of sexual violators in any conflict. Second, this practice is increasingly reported upon by the international media. Third, female victims of sexual violence tend to carry greater outward signs of violation compared to their male counterparts. Fourth, females are more vulnerable to such attacks than males. Fifth, one could posit that, since war is conducted mostly by men, women by default become attractive targets for violation. Sixth, a somewhat controversial aspect of this violence rests with the biological explanation of sexual violence, which suggests that men are more likely to engage in such undertakings than their female counterparts. Seventh and finally, there exists a form of self-denial among male victims about their violation, further consolidating the position of women as the sole victims in this narrative.

What is the effect of the gender bias we have identified? Insofar as impact assessment is concerned there are two ways of viewing it.

First, what impact does such a skewed or lopsided understanding have on the male victim? Second, what are the effects of non-recognition of the male experience on the immediate family of the male victim?

To address the male experience first, as I have stated in several other contexts, the victim is twice victimised, first by the act itself and second owing to society's refusal to acknowledge it or view it in the same category as the female experience of violation.

Second, according to some critics 'silence about male victims reinforces unhealthy expectations about men and their supposed invulnerability' (Stemple, 2011: 25). In other words, since society considers them invincible those who are affected by such violence end up suppressing their victimhood and, consequently, their trauma can find manifestation in aggression against the victim's immediate female companions such as wife, girlfriend, partner and daughters.

Third, gender-bias or sex-specific stereotypes about the male experience or absence of it, in turn conditions the international community's response towards the victim. To put it slightly differently, the international community is more likely to address the female experience over that of the male experience because of this inherent bias and stereotype.

Fourth, this bias also contributes to a gap in the medical treatment of male victims. For instance, the sexual component of abuse of males may not be taken into active consideration either by health workers/professionals or aid workers. For Stemple, 'doctors and emergency aid workers are rarely trained to recognise the physical signs of male rape or to provide counselling to its victims' (Stemple, 2011: 25).

Institutional bias

The gender bias that exists in the context of approaching and appreciating the experience of male wartime sexual violence from an academic and institutional perspective afflicts to a similar degree various policy-making bodies. If international legal and political institutions are reluctant to engage with the issue, governmental and non-governmental organisations working in the field and specifically looking at wartime sexual violence are averse to the idea of taking on the cause of male victims.

As I highlighted earlier in the introduction of this book, in 2002 a quantitative inventory of information materials of 4,076 NGOs addressing sexual violence in armed conflict and wars found that only 3 per cent of the organisations concerned specifically mentioned the experience of male victims in their programming literature (Del Zotto & Jones, 2002; OCHA, 2008: 3). And, that too, only in passing reference—as an afterthought in their advocacy and policy literature. This overwhelming unwillingness to engage with the issue has unsurprisingly had a detrimental effect on addressing the suffering of male survivors: why this apathy? What are the factors that feed into this bias?

What was true of the 2002 finding is still true in the year 2014. This inability on the part of most of these NGOs and INGOs to address this issue or even recongise its prevalence, stems from a set of complex cultural as well as strategic factors. In fact there are two key factors which work towards and contribute to the consolidation of this bias from a policy perspective. One could identify these two factors as fear of sustainability and strategic anxiety.

Often there is fear among the NGO community that dealing with victims of sexual violence from the perspective of gender inclusivity stems from the issue of sustainability of their endeavour. In the view of some researchers working in the field, the donor community is often to be blamed for this. Very often they consider that the funding they have made available to the agencies working for the victims has a certain gender-exclusive agenda. And if they start talking about male victims alongside female victims the issue is going to drain their limited resources, thereby taking away a 'big chunk of the cake that has taken them a long time to bake' (Storr, 2011: 7).

Such fears about sustainability receive credence if one were to assess the guidelines of some of the donor bodies. The Dutch Oxfam, for instance, in the year 2010 refused to provide any more funding to the Refugee Law Project (RLP), a partner organisation of Christian Aid working in Uganda and openly addressing the issue of male survivors, stating that the RLP would not receive funding from the former if it did not make amends to its operations. In other words, Dutch Oxfam wanted RLP to have a gender-exclusive approach where 70 per cent of its client base had to be women or else there was no funding (Storr, 2011: 7). Similarly, many male survivors of this violence have gone on record to highlight that when they approached bodies such as UNHCR for medical help for their condition its officials refused them the treatment suggesting they 'have a programme for vulnerable women, but not men' (Storr, 2011: 7).[1]

On the face of this discrimination the most relevant question that one is forced to ask is: why are not individuals, communities, societies, and states contributing to a fund for male survivors as well? Interestingly, there exists a significant apathy ranging from individual donors to states when entertaining such a task. There exists very little or no interest in picking up the case of males. For instance, personal interviews with some of the volunteers working with the victims of sexual violence in the northeast of England revealed that two parallel organisations set up to address the needs of male and female victims of peacetime sexual violence produced a startlingly disproportionate picture.

Interestingly, while there were many volunteers, counsellors and donors supporting the work of the body responsible for looking after female victims, none of that was forthcoming for the parallel body that made the male victims its stated cause. In fact, this body was run by one single female charity worker who often put in her own money and resources to keep the organisation afloat while there was no monetary help from the donors. If such a lackadaisical response and bias can be found in the twenty-first century in the developed West, then its prevalence in conflict ravaged non-Western societies should not come as a surprise.[2]

The second dominating factor in perpetuating this bias stems from a strategic anxiety. Many of the NGOs and INGOs addressing the issue of wartime sexual violence often operate in societies and states that consider male experience of this abuse as taboo. Plenty of these states in fact censure any male-male sexual interaction in peacetime and maintain openly homophobic policies when it comes to handing out verdicts against those found to be in such a relationship. Thus NGOs' and INGOs' reluctance and refusal to address the issue is often couched in strategic thinking.

In Uganda, for example, 'businesses or non-governmental organisations found guilty of the promotion of homosexuality would have their certificates of registration cancelled and directors could face seven years in jail'.[3] Interestingly the charge of homosexuality in such circumstances may include addressing the issue of male-male rape. Uganda is only one of the extreme examples. Three quarters of African countries, in fact, have variations of similar rulings. Therefore the implications for the NGO and INGO workers can hardly be underestimated. Very often they have ended up taking a policy approach which can be summed up as follows: 'Don't ask, don't tell, and don't pursue'.

Policy loopholes

Owing to these inter-related narratives it would not be wrong to argue that this lack of institutional recognition of the male plight has a direct bearing on the post-conflict human security discourse and agenda. The far-reaching dissemination and institutionalisation of this narrow construction of victimhood is again picked up by political elites across the globe who wish to be viewed among their electorates and fellow leaders as 'exceedingly compassionate' visionaries who are conscious of their moral responsibilities (OCHA, 2008: 7). All these factors contribute to silencing male wartime experiences of sexual violence and, in turn, promote a highly selective human security agenda in the post-conflict policy framework and agenda.

From a policy perspective, in order to establish some form of equity in terms of victim grievance redressal, male victims of such violence must be accorded the same degree of concern and protection as their female victim counterparts. Moreover, one ought to acknowledge the fact that male victims may be specifically targeted for violation in armed conflicts and wars just like female victims in some theatres of conflict. Men and boys deserve protection against these abuses in their own right (Carpenter, 2006). Their victimhood should not be weighed as less or more than the victimhood of women.

How is one to address this problem from a policy perspective? There are two parts to this undertaking—one is domestic and the other one is international. Making male victims a part of an overarching human security agenda, however, must start with addressing the gaps in the organisational strategy at the domestic or grassroots level. For instance, one needs to place expectations on organisations (such as NGOs and INGOs) operating in conflict locations to actively pursue efforts at identifying both sets of victims from a gender-neutral framework; strengthen efforts to identify male victims in particular where cultural taboos prevent the population in coming forward to volunteer such information; and prioritise their efforts at seeking ways that could allow these specific victims to be reintegrated into society rather than be ostracised (Russell, 2007).

The second part of this policy undertaking has a larger international dimension. If the organisations dealing with this particular issue can represent these cases transparently and objectively in various international institutions, it would help redress some of the victims' grievances. Needless to say, the discrepancy at the international level that exists when it comes to addressing male victims of sexual violence in armed conflicts has to do with a lack of understanding and under-reporting. If the organisations working on the ground can publicise the issue then the challenges would gradually recede.

The reason why male victims of sexual violence are not included in any serious post-conflict human security undertaking in many of these societies is also due to the fact that the leadership responsible for bringing about this reform often happen to be conservative and hold a rather negative view on the male victim's condition. Therefore, if external as well as internal bodies can make a case for these victims and bring the issue out of the closet then the leadership might be more attentive to the victims' condition and needs. Full representation of male victims both in the local human security framework as well as within the international systems of justice is very much dependent on the manner in which the organisational bodies working in the conflict zones denote them and their cause.

Homophobia, the state and the legal limits

Even if one succeeds in introducing a gender-neutral international legal covenant that treats male wartime sexual violence victims on a par with females, this would not necessarily mean the end to the 'male plight'. This has to do with the inadequate legal provisions at the national level. A majority of nations in contemporary international society do not recognise sexual violence against men. The International NGO War Child, following a review of 189 Penal Code Provisions on Rape found that 90% of male victims in active conflicts today do not have access to justice (http://www.warchild.org.uk/news/shocking-scale-sexual-violence-against-men-and-boys last accessed 23 October 2014).

It is imperative, therefore, that we inquire why this is the case. To answer the first question (about the absence of legal recognition of the male victims' victimhood), the societies or states where such a lopsided framework is prevalent are inherently homophobic. These societies view any form of male homosexual act either in wartime or peacetime with extreme abhorrence. Such discomfort and anxiety on the part of the state and society has its basis in deep-seated psychological factors. Joseph Daniel Unwin, in his controversial but highly influential study, *Sex and Culture* (1934), argued that for some cultures' acceptance of sexual taboos as mainstream subjects can lead to gross social decadence. According to this principle, societies with strict rules for sexuality have 'high' cultures. Consequently, they fear by admitting to these acts that the society at large would somehow be tainted by homosexuality and by extension primitive.[4] This fear of being labelled as primitive owing to the acceptance of loose sexuality and eventual decadence leads many of these societies either to proscribe it or engage in collective denial when it comes to wrestling with this issue.

This form of non-engagement eventually facilitates state-sanctioned heterosexuality as the structure within which mainstream cultural identity and political ideals are housed. Here heteronormativity and more specifically heterosexuality becomes a means by which to discipline both subjects and citizenry. Unsurprisingly, the justice system reflects the prev-

THE LANDSCAPE OF SILENCE

alent anti-homosexual mood. In many instances this prejudice of the society and the complicity of the judiciary in that bias leads them to evolve a symbiotic relationship where each reflects the other's bias and discomfort in dealing with the question.

Many sub-Saharan states where homosexuality is treated with derision reflect this symbiosis. In Uganda, Tanzania and Zimbabwe, for instance, where homosexuality is banned by law, the violated victim finds himself at the other end of the justice system. On 24 February 2014, for instance, the Ugandan president signed into law a bill toughening penalties for gay people and those found to have had a homosexual experience. The bill, which originally sought the death penalty for male-male sex or homosexual encounters, was later watered-down to life imprisonment. It also made non-reporting of such acts a criminal offence.[5] Thanks to the overwhelming prejudice against this 'experience' the victim cannot afford to take recourse to the legal system to redress his suffering. Even if he dares to approach the judiciary he ends up facing the full force of the law that bans homosexuality. Put simply, our victim is doubly punished: first, by the violator and for the second time by the judicial system that considers his very being as an act of homosexuality and therefore subject to the penalties of the state.

What about those states and societies where there exist forms of legal recognition of such violence? Is our victim better protected in these systems? Here is a snapshot of that state's treatment of the male victims. An overview of the ICTY, which looked into wartime sexual violence both against women and men suggests that the sentencing patterns of this court were highly imbalanced. The perpetrators of sexual violence against women received stricter sentences than those who committed such violence against men, who were let off with lighter sentences (King & Greening, 2005).

Then there are states such as Guatemala. Here, even two decades after the civil war the state is reluctant to acknowledge that rape was used as a form of warfare. According to some conservative estimates over 100,000 women were raped across the country during the period. Although small in number by comparison to their female counterparts, male victims of such violence ran in to the thousands. However, successive Guatemalan governments, since the beginning of the peace process in the 1990s, have refused to acknowledge such violence. For the new democratic regimes, officially this sort of violence never happened. Consequently the refusal of the state to recognise this atrocity during the civil war years has often 'led the violator to walk freely through the streets and live in the same villages as their victims' (de Pablo, Zurita & Tremlett, 2011: 13).

Such callousness on the part of the regime and the impunity that is automatically awarded to the violator in the wake of its refusal to acknowledge the violated only heaps a further load of humiliation on the victim. It condemns him to a world of impotency and helplessness that he first encountered when he was violated. Needless to say, in the absence of state-sponsored measures to address this grievance one ought to look for avenues at the international level to redress victims' sufferings.

Some observers may refer to the 2014 *Global Summit to End Sexual Violence in Conflict* as a benchmark in addressing the issues I have already highlighted.

The Chair's Summary of June 2014 London Summit outlined that: "Definitions of sexual violence domestic legislation should confirm to standards and definitions in international law, and should also ensure that crimes against men and boys can be prosecuted."

However, according to Lesley Wexler, a professor of Law at the University of Illinois College of Law,

What this declaration does not do is create a binding legal obligation for states to follow through on their "commitment". By their very nature, declarations are aspirational, expressing what states hope to achieve rather than what they will or must do. In crafting the declaration, states chose not to include binding obligations or enforcement mechanisms to make themselves accountable for implementing any of the recommendations (Wexler, 2014).

The Summit was an expression of great sentiment without the requisite aspiration to follow through the recommendations. Wexler further argues, declaration such as the London Summit, "does not commit states in any binding sense to ending the culture of impunity for sexual aggressors or to funding prevention and response efforts or even to improving our knowledge on the subject (Wexler, 2014)."

Towards an holistic response

Earlier we saw how the world of male sexual violation is determined by a number of other relations: of race, religion, political atmosphere and particularly that of the dominant culture. This demonstrated how different groups endorse different perspectives on male sexuality. While in India a Muslim male faced a constant harangue of verbal sexual violation from his Hindu counterpart in an atmosphere of perpetual distrust and enmity, in other prominent conflict locations such as Afghanistan boys dislocated by the ravages of war and carnage simply became objects of sexual slavery to warlords and strongmen. These examples amply demonstrate different conceptions of violation and different views of what actually constitutes violation. This would imply that we seem to inhabit a world of conflicting value systems.

If one were to suggest an holistic response to this problem then what is needed is a broad-brush strategy. It is clearly established that sexual violence causes long-term physical, emotional, as well as moral damage not only to the individual but also to those around him and often entire societies (where memories of violation undermines national self-worth). While we need mechanisms of law to prevent such violation from taking place in the first instance, we also need to devise ways to reduce its promotion and advertisement. For promotion of such violence either in popular verbal form (as we saw in the case of India) or valorisation of it through dissemination of offensive images (as with Abu Ghraib) can act as triggers for such violence in future. Put simply, a form of sexual behaviour which flirts with power and domination or, worse still, humiliation of the enemy can sustain a discourse and intention for similar activism in future among potential violators.

One of the key hurdles that we face in getting to grips with such violence has been the victim, the violator and the society's reluctance to engage with the issue openly. A politics or popular culture that denies this violence, which shies away from it or feels ashamed of it and, worse still, blames the victim for his violation will not be in a position to defeat this problem.

If we are to attack the root causes of this problem and make sure that there is no scope for it in the pre-conflict stage or during the conflict, then we have to bring the topic out from the closet. For far too long it has been brushed under the carpet. We as a society have had little courage to confront it headlong. Thus, if we are looking for ways to combat it both in the context of actual violence as well as its promotion (clandestine and otherwise), then we need to display a mature attitude towards the whole issue and acknowledge that such a thing exists—that boys and men suffer the same fate and deep physical pain and trauma following their violation. In the first instance we need to take stock of the issue and generate a self-acknowledgement and then work for ways to combat it through policy mechanisms and popular intervention.

This is the point where sexual politics returns to its wider international context. To weed out this problem we not only have to pass laws at the local level but make ways for the condemnation of this violence at the universal level as well. If there were to exist a punitive international regime that recognises such violation (even in verbal and cultural contexts) as a crime against humanity, then we can effectively see this violation becoming scarce.

Moreover, confronting this challenge also necessitates that we not only recognise the crime but also make efforts at successful rehabilitation of the victims. Some critics have argued that the civil society in general and civilian community associations in particular can fulfill their duties by creating an atmosphere whereby the perpetrators are not only castigated but the victims are treated with empathy and respect. Once the civilian community embarks upon encouraging victims of this form of violence to break their silence and address their socio-medical needs, other areas of victim redressal such as reparations and rehabilitation will follow (Zawati, 2007: 40). Once the civil society picks up the issue it would lead to greater advocacy and formation of interest groups, eventually shaping and forming pro-victim public policies.

Some critics have even gone to the extent of suggesting that to further enhance the protection of vulnerable individuals in armed conflict settings 'policy makers should incorporate men explicitly into international instruments pertaining to sexual violence, and promote a *jus cogens* norm that encompasses all forms of sexual violence against men as well as women' (Lewis, 2009: 2).

To have a wider application of international law the policy makers and drafters of these laws should go beyond the traditional gender division in order to lay down specific laws for their protection during armed conflict and war. Since in such situations, those with transgender sex and those with same-sex preference (homosexuals) are singled out more frequently by their aggressors, the law should be devised in such a way that protects these demographics from harm. As one critic points out, 'Criminalizing attacks targeting an individual's sexuality would work toward delegitimizing the destructive stereotypes attending heterosexuality and homosexuality in wartime, stereotypes that provide some of the

motivation for men (and women) to commit sexual violence against men'
(Lewis, 2009: 49).

External involvement

On another level, if one were to introduce far-reaching reforms that oversee the uplifting of victims from the mire where they are currently found
then one needs to turn one's attention in the direction of the international community. In some post-conflict societies, the long-term engagement of national authorities and international donors is fundamental in
overseeing the introduction and implementation of policy programmes
for the violated and surviving victims. Without this partnership participation it would be very hard indeed to bring about any meaningful
change in the victims' lives.

This partnership is crucial in the sense that even when some national
governments are aware of their role in the context of victim support they
may not have the required resources to oversee it. And we might have
some governments that are reluctant to enter into any policy programme
of victim support because of its own prejudices. In both these instances
the involvement of the international community can have a significant
impact on the way the national government behaves in terms of its
approaches to the issue of male victims of sexual violence.

A case in point is Ugandan President Yoweri Museveni's decision to
criminalise male-male sex in February 2014. Responding to it the US
President Barack Obama cautioned his Ugandan counterpart that the
bill would be a backward step for the country and the society. More
importantly, he warned that the Ugandan government's move in that
direction could 'complicate'[6] Washington's relations with Kampala, which
receives £400 million in annual aid from the United States.[7] What was
being proposed here is a soft power approach. The US in this context
would appear to be using both carrot and stick options to address the
challenge to the victims in a specific country.

We not only require such tough words followed by action but also a
renewed commitment to do something. There needs to be the building
up of a consensus against these discriminatory practices across the international community. Similarly, fiscal incentives provided by the international donor community are critical in motivating national governments
to turn their attention to this neglected area.

Economic exclusion

When men are put through this form of degradation, it not only affects their own sense of self-respect, but it also affects their economic well-being and their place in the community. Leaving aside some extreme examples from Africa, we may have occasions when some national governments feel they ought to do something to care for male victims of sexual violence financially and medically. However, they may not be well equipped enough to see through this initiative. It is in these situations that the role of international organisations and the donor community assumes increased importance. The partnerships between national governments and these external bodies are crucial in overseeing various issues surrounding victims' needs.

Similarly, there might be some governments that are reluctant to enter into any policy programme of victim support because of their own prejudices and cultural taboos found within the larger society. In both these instances the involvement of the international community can have a significant impact on the way national governments behave in terms of their approaches to the issue of male victims of sexual violence. This is very obvious in those instances where the victim is physically unable to work following a severe attack on his genitals. Below is a typical example of one such case from eastern DRC.

Today I cannot work. I have to keep a cloth over my genitals like a woman. Only hot water seems to calm the pain. My wife looks after everything now, and I'm beginning to lose hope. I have no future (Amnesty International, USA, 2008: 8).

Clearly the fifty-year-old man who was raped and stabbed in his genitals by combatants in DRC in 2002 was physically not in a position to work even if he wanted to.

Yet, even in those situations where victims are capable of doing work and do not suffer from physical pain their experience renders them economically unviable for their employers. Such is the stigma associated with the violence they are often denied work by the immediate neighbourhood society into which they belong. In some non-Western societies some employers even refuse to keep them in employment for fear of drawing attention to their business.

Being shunned by the society the victims of such violence are forced to find their own way and suffer from deep economic hardship (MSF, 2004: 6).

Typically, a victim that has been economically ostracised generally has three options. Unable to go back to the profession he previously held or make a living through self-employment, in some contexts the victim is forced to beg or worse still resort to prostitution in order to survive.

According to some NGOs, the road to victim recovery, therefore, should not be limited to psycho-medical help and moral societal support. A true and meaningful road to recovery in the view of MSF should aim at providing full economic support as part of the holistic rehabilitation programme for the victim. According to MSF, 'the stigma attached to rape victims must be fought and socio-economic support provided in order for them to maintain their livelihood with dignity' (MSF, 2004: 32).

Moreover, while they may share a specific gender identity, male victims of sexual violence often have different needs depending on their cultural contexts. For instance, a Bosnian male survivor of such violence would find himself in a very tricky cultural terrain compared to his Northern Irish counterpart. Using the yardstick of comparative tolerance one could suggest that while the Bosnian victim is more likely to face social isolation, his Northern Irish counterpart might receive greater degrees of communal empathy and support. Therefore, expert discussion both within and across cultural contexts would help programme managers formulate effective strategies on responding to the victims' needs and post-conflict rehabilitation (Russell, 2008: 23).

While we have seen a slow rise in interest in policy circles in the male victims of such violence in recent years, the thinking and initiatives in this direction are rudimentary. In order to establish a comprehensive mechanism of ways to assist these victims, expert discussion needs to be initiated across cultures and societies involving various actors, from health professionals on the ground to donors. For some critics, given the extraordinary sensitivity of the issue for victims, communities and cultures alike, one ought to prepare some very careful strategies in order to respond to the victims' needs (Russell, 2008: 23).

Moral sanction

So far, we have assessed the role of external agents in tackling this form of violence. What is missing in the discussion is the role of violators and would-be violators. I want to ask whether one could use moral arguments that would prevent violators from violating in the first place. Can such behavior, based as it is on multiple sets of causes and reasons, be controlled by promoting self-regulating behaviour?

Unfortunately, conflict conditions presuppose a total breakdown of state-sponsored order and, of course, there is a short supply of self-sanctioned moral authoritarianism in armed conflict zones. The worst effect of armed conflict and war is that it destroys civility, erodes deeply held cultural values, wrecks formal individual restraints and undermines a society's beliefs in 'right' and 'wrong'.

Furthermore, the moral commonplaces of our age, such as that violence and torture are wrong, are grossly undermined in such contexts (Pinker, 2011: 838). In close combat the moral resources of those fighting that guards them against excesses of violence slips away from their consciousness. War, to some extent, facilitates eschewing all ethical restraints: 'the restraints of human responses or of moral identity on such occasions may be overwhelmed by an emotional explosion in which the aggressors' "mind just went", either caused by impulses of vengeance or by a reaction to some form of pre-existing humiliation' (Glover, 1999: 113).

If that is so, how can one persuade or pre-condition the behaviour of those participating in such conflict not to undertake certain forms of violence that can be placed in the category of less than human? If war and the fallout of war can be addressed through acculturation then we need to act on this fact. In his seminal essay *Neither Victims Nor Executioners* Albert Camus suggested 'the use of violence as an instrument of individual action can only be abandoned if the frame of mind that legtimises such violence is rejected' (Camus, 1986). What is in order here, therefore, is a socially sponsored mechanism of prevention addressed at the individual level. The simplest and the most practical approach would be to introduce a form of liberal educational process in peacetime in every society, which would, in turn, act as a self-regulating principle when these very individuals (potential violators) find themselves in times of war or in both intra-state and inter-state conflict situations.

Many of us in the West are heirs to an absolutist tradition when it comes to matters of sex. According to some critics this absolutist tradition means that the 'disruptive powers of sex can only be controlled by a clear-cut morality' (Weeks, 2003: 106). This particular morality, in turn, is intricately embedded in a given set of social institutions, which again derive their basis from religion. This is true of societies based on Judeo-Christian principles (as in the West) as well as those deriving their values from Islamic beliefs. In other words, such religiously sanctioned moral absolutism has deeply influenced our general culture, and in particular the forms of legal regulations, many of which we hold dear and follow (Weeks, 2003: 106).

If these traditions can inculcate absolute standards (such as that incest is morally reprehensible and that murder is beyond redemption) then surely sexual violence against boys and men can be put on an equal footing.

While it cannot be denied that this line of argument has obvious merit there are some practical problems associated with it. We cannot ignore the fact that there exists a fundamental difference between a peacetime moral posture and the lack of it during war or conflict conditions. If that is so, what is morally reprehensible can easily become the norm during war. In other words, murder may be 'beyond redemption' during peace-time but in the thick of a civil conflict such views or self-sanctioned moral understanding may lose some of its relevance. War, in other words, can rob the society of some of its pre-conceived values. If that is so, how did our earlier moral prohibitions on sexual violence against boys and men work during such upheaval?

Nevertheless, one could talk of inculcating a form of private absolut-ist individual moral standard in people's minds early on. 'I am that sort of person, I belong to that strata of humanity, which would not do such a thing,' is the sort of homily that can have a lasting effect. If churches, mosques and temples could strive to tell people how to conduct them-selves in private as well as public they can also serve as the fora to impart and disseminate a value system that considers such acts as reprehensible and unbecoming of a moral human being. When brought up in this tra-dition, individuals or potential violators are less likely to deviate from the proscribed path. In this context the reflection of sociologist Norbert Elias makes perfect sense. Elias argued that a desire to harm and see harm done to others was very much a part of mediaeval European civilisation. Over time, European society came to associate these impulses toward violence as negative values with the result that 'socially undesirable expres-sions of instinct and pleasure were threatened and punished with mea-sures that generated and reinforced displeasure over these actions even-tually leading to a near-absence of such behaviour' (Elias, 2000: 204).

While such moral enforcement is critical, one cannot discount the need for some form of interventionist strategy or policy framework from a power holding authority (for example, the state) to oversee it.

In order to provide a further bulwark against this violence the state needs to adopt certain policy measures. As we saw during the course of the discussion in previous chapters even the most conscientious of states fail to own up to the guilt of the violators. In fact it is the collapse of the external authority of morality that in turn facilitates individuals to abandon their private morality. Hence, one could argue, such undertakings by soldiers, militias or renegades who represent the state or work against it, in the ultimate analysis capture the personality of the state and reflect its ideology through their particularised forms of behaviour. The classic example in this regard comes from the reaction of the Bush administration to the sexual violation of Iraqi prisoners in Abu Ghraib. As we saw, the government at the time not only refused to own up to its moral failings but also patently failed to convincingly condemn the actions of its soldiers.

What I intend to put forth in this context is that the state needs to make it very explicit to those who are participating and would-be participants in a conflict that such actions are not only morally reprehensible but that anyone be found engaging in them will be severely judged and retributive justice that will be meted out afterwards.[8] Such a harsh pre-conflict declaration or legal ambit of the state towards the violators is more likely to reinforce the moral absolutism against such violence as suggested earlier.

If one were to make space for retributive justice to take hold then this form of punishment should have both physical pain inflicting attributes as well as some symbolic moral condemnation built into it. As one critic reminds us, this last aspect is particularly important, because 'recognition of one's sin in public in some form or other is a necessary condition of moral regeneration, and the formal and impressive condemnation by society involved in punishment is an important means toward bringing about this recognition on part of the violator' (Honderich, 1984: 89–90).

Responsive society

There is unanimity among scholars that the 'victims of rape who physically survived the Rwandan genocide in 1994 were psychologically destroyed' (Taylor, 2002; Dallaire & Beardsley, 2004; Fox, 2014: 24). As underscored in the previous chapter, the community and the society's inability to empathise with the victims' misfortune in the post-conflict stage creates a condition of self-loathing in the latter. There is a widely

prevalent and mistaken belief shared across all cultures and geographical regions that those men who were violated were somehow 'less than
men'. This construct also proposes that a real man endowed with appropriate masculinity should have been able to repel such violation. Such
attitude further seeks to reinforce the fallacy that every man is naturally
capable of warding off such threats and those who fail to prevent this
violence happening to them are somehow culpable. The prevalence of
this hyper-masculine ideal not only conditions the society to maintain a
self-imposed silence about the victims' experience but also encourages it
to ignore the latter's plight.

Furthermore, such biased understanding puts the victim under a specific spotlight by feminising his identity and consequently strips him of
all moral and legal recourse. Such is the power of this mode of thinking
and the prevailing discourse that even wives and girlfriends of certain
victims come to associate their partner's victimhood with a certain amount
of shame. One of the victims from the DRC revealed during the course
of an interview that his wife, following his violation at the hands of enemy
soldiers, rather than sympathise with his abuse constantly harped on
about the fact that he could be effeminate and treated him with contempt. Our victim, Mr K., could not make his wife believe that enemy
soldiers raped him. The fact that one of Mr K.'s companions could run
away fast and escape this misery did not help his own condition. For his
friend became an example of a 'real man' before his community for having escaped the same fate as Mr K., while the latter was consigned to a
world of blame. Given the enormity of the societal attitudes that depict
the victim's misfortune in a certain light, the latter is forced to retreat
into a world of self-blame from which he is never able to escape.

Although earlier I suggested how law and the state can be catalysts in
putting a lid on this violence, their intervention can only go so far. One
can never prescribe laws as to how a society should think. Understandings
of right and wrong, just and unjust, good and evil, predictable and unpre-
dictable, are cultural inheritances that societies adopt and subscribe to.
Very often the victim, for these societies, is a visible reminder of the violation of cultural norms they hold dear. Thereofere no amount of external pressure or legal imposition will force a society to change its values.
Such change has to come from within. What is an urgent necessity is a
revelatory awareness surrounding victims' conditions and the ability to
share that pain both at an individual as well as collective level.

Although rare there are occasions when such humanity breaks through. After absolving itself from such crimes committed against Kenyan freedom fighters for six decades, finally in 2013 Mr William Hague, the then British Foreign Secretary went on record by telling fellow MPs in the parliament: "I would like to make clear now, and for the first time on behalf of Her Majesty's Government, that we understand the pain and grievance felt by those who were involved in events of the emergency in Kenya (quoted in Chorley & Watson, 2013)."

What can be done in this particular context is to educate and reorient the members of the society to new forms of thinking. This can be done best by community leaders, teachers, doctors, religious preachers and, above all, law and order forces. If these actors join hands together their combined effort and contribution towards repelling the stigma associated with our specific victim of such violence can bear fruit. As the old saying goes 'charity begins at home'.

Surrogates' sorrow

While much of the aggression and violence against the male victim remains untold and ignored there are occasions when it becomes a part of communal experience. There may be situations when a friend of the victim finds himself in the position of witnessing the violation. What impact does it leave on him? How profound is his sorrow on experiencing this second-hand indirect violation? Does he feel repulsed by the event? How does he react? If he reacts at all, is it immediate or delayed? How does he channel his frustration and anger at witnessing such a sordid event?

While confronted by these life-changing events 'people make choices in pursuing goals that give their lives meaning' (Morris, 1993: 266). In these situations the enormity of the violence they are confronted with can mean that they themselves assume a sense of victimhood (albeit indirectly).[9] Their pain on being witness to this horror is so overpowering that they end up making interventions with far reaching consequences.

In his preface to Frantz Fanon's *Wretched of the Earth—A Negro Psychoanalyst's Study of the Problems of Racism and Colonialism*, fellow intellectual Jean-Paul Sartre wrote, 'the rebel's weapon is the proof of his humanity' (Fanon, 1963). What Sartre was proposing was that the society may take a rather sympathetic view if a victim or someone indirectly affected by an act of inhumane aggression takes recourse in open violence against the identified aggressor. Closely examined this form of individually mediated retributive violence would appear to have its basis in vengeance undertaken specifically to right the wrong.

But this raises several moral questions. Should there be a clause allowing the individual affected by this experience to pursue a private vendetta? Some tentative answers to this line of inquiry could be along these lines. If punishment is the sole objective here, 'The only humane motive, the only possible moral justification for punishment is to reform the criminal and/or to deter others from committing similar crimes' (Armstrong, 1969: 139). But the affirmation towards retribution need not always be violent.

The man born Cassius Marcellus Clay Jr. is perhaps the greatest boxer of our time and will remain so for a long time to come. His fame as a boxer is only incidental to his personality. He is more of a hero for the stand he took early on in life. He lived a better part of his life suffering from a damaged brain condition owing to the great many bouts and punches he received in his long career. Cassius Clay's decision to become a boxer, however, was not premeditated. He did not choose it in order to seek fame and fortune. His participation in it and sacrificing his body to this cruel and inhumane sport was a result of his own deep scars received early on while witnessing the violation and suffering of his friend.[10] What Cassius Clay, later reincarnated as Muhammad Ali, was expressing was a tragic pain that he harboured for being a witness to such violence.

If such decisions belong to the domain of revenge they can take a most violent turn. On such occasions a witness to the horror (an indirect victim) may take recourse in introducing direct violence in order to avenge the violation of his comrade or friend. In the absence of a real life example to demonstrate that to be the case, I use a fictionalised/cinematic representation of such an event.

Deliverance

Take the James Dickey-authored and John Boorman-directed 1972 Warner Brothers' film *Deliverance*, for instance. It is one of the earliest Hollywood films to dwell on the issue of male–male sexual violence and rape, and it does so extremely graphically. The film can be read in various different contexts. When it was released critics read the rape as a metaphor for the rape of the environment. Other subtle issues such as the victim's sense of victimhood and how he and his friends subsequently deal with the question of justice tended to be lost on audiences.

The plot is at once simple and at the same time extremely complex from a victim justice-vengeance perspective. Four thirty-something male city dwellers make an adventurous canoe trip of a lifetime down the Chattooga River in the Appalachian mountains that is going disappear under a proposed hydroelectric project. While one of the parties briefly comes ashore to the river bank to wait for their other two friends they are taken hostage by two rifle-wielding mountain men/trackers. While one of the adventurers Ed (Jon Voight) is tied to a tree stump by his belt and cut with a knife, his friend Bobby (Ned Beatty) is forced to mimic a sow by one of their captors and then brutally raped. The rapist then returns to the tree stump to help his friend initiate the rape of Ed.

While the second tracker is undoing his zip to begin his rape of Ed, the remaining two friends arrive on the river bank in a separate canoe and Lewis (Burt Reynolds), who is witnessing this unfolding event from a distance, aims and shoots an arrow from his bow. The arrow goes straight through the first rapist. While he lays bleeding and dying the other would-be violator escapes into the thick of the forest.

Following the slow and agonising death of the violator, however, begins the real moral and legal dilemma between the four friends. What do they do with the dead violator? Do they report the incident to the highway patrolman/sheriff up river in Aintry, where they are heading? What are the consequences of having murdered a sexual assailant? Did the chubby-looking Bobby invite the catastrophe on himself for his own slightly effeminate physicality? Can they convince the law that it was justifiable murder? Would the law and the jury be sympathetic to their horrendous experience and traumatic ordeal and issue a not-guilty verdict? What about the victim(s) of the homosexual violence themselves? Can they go through the parade of public interrogation of homosexual rape and the attendant double humiliation? So the four friends angrily debate on the forest floor.

While a conscience-stricken Drew (Ronny Cox) is for informing the law about their killing, the actual killer Lewis is not so sure. He feels the law is going to be unsympathetic to their cause. So, Lewis proposes a vote in which the actual victims decide the matter. A brutalised, shocked and mangled Bobby is the first to react. He says, 'I don't want this story to get around.' His solution therefore is, 'Let's bury him.' Faced with this potentially devastating verdict the conscience-keeper of the group Drew now turns to the other victim Ed, hoping he will see reason, be a law-abiding citizen and take the matter to the authorities for conferment of eventual justice. After a brief contemplation, however, Ed declares, 'I am with Bobby. We bury him.'

Their plight is not over, however. The other escaped mountain tracker shoots Drew with his rifle from a cliff above and pursues them on the bends of the river. This time Ed, who was about to be molested/raped by this man earlier, pursues him and kills him. In this scene we are shown an indecisive Ed who struggles to aim (as he is not capable of killing as shown earlier from a failed deer-shooting incident).

Both our victims, Bobby (who has been raped) and Ed (who narrowly escaped that fate), appear to entertain an unbridled disgust towards their violators and do not mask their intention to avenge their violation. Bobby even tries to physically assault the rapist while he is bleeding to death. What Bobby lacks in raw physical power to defend himself is amply compensated for by his use and choice of emotions and words. While Ed lowers the second violator into the river, Bobby tells him, 'You did it,' (you succeeded in avenging our dishonour and my defilement). And, 'It is good!'

While Bobby (the primary victim) cannot avenge his violation, unsure about the legal outcome and uneasy about seeing his violation made public, he falls upon those next to him (his comrades in arms) to dispense with swift retributive justice and in fact is the first to condone it. Ed is less direct in his expression of emotions surrounding vengeance but nonetheless is clearly determined to avenge the dishonour.

For Brownmiller, 'what is presented as heroic in *Deliverance* is the justifiable murder of one of the rapists by the victim's buddy, a revenge' (Brownmiller, 1975: 304). She seems somehow unable to appreciate the plight of the male victims of such violence. She argues that female victims are never portrayed as taking vengeance in the same way (Brownmiller, 1975: 304). But her focus on this gender issue deflects her attention from the inner conflict that the victims and their friends go through while seeking a way out of their situation. She seems oblivious of the overarching legal ambiguities that surround such an event as male-male rape.

In more ways than one *Deliverance* dealt with the same sorts of anxieties, challenges, apprehensions and legal conundrums that male victims of sexual violence encounter today. While both our victims are consumed by this duality of private violation and private vengeance there is also tension in their own undertakings. While sending the dead body of Drew to the watery grave of the depths of the river, Ed pronounces, 'He [Drew] was the best of us.'

Drew—the one who did not kill, who opposed dispensing with the violator's body without informing the authorities—is singled out as the best of them for the simple reason that he stood for law, for morality, for openness and transparent justice. But under the circumstances our victims could not entertain such a line of action and ended up seeking out a form of retributive justice over restorative justice. In fact the parting shot of *Deliverance* where Bobby tells Ed that he would not be seeing him for some time (although they are close friends and have gone through this nightmarish hell together) again brings up the victim's inability to come to terms with his victimhood—even though the violator has been dealt with.

Taken together, both the narration of Cassius Clay and *Deliverance* point in one particular direction: the victim cannot stand up in his own defence and is instead aided by others. In these instances the 'defender' often becomes a surrogate victim. He carries a certain amount of the pain of the violated and that pain instigates him to take a particular stand, either in the form of immediate retributive violence, or in a form of internalised offensive defence that leads the surrogate to become a violated as we witnessed in the case of Cassius Clay.

Conclusion

We, as a community of responsive individuals, have not yet succeeded in facilitating an environment where victims' tragedies could be brought to the fore without him or his family being cast in some negative stereotypes.

In the end, coping with this particular violence is dependent on changing the conditions that cause it. While we can identify the conditions we are not in a position to change them altogether. What we can do is to be conscious of them. It is the traditional social constructionist conceptualisation of the 'role' of the male which puts the victim at a disadvantage when we talk about societal response to his victimhood. There needs to be an expression of courage and conviction to move away from that stereotype. It is only when the wider society openly and without bias confronts this issue that the victims can find justice and the violators feel less inclined to undertake their sordid enterprise. Thus, it is imperative that these (in)visible victims and their private tragedies become fully recognised at the societal as well as institutional level, and structures be put in place in order to deal with the the their long-term emotional, economic, psychological and physical needs.

Equally importantly we also need to treat male victims as being in need of the same degree of protection and empathy as their female counterparts. Being understood without being judged is perhaps the greatest need of male victims of such violence. There is also a need for abandoning the currently prevalent hierarchy of concern. Addressing one group of individuals' needs while refusing to acknowledge the victimhood of another group because of gender differences sets a bad precedence. If society as a whole can move away from its current mindset it can go a long way in alleviating the suffering of the victim.

CONCLUSION

> To speak is to act.
>
> Tzvetan Todorov, *The Morals of History*, 1995: 156.

War is a state of exception. War 'oversees interruption of subjective continuities, the alienation of persons from the structures of meaning which defined them in times of peace' (Levinas, 1969; Brighton, 2011: 103). It is an enforcer of exceptional conditions. 'War forces the unmaking and remaking of individual, social, and political meaning in ways which defy prediction' (Brighton, 2011: 103). It is a great theatre for individual experimentation. War both enables and offers the possibility to explore unexamined sexual boundaries. War unhinges restrictions imposed by conventions, morality and law.

Armed conflicts and wars are very much about direct physical intervention. Beyond the claims surrounding 'virtuous wars' that promote a vision of bloodless hygienic encounter, wars have always been and continue to be lo-fi, intimate, and messy (McSorley, 2012: 48). In these physical encounters civilians have increasingly become the targets, with warring factions across the world successfully destroying individuals and communities both physically and mentally by employing particularised forms of violence (Hargreaves, 2001: 737). The arena and ambit of this process of destruction is very large and varied indeed. Conflict related sexual violence 'occurs in homes, agricultural fields, forest, places of detention, prisons, military sites, and camps for refugees and displaced persons. It occurs at the height of conflict, during population displacement and continues after conflict' (Bastick, Grimm and Kunz, 2007: 13).

There are several conflict conditions that ultimately contribute to the introduction and enactment of such forms of physical encounter. Sexual violence against boys and men in armed conflicts and war is a product of complex political, social and biological processes—ranging from skewed atavistic nationalism to predatory opportunistic responses by the transgressors. In conflict settings, custodial situations and mass displacement can facilitate abuse on a larger scale (Lewis, 2009: 16). Since the absence of general law and order is a given in these circumstances, the problem is exacerbated.

A persistent conflict scenario also leads to predatory sexual violence against the civilian population. In these settings the condition of anarchy or near-anarchy provides a perfect incentive for irregular actors such as rebel leaders, warlords and even the general populace with economic and physical power, to impose forms of sexual violence upon their hapless victims. At the height of the Sierra Leonean civil war various armed factions, in particular the Revolutionary United Front and the Armed Forces Revolutionary Council, carried out a systematic retaliatory orgy of sexual violence against both sexes. To those embarking on this path, such strategic violence became an accepted face of the overall armed interaction with the enemy.

Sexual violence against an antagonistic rival or traditional enemy is a historical and social process that is carried out collectively and, thus, has a collective meaning (Seifert, 1996: 36). An endemic intra-ethnic and intra-religious divide provides cover for ultra-nationalist leaders and bigots to direct such forms of violence against a section of the population. When the symbolic identity of the targeted male is coupled with their cultural and religious identity the punishment becomes all the more severe and horrific. As discussed in several places, the central objective behind such undertakings is not only to satisfy at times one's perverse carnal desires but also to exploit the occasion to engage in various forms of hegemony, ethnic cleansing, emasculation of the opponent's nation and so on. Put simply, it is aimed at the destruction of a people: it is a form of torture preceding death (Allen, 1996: 100–1).

Warfare 'proper', which signifies a confrontation that takes places between soldiers to seek a political outcome, is rather an outmoded concept. Contemporary study of armed conflicts and wars is about much more than bombs, the number of dead and who ultimately wins. It is about the study of entire societies and their peculiarities. For war and society are entwined in mutually constitutive relations. War is shaped by, and shapes, social contexts (Barkawi & Brighton, 2011: 132). An examination of war, therefore, requires us to look at the war outcome in its entirety—in the battlefield as well as in a societal context. Once we have that framework of assessment we can better understand why some societies in the midst of a perpetual warlike condition facilitate an abhorrent practice where abduction and forced sexual violence against boys and men can become an accepted norm.

Yet, sexual violence as a war undertaking is not a universal norm. Ethnological research reveals that sexual violation of the rival or enemy is by no means equally common in all societies. Rather, there are sexual violation-prone and largely violation-free societies (Seifert, 1996: 36). Hence there exists a wide variation in conflict-related wartime sexual violence against boys and men. While it is widespread in some civil war locations such as the DRC and Afghanistan it is conspicuous by its absence in other theatres of conflict such as Israel-Palestine and Somalia. While '[i]n some conflicts, the pattern of sexual violence is symmetric, with all parties to the war engaging in sexual violence to roughly the same extent; in other conflicts, it is very asymmetric' (Wood, 2006: 308).

While an overwhelming majority of rebels and militias in various contemporary armed conflicts appear to have engaged in such violence, others display a separate set of dynamics. In fact some armed groups are found to prohibit wartime sexual violence (Wood, 2006: 308; Cohen, Green & Wood, 2013: 13). The feared Liberation Tigers of Tamil Eelam (LTTE), which fought a quarter-of-a-century long civil war with the state authorities in Sri Lanka and experienced regular wartime sexual violence against both its civilian and military male and female members was remarkably restrained in its reprisal attacks when it came to the use of such violence against its opponents.[1]

Interestingly, while we witness restraint in some localised conflicts it may be very widespread in other contexts. In fact these forms of violence can have both international and non-international dimensions. These could be isolated but sporadic events, where such violence becomes an all too frequent occurrence (cases of sectarian or religious conflict), race-inspired sexual vigilantism, as well as incidents of isolated sexual violence in post-conflict settings (as is the case with UN peacekeepers and various NGO workers in central Africa, the Caribbean and the greater South Asia). Although wartime sexual violence is often seen to be perpetrated primarily by unruly and undisciplined rebel forces, it is found that state-based armed forces are far more likely than rebel groups to engage in such undertakings (Cohen, Green & Wood, 2013: 4). In addition it could also be opportunistic and predatory.

What makes the exploration of male sexual violence so important, yet so difficult is it seems to be present in most conflicts from ancient times to the present and yet it scarcely makes the headlines. If the topic of sexual violence against women in times of war has been uncomfortably pushed to the side of mainstream debate, then this particular issue concerning such aggression against men has been treated for the most parts as taboo (Carlson, 2006: 16).

With violation come categories of emphasis and distinction, labels and discourse. Often times we have a binary understanding surrounding gender and the consequent security needs of gender groups. Note, for instance, a Red Cross video that was aimed at the former Yugoslavia. The homily in the video went like this: 'A warrior does not kill prisoners. A warrior does not kill children. A warrior does not rape women.' (Ignatieff, 1997: 157.) But what about all those men who were brutally raped, castrated and left to die of their wounds? Should not there have be an additional sentence like 'A warrior does not sexually violate men'?

While the social basis of combat behaviour is to be found in the construction of what it means to be a soldier and a warrior (Barkawi, *et al.*, 1999: 183), for all intents and purposes it remains partial in its overall remit. In Sanskrit there is a value-laden phrase surrounding the female body; it refers to *abala durbala*. Examined in a socio-political context it highlights the fragility and vulnerability of the female physical self, incapable of protecting herself from likely transgressors.

Consequently we have a whole genre of formal and informal cultural and social constructions that requires the combatants to foster a warrior ethic that treats women in a particular way: 'women are to be protected from the realities of war because, while virtuous, they are weak' (Barkawi, 1999: 184). Needless to add, we have no such aphorism or war ethic which underscores the fact that men could be equally vulnerable and may require restraint if not protection.

Moreover, our understanding surrounding this phenomenon is governed by a disordered state of knowledge and response. The knowledge surrounding violence in general and sexual violence in particular in armed conflicts and war is primarily based on a constructivist theory of gender.

In fact much of the 'human security discourse in international institutions is based upon a highly gendered understanding of who is to be secured, characterised by the exclusion of civilian males as well as war combatants as subjects of "protection" or as victims of "gender-based violence"' (Carpenter, 2006: 85).

Furthermore, evaluated against sexual violence towards women in armed conflicts, the situation of male victimhood establishes hierarchies of suffering that treat some victims as more in need of sympathy than others. Second, it perpetuates 'false' norms that essentialise women as the 'only' victims. Third, by ignoring the fact that boys and men could be equal victims of such forms of violence, society imposes unhealthy expectations about masculinity on the male sex whereby they are expected to keep quiet about their victimhood (lest it damage their masculine pride) (Stemple, 2009: 606).

It is this one-sided approach towards assessing wartime and conflict-related sexual violence, that overwhelmingly considers females as the 'sole' victims, that does most harm to the 'male condition'. On the whole there exists not only a lack of knowledge about these victims' particular situation but also the consequent absence of methods to redress their personal tragedies in social, political, legal, medical and post-conflict contexts.[2]

This mode of violence cannot receive the attention it deserves and will not be deterred unless, and until, the victims' experiences are retold and the public develops an appetite to confront these individual and communal tragedies. As one critic put it, 'people must hear the horrifying, think the unthinkable and speak the unspeakable' (Tompkins, 1995: 852). To acknowledge the suffering of these victims requires more than a reminder of the cruelties they have experienced—it requires a leap of imagination. Only then will the intelligentsia, policy makers, jurists and the masses sit up and take notice of it.[3]

In light of the brutality suffered by the victims in all these contexts it is worth pondering how one is able to redress their misfortune. Owing to the nature of this violence outlined in previous chapters it is but natural for the reader to expect a meaningful cognitive framework that addresses it. Addressing violence in the context of armed conflict and war needs to be approached within an ethical register, with a concern for overcoming it (Barkawi, 2011: 703). When such atrocities are found to have been committed there are two things to do, 'one centered on thinking and one on emotion. We can try to understand why it happened, and we must find the right attitude to it, one that acknowledges its horror' (Morton, 2004: 104).

However, given the complex dynamics of this particular form of violence, there is no single path to addressing the issue or the needs of the victims. Given the enormity of the challenges involved one can only put forward several different measures to deal with this problem. These may range from greater legal protection for victims, to the introduction and codification of a credible set of universal legal mechanisms which would serve as a deterrent for would-be violators.

One could also explore the possibility of some form of compensation. For the yearning to compensate the victims of such personal tragedies would appear to be universal. But it is not entirely clear how one should go about finding an effective mode of compensation. In situations where females have gone through such forms of violence there have been financial reparations, but given the reluctance of the male victim to come forward it is doubtful if such a compensation strategy could have any effect. Apologies would seem trifling for two reasons. First, who should have the moral responsibility to extend such an apology? Second, how does one prove that the apology is a result of the moral burden that the perpetrator or the state in question felt?

My personal experience of dealing with this subject has been quite varied. I have received hostile after-seminar remarks from many fellow academics who did not think 'the subject worth talking about'. Known violators have sneered at the mention of their horrific violence. Victims, being asked to narrate their experience, have sulked in helpless silence. And, then there is the general mass that expressed its complete ignorance of the subject. What I have tried to do in this study is unearth and document scraps of horror.

This search has led me to interpret mainstream cinema, record wartime experiences, bring aboard hitherto lost bits of information and so on. As Visvanathan suggests, 'political theory often heals itself not by acts of exorcism which create its own violence but by acts of re-reading' (Visvanathan 2006: 537). If anything this study has underlined that particular aspect.

With the end of this study now fully in sight the inevitable question is: what does it all add up to? What have we learned about sexual violence against boys and men in armed conflicts? How does this normative explanation contribute to the reordering of our knowledge?

CONCLUSION

What this study underscored is the fact that our political reflection has lagged far behind empirical events. The exploratory journey that this undertaking offered was as much about unearthing those events as it was about contemplating those events themselves. What I argued amounts to the claim that such sexual violence in armed conflicts and war has been a persistently contradictory aspect of human history. While we as a community of individuals are partially aware of it, we have not yet fully comprehended its scope and the tragedy it inflicts upon individuals and communities.

NOTES

INTRODUCTION

1. According to one observer while both groups are vulnerable to sexual violence in detention, in some places over 50 per cent of the detainees can experience sexualised torture (Russell, 2008: 22).

2. Although not publicised, these forms of violence have been regularly reported to agencies in the humanitarian community. In fact, over the past decade various international humanitarian and civil society organisations and non-governmental organisations (NGOs) have reported incidents of sexual violence against boys and men in the context of violent intra-state or inter-state conflicts. Notable among these identified conflict locations are Afghanistan, Algeria, Burundi, Chechnya (Russia), the Republic of the Congo, the Democratic Republic of the Congo (DRC), East Timor, Egypt, Guatemala, Guinea-Bissau, Iraq, Israel/Palestine, Kenya, Liberia, Rwanda, Sierra Leone, Sri Lanka, Sudan, Syria, Turkey, Uganda, Uzbekistan, Yemen, former Yugoslavia, Zimbabwe and United States' detention centres across the world (Sivakumaran, 2007; Russell, 2007: 22).

3. The first recorded statement in this regard can be found in the Old Testament. In the *Book of Isaiah*, for instance, there exists vivid description of such undertaking. While commenting on Babylon and the vanquished Babylonians, Chapter 13, Verse 16 suggests: 'Their children also shall be dashed to pieces before their eyes; their houses shall be spoiled, and their wives ravished.' (Isaiah 13: 16). We find similar sentiments and violent sexual undertakings against the enemy's women during Alexander the Great's military campaigns into the known world. The Romans pretty much followed this practice and by the Middle Ages it had become an established norm in warfare. Interestingly while the Old Testament did not see any problem with sexual violence against enemy women during armed conflicts and war, it certainly was uncomfortable with sanctioning something similar against male enemies. It detested any male-to-male sexual undertaking. This particular view found its ample manifestation in the context of Sodom and Gomorrah, where it condemned the inhabitants for their homosexual practices and sanctioned utmost

punishment. Although we have this overwhelming evidence against homosexuality it would be wrong to assume that boys and men were not subjected to forms of sexual violence.

4. To the classical Greeks, 'the sexual nature of every human being combined elements which were as much homosexual as heterosexual' (Puig, 1984: 152).

5. In the view of some critics, homosexual rape perpetrated by victors upon the vanquished was a sure and certain way of feminising enemy officers as well as soldiers. At times such violence took a different turn in the form of the castration of conquered enemy males. Such forms of violence were common among the Amalekite, Chinese, Egyptian, Persian, and Norse armies (Goldstein, 2001: 357–60).

6. Steven Pinker, in his acclaimed work *The Better Angels of Our Nature*, reminds us: 'Warriors often reward themselves with trophies, especially heads, scalps and genitals' (Pinker, 2011: 53).

7. The possible reason for this undertaking, Tacitus suggests, is that 'he was a possible challenger to the imperial power' (Tacitus, *Annals* xii: 17). The brief reign of Nero was indeed synonymous with untold and gross sexual abuse of both men and women who he considered a threat.

8. Bosnian Serb Commanders during their genocidal purge against Bosnian Muslims and Croats 'reportedely encouraged their soliders to rape the enemy civilians claiming such actions would boost their morale'. According to some violators' testimonies, often they 'were ordered to rape so that their morale would be higher. They were told they would fight better if they raped the enemy women' (Kressler, 2002: 33).

9. Reflecting on Nazi experiments with *Versuchspersonen* or human guinea pigs, Giorgio Agamben describes such undertakings as being 'merely sadocriminal acts with no relation to scientific research' (Agamben, 1998: 146).

10. As reported by the BBC: http://www.bbc.co.uk/news/world-latin-america-14796970; http://www.bbc.co.uk/news/world-latin-america-17351144

11. Documentary evidence on the Sierra Leoneian civil war suggests sexual violence was committed by female combatants against men and boys (Bastick, Grimm and Kunz, 2007: 58).

12. A recent study asks: Why is it that the research community has been ignorant of the fact that female rebels, militias or armed forces personnel could also be perpetrators of such violence? To unravel this mystery this study argues it may have to do with the way the question itself was framed: 'researchers typically have not asked respondents about the sex of their perpetrators, instead assuming that the perpetrators are always male' (Cohen, Green & Wood, 2013: 4).

13. In addition, this debate mistakenly implies that men are the only culprits who undertake such violence. That forms of sexual violence in armed conflicts could be undertaken by female transgressors both against women as well as men is often ignored.

14. In this particular instance, at least, one could argue because of private prohibitions and methodological differences prevalent among researchers there are occasions when the truth is left buried.
15. Also see: http://adamjones.freeservers.com/malerape.htm

1. THE BODY

1. They all hold a certain amount of value. Just like virgin women, boys with innocence still intact, rank as high prize loot in many theatres of conflict. This was the case in ancient times and still dominates the thinking in contemporary conflict situations (such as Afghanistan, Sudan, Sierra Leone to name a few hotspots). Similarly young political prisoners with commitment to a given ideology and conviction about their beliefs are considered high-value victims. They are the ones who often are picked up by the opposite side in a conflict and forced into the most humiliating and at times violent sexual violation and torture.
2. Similarly, 'there were some Iranian prisoners who, in return for privileges from their Iraqi captors, would actually search for young Iranian boys in the camp and pick them out for their Iraqi captors. These mercenaries—one of them had the nickname "Mohsen Amrikaie"—would clothe the boys in Arabic garments, put make-up on them and hand them over for the sexual pleasure of the wardens' (http://www.iranian.com/Nov95/POW.html#Abuse).
3. 'Afghanistan's *mujahideen* warlords, who fought the Soviet invasion and instigated a civil war in the 1980s, regularly engaged in acts of pedophilia. Keeping one or more "*chai* boys," as these conscripts are called, for personal servitude and pleasure became a symbol of power and social status. When the former *mujahideen* commanders ascended to power in 2001 after the Taliban's ouster, they brought with them a rekindled culture of *bachha bazi* and *chai* boys.' Chris Mondloch, 'Bacha Bazi: An Afghan Tragedy', *Foreign Policy*, 28 October 2013.
4. 'One of the colonels that we both knew had been accused of raping a *chai* boy, badly. The all have *chai* boys. It's not some perverted thing, it's just what they do. Women are for juma. The only time you interact with your wife is on Friday, the rest of the time it's *chai* boys.' Thomas E. Ricks, 'Tales of the Afghan military: Honestly, which officer here hasn't raped a tea boy?' *Foreign Policy*, 11 April 2013.
5. As Chris Mondloch in his analysis points out 'the lawlessness that followed the deposing of the Taliban in Afghanistan gave rises to violent expressions of pedophilia. Boys were raped, kidnapped and trafficked as sexual predators regained their positions of regional power' (Mondloch, 2013).
6. Médicins Sans Frontièrs (8 March 2005); Physicians for Human Rights (October 2004); Amnesty International (2006)
7. There exists a whole tome of scholarly/conspiracy literature that question this experience. Here my intention is not to examine the veracity of these claims and counter claims. What I am interested in is to build up a line of argument based on Lawrence's work and take on the subject.

8. According to Giles Deleuze, the bodily violation of Lawrence projected two sets of contradictory emotions in the victim. Lawrence's 'private shame at being raped by his captors' at Deraa coexisted and intermingled 'with his sense of personal glory' (Deleuze, 1998: 124).

9. 'I believe he's taken a shine to you old man', one of the key characters Captain Lawrence tells the David Bowie character.

2. BIOPOWER

1. Incidentally Shiraz had gone home directly after his release but his father 'did not let him in' (Poorgiv, 2009). According to another victim of such state-sponsored violation '…rape is not just a blow to one person; it is a blow to the whole family. A victim of rape is never healed with the passing of time. With every look given by a father, the wounds open again' (quoted in Allen, 2010).

2. See, http://www.bbc.co.uk/news/world-asia-21577866, last accessed 26 Feb. 2013.

3. Note, for instance, Robert Mugabe's condemnation of homosexuality as an 'evil' that 'destroys nations' during his 7th presidential inauguration speech on 22 August 2013.

4. As reported in *The Mirror*: http://www.mirror.co.uk/news/world-news/muslim-mutilated-central-african-republic-3123452, last accessed 25 July 2014.

5. http://www.bbc.co.uk/news/world-africa-25946920, last accessed 24 July 2014.

6. Removing the genitalia of the enemy in order to gain potency has a long history and is a common occurrence in some contemporary conflicts. The Mai-Mai (Mayi-Mayi) rebel fighters in eastern Congo, for example, often drink the blood of their slain enemy and ingest their heart or genitals to gain the power of the warrior.

7. Note, for instance, the killer Christian mob in Central African Republic: 'people were filming … [the genital mutilation] on their cell phones and many were laughing. When we [the reporters] left the scene, they said: "Keep on filming, because we're not yet done."' (http://www.bbc.co.uk/news/world-africa-2594 6920)

8. This experimental dimension to sexual violence can be found in some philosophical/fictional writing. In Georges Bataille's *Story of the Eye* a priest in a Catholic Church is subjected to elaborate sexual torture by two violators, Sir Edmund and Simone. The torturers want to sacrifice the victim through hanging, while he is being tempted into having sex with Simone. The attempt here is to find out whether or not it is true that, as is rumoured, a man who is being hanged ejaculates at the same time. Sir Edmund declares to the victim prior to his execution: 'You know that men who are hanged or garroted have such stiff cocks the instant their respiration is cut off, that they ejaculate. You are going to have the pleasure of being martyred while fucking the girl.' (Bataille, 1982: 64).

9. This argument gains much credence in the context of Pashtun male populace in Afghanistan. According to one critic, 'a significant percentage of the country's Pashtun male population bears the deep psychological scars of sexual abuse from

childhood. Consequently many of the prominent Pashtun men who currently engage in *bacha bazi* (which we discussed in chapter one) were likely abused as children; in turn many of today's adolescent victims will likely become powerful warlords or government-affiliated leaders perpetuating the cycle of abuse'. Chris Mondloch, 'Bacha Bazi: An Afghan Tragedy, *Foreign Policy*, 28 October, 2013.

10. Interestingly there are, as yet, no official victims in this tit-for-tat violence. The Guatemalan state does not recognise any such violence. Officially, the rapes either against female or male Guatemalans during the conflict 'never happened' (de Pablo, Zurita and Tremlett, 2012: 13).

11. As reported by the BBC: http://www.bbc.co.uk/news/world-africa-15390980, last accessed 25 July 2014.

3. IN THE NAME OF THE NATION

1. Note, for instance, the symbolism of the hand-physical relationship across all modern ideological frameworks—hand salutes in Nazi Germany; the hand of Uncle Sam stretching out to command allegiance from the citizenry in the US post-war posters; and the ubiquitous Soviet-era motifs of muscular hands of workers signifying a stronger state.

2. Taking a Hobbesian imaginary leap one could argue, if the Leviathan's body is formed out of all the bodies of individuals, then by violating one single body or a group of bodies one is, in fact, corrupting the entire body politic. Or, how could a body of violated men constitute the covenant of a sacred Social Contract?

3. Very often the violator is very much aware of the consequential effects of his actions on the victim. By forcing him to undergo such violation the violator is effectively condemning the individual to an inescapable cycle of moral degeneration. The awareness of violation-led-moral-degeneration not only prevents the victim from speaking out for his nation it also effectively seals his participation in any future nationalist or nation-building projects.

4. This is a slightly altered model devised by Flora Anthias and Nira Yuval Davis, to contextualise women and nationalism. For details, see Anthias, Flora and Nira Yuval Davis, *Woman—Nation—State*, London: Macmillan, 1989, pp. 6–11.

5. Very often 'full and semi-castrations were performed either by cutting the victim's scrotum or penis using a knife or another sharp object or by tying up the penis with rope or wire, followed by pulling the rope by hand, pliers, or other suitable objects' (Loncar et. al., 2010: 197).

6. Although a pioneer in this method Dr Schumann, however, was sceptical of its wide use. He would argue that castration of the subjects of 'inferior race' was cheaper and took less time. However, he cautioned that such method could not be adapted to large numbers of subjects for the amount of time required and the presence of physical evidence in the victim afterwards. For an exhaustive discussion, see Kogon, 1950, pp. 152–6.

7. Coarse imagery, perhaps. But in the highly charged environment of contested

nationalism such sentiments at times find an actual outlet when the enemy is treated very much in the manner expressed in the sentiment. For a related discussion, see Ignatieff, 1994.

8. In an orchestrated orgy of violence they both raped and impregnated Bosnian Muslim women in order to produce a new generation of Serb offspring. Or, as one critic pointed out very shortly after these undertakings: 'the purpose of systematic rape of these women were to "clean" them of their ethnic identity and humiliate their male kin' (Olujic, 1998: 42).

9. These violators often live marginal lives, facing a constant contingent of threats to their very existence at every twist and turn in their lives. And in some instances their lives may have been marked by an absence of sexual company from the opposite sex. When presented with an enemy who clearly has everything in life that the perpetrator lacks, the result may be an outburst of anger leading to gross sexual violence against the hapless victim. In such situations, accumulated insults, rebukes and disappointments of life come out in a cathartic release of rage and fury.

10. The other subset of the question has a slight variation. It can be framed along these lines: What if the female perpetrator undertakes a form of sexual activity that does not involve any of the above categories, but in fact makes herself the subject of sexual interaction with the captive? For instance, if a female perpetrator undertakes forcible sexual intercourse on her male captive, opponent or victim could it be a clear case of sexual violence?

11. In mediaeval Europe castration in the hands of the enemy forced the victim into a sate of abjection. Being incapable of producing children for your country which feared depopulation in the face of wars, castrated men could not be tolerated and invariably ended up despised by their own community and the country and punished with ridicule (Wagner, 1987: 58).

12. In *The Tears of Eros* Bataille calls it 'the little death' that follows sexual climax. 'This photograph had a decisive role in my life. I have never stopped being obsessed by this image of pain, at once ecstatic and intolerable' (Bataille, 1992: 73).

13. Having said that, I ought to stress that the male body has essentially been a denominator of difference rather than unity. The external attributes of the body and its representation in terms of colour, ethnicity, lineage and location has been a natural agent of division. In times of calm and civility the tendency happens to favour a policy aimed at accommodating various shades of bodies under a common umbrella of governance and forged some degree of national unity. This was the case during the Roman empire and it is true today when President Barack Obama talks about various bodies—'Whites, Blacks, Hispanics, Asians, Gay, Straight, Native American, Asian, able bodied and disabled' (Obama, 2008: Victory Speech Chicago)—all forming a unified American body representing a unitary nation.

4. THE TORTURER'S SOUL

1. While the admission of this violence on the part of the victim and the resultant effect on his body and psyche is hard to gather, the interlinked effect on the perpetrator is harder and rarer still.

2. One can, of course, strongly disagree with this mode of interpretation of the violators' neuro-psychological status. But it is impossible to deny that some degree of erotic desire plays some part in such undertakings.

3. In the view of Bataille, however, such 'transgressive sexuality, in even its most extreme variant is a part of "normal" human sexuality'.

4. According to some observers, the absence of character-forming traits in the violator is 'mainly because of unsatisfactory emotional environments or simply inconsistent treatment in early life, no adequate Super-Ego or conscience has been developed' (Honderich, 1984: 96). This argument has some merit owing to the fact that we have situations and instances where some aggressors have undertaken this particularised forms of violence while their companions have refrained from it.

5. Contrary to the general view and the reports peddled by the media, the violators on these occasions may not exclusively belong to the rebel groups, militias or government soldiers. The perpetrator could equally be an intimate member of the community to which the victim belonged. He could be a friend, partner, acquaintance or a simple non-combatant.

6. *Why I Killed So Many Liberians, The Demonic Confessions of General Butt Naked* (http://www.youtube.com/watch?v=QKQ1O_HMvHs, last accessed 25 July 2014).

7. 'Hindu-Muslim violence in India is usually described as "communal," with the term "ethnic" reserved for racially and linguistically distinct groups' (Dhattiwala & Biggs, 2012: 487).

8. This point comes alive in Suketu Mehta's magnum opus *Maximum City*. Commenting on the Hindu-Muslim communal riots in India, Mehta stresses, 'that little flap of skin that the Muslims lacked could cost them their lives…' (Mehta, 2005: 45).

9. *Kattu* is not only different from a non-*Kattu* but the former's very presence and existence is an affront against the latter. A non-*Kattu* perpetually harbours two set of contradictory images about his own sexuality vis a vis that of the *Kattu*. First, a non-*Kattu* takes pride in his supposed purity (for not having gone through the abominable act of circumcision). Second, at the same time, he (the non-*Kattu*) constantly envies the *Kattu* for the latter's alleged sexual excesses.

10. Explained within the Freudian trajectory, 'the very skin is an erotogenic; a source of, and object for, a drive to touch; a site of contact and contagion; a boundary layer representing protection and vulnerability'. Such an erotogenic drive becomes the site of intense desire and objection when the skin in question is the rival's genital without its foreskin.

11. Interestingly, expression of this fury is not limited to times of communal carnage alone. In peacetime the same constituency engage in linguistic violence. In the run up to the Indian general election in May 2014, for instance, among the articulated middle-class supporters of the BJP, the unofficial message doing the rounds was: 'When Modi comes to power it is time to cut the *kattus*' (note the rhythmic assemblage of English and Hindi). I thank Mark Lacy for bringing this to my attention.

12. Interestingly the post-partition Indian government was engaged in a massive 'recovery operation' with its Islamic counterpart Pakistan in order to recover Hindu and Sikh women who were abducted to this new country by Muslims following Partition in 1947. For an interesting overview, see Menon and Bhasin, 1998.

13. The then Chief Minister of the Gujarat state, Narendra Modi, is reported to have cited Newton's third law—'Every action has an equal and opposite reaction'—to justify the killings of Muslims in the 2002 riots (quoted in Dhattiwala & Biggs, 2012: 486–7).

14. In another conflict location, Kosovo, the minority Serbs often cited the Kosovo Albanians' high birthrate as a proof of this particular Muslim community's 'abnormal sexual drive' (Diken & Laustsen, 2005: 114).

15. If rape of Muslim women by Hindu men is considered a form of male empowerment at times Hindu women push them in that direction. It is not uncommon to come across references of Hindu women actively assisting the Hindu mob in the gang rape of Muslim women in some riots (Hansen, 2001: 123).

16. A rather disturbing audit of such atrocities can be found in the Human Rights Watch report on the Gujarat Riots of 2002. '"We Have No Orders to Save You": State Participation and Complicity in Communal Violence in Gujarat', 14, 3 (C), (2002), pp. 1–67. http://www.hrw.org/reports/2002/india/gujarat.pdf

17. There is an interesting comparative variation here. During the height of the Bosnian civil war, Serb militias were engaged in a similar project, i.e. the reduction of future generations of Muslims. Thus they went about impregnating Muslim women with the aim of producing a new generation of Serbs that replaced Muslims (Stiglmayer, 1994; Sells, 2003; Snyder et al., 2006). Our violators, however, were not pursuing any such logic.

18. This is how the real-life character Michael Bernhardt (the Charlie Sheen character in *Platoon*) who refused to join the killing against the orders of his superiors reflected on the My Lai massacre: 'What people think of you back home don't matter … What matters is how the people around you are going to see you. Killing a bunch of civilians in this way—babies, women, old men, people who were unarmed, helpless—was wrong. Every American would know that. And yet this company sitting out here isolated in this one place didn't see it that way. I'm sure they didn't' (quoted in Bilton & Sim, 1992: 18–9).

19. Note, for instance, the parallels between many Nazi leaders, who were doting fathers and husbands in the evenings and weekends, but committed butchers

during the weekdays in office. Or, the prison warden in the now (in)famous movie *The Midnight Express*, who, while walking his sons to the school stops at the prison in order to rape the protagonist, and after the violation simply walks back to his waiting children to accompany them to school.

20. Otto Adolf Eichmann, the Nazi responsible for sending millions of Jews to gas chambers, argued during his trial in Jerusalem, 'I was never an anti-Semite… My sensitive nature revolted at the sight of corpses and blood… I personally had nothing to do with this. My job was to observe and report on it'. Whatever he did, Eichmann argued over and over again, 'he did, as far as he could see, as a law-abiding citizen. He did his *duty*. A duty based on Kantian moral precepts' (Arendt, 1965: 135–36).

21. Note, for instance, the violator's insolence. Appearing in his trial at the International Criminal Tribunal for the Former Yugoslavia (ICTY) in the Hague on 16 October 2012, the former Bosnian Serb leader Karadzic claimed 'instead of being accused of the events in our war, I should be rewarded for all the good things I have done' (http://www.bbc.co.uk/news/world-europe-19952899, last accessed 16 Oct. 2012).

5. THE LEGAL CONUNDRUM

1. Note the long running civilisational prejudice: 'If a man has sexual relations with another man, they have done a disgusting thing, and both shall be put to death. They are responsible for their own death.' Leviticus, 20:13, *Good News Bible*, London: Collins, 1976, p. 122.

2. Using this framework one could argue the Bush government that shirked its responsibility with regard to Abu Ghraib could be brought under the full force of justice for the crimes committed by its personnel.

3. We have exceptions to this rule, however. Stalin turned a blind eye to the organised rape of German women by the Red Army during the Second World War. In East Pakistan (now Bangladesh) the West Pakistan (now Pakistan) general in charge of the military campaign against the secessionist war General Niazi ordered his troops to especially employ the tactics of rape and other forms of sexual violence to curb the uprising.

4. In places like Northern Nigeria Islamic jurisprudence requires 'four witnesses to testify they saw a homosexual act being performed before it could be addressed by the shari'a court', as reported by the BBC: http://www.bbc.co.uk/news/world-africa-26065392, last accessed 6 February 2014.

5. 'Convictions against UN peacekeepers in Haiti do not serve justice', Amnesty International press release, 15 March 2012: http://www.amnesty.org/en/for-media/press-releases/convictions-against-un-peacekeepers-haiti-do-not-serve-justice-2012–03–15, last accessed 25 July 2014.

6. '[D]uring trials, survivors of sexual violence are reported to have received inadequate witness preparation, and experienced aggressive cross-examination, which

left them feeling revictimised and humiliated. Furthermore, a decision by a survivor to testify sometimes led to their abandonment by their family or explusion from their community' (Bastick, Grimm and Kunz, 2007: 156).

7. While there is a clear absence of legal provision that specifically calls to attention the plight of adult male victims, it would be wrong to suggest that this constituency completely falls foul of the existing international law, abandoned to its fate and existing in a legal black hole. To be fair, various rulings in international human rights law, international humanitarian law and international criminal law provisions are applicable to sexual violence against men in armed conflicts and war. However, despite the clear convergence of these three areas of law, the question of their application in relation to victims' rights differs significantly (Mouthaan, 2012: 7).

6. MAPPING MEMORY

1. One who has lost a parent is never a part of the collective. Even though others have gone through similar experiences, for the person with that bereavement, their loss is unique and can never be a part of a collective experience.

2. As Tannahill argues, after the first shock of pain and revulsion, victims of such violence like Ssu-ma Ch'ien had some escape into the private refuge of the mind for he contemplates how best to live the remainder of this ignoble life. 'I should hide away in the farthest depths of mountains. Instead I go on as best I can, putting up with whatever treatment is meted out to me, and so complete my degradation' (Tannahill, 1980: 253).

3. Note, for instance, T. E. Lawrence's constant preoccupation with his violation by the Ottoman Turkish military commander. In his autobiographical/historical work *Seven Pillars of Wisdom*, Lawrence repeatedly returns to the topic and 'wonders whether it was actually a real occurrence or bad dream'.

4. Societal and state sanctions against homosexuality are common in Africa. In fact many of its post-colonial leaders, belonging to a variety of ideological persuasions, have one time or another publicly condemned it. This 'political project' has often contributed to social responses. For an exhaustive discussion, see Hoad, 2007.

7. COMING TO TERMS

1. As has been noted time and time again over the past decade, psychosocial and medical aid for male survivors of such violence in conflict situations are nearly non-existent (Ward, 2002: 4; Carpenter, 2006: 95; Sivakumaran, 2010). In the current context most of the NGOs and INGOs focusing on victims of wartime sexual violence exclusively concentrate on the victimhood of women.

2. Some critics are of the opinion that such a disproportionate response may be the result of 'the tension between addressing sexual violence against boys and men and combating sexual violence against women and girls. At a practical level,

resources may be limited and to consider one may be to take away from the other. At a political level, proposals to widen the focus away from girls and women may be seen as a bad faith attempt to hijack the debate.' (Sivakumaran, 2010: 276.)

3. 'Ugandan President Yoweri Museveni signs anti-gay bill', http://www.bbc.co.uk/news/world-africa-26320102, last accessed 25 February 2014.

4. Homosexuality as representative of a primitive culture is an external import. The Victorian attitudes toward sex at home were exported to British colonies in the nineteenth and twentieth centuries and hammered into native cultures. Hence we have states like India and Uganda proscribing homosexuality in the twenty-first century while using the cultural arguments provided by their colonial masters in the past.

5. 'Ugandan President Yoweri Museveni signs anti-gay bill', http://www.bbc.co.uk/news/world-africa-26320102, last accessed 25 February 2014.

6. As reported by Reuters: http://www.trust.org/item/20140224043841-uw9vt, last accessed July 25 2014.

7. There was an immediate international outrage to President Museveni's policies and swift aid threat responses against his government. A day after this law was passed in Ugandan parliament 'Sweden's Development Assistance Minister Hillevi Engstrom called Mr Museveni's decision "terrible" and said that direct aid to Uganda, worth about $10.8m, could be withdrawn. As a result of the new law, the Netherlands has stopped a $9.6m subsidy to Uganda's judicial system Similarly, Norway and Denmark said they would transfer direct aid—together totalling about $17m—to non-governmental organisations.' A few days later the World Bank postponed $90m loan to the country in protest. For details, see http://www.bbc.co.uk/news/world-africa-26338941, last accessed 25 February 2014.

8. While receiving an award for promoting women's rights from the former US Secretary of State Hilary Clinton, the then British Foreign Secretary William Hague recognised the fact that rape as a weapon of war is used by various military machines in armed conflicts around the world. He also sought ways to address it by 'writing action against sexual violence into military training and doctrine'. 'William Hague calls for end to rape as weapon of war', http://www.bbc.co.uk/news/uk-politics-26349198, last accessed 26 February 2014.

9. Mamie Till's decision to leave her tortured, mutilated fourteen-year-old African-American son Emmett Louis Till's coffin for four days on public display in Chicago could be seen as an exercise in another form of revenge. It was aimed at generating public indignation and a collective sense of moral outrage (which incidentally was instrumental in launching the Civil Rights Movement in the United States).

10. See the opening quote in this chapter, 'I saw Negroes being hung, a boy named …' (quoted in Morris, 1993: 266).

8. CONCLUSION

1. One is obviously confounded by the simple question: Why are men sexually violated in some conflicts and some contexts but not others? Answering such complex questions warrants a separate ethno-cultural study, which may be able to throw some light on this paradox. For a general discussion, see Weinstein, 2006.
2. Critics like Barkawi argue that 'in a world made in no small measure by ongoing histories of organised violence, we lack a social science of war'. More importantly, 'war is radically underdeveloped as an object of inquiry' (Barkawi, 2011: 704).
3. While there is plenty of room for exasperation and frustration about the societal response to male experiences of wartime sexual violence, it is not a completely lost cause. For some observers, the fact that 'most nongovernmental and intergovernmental organisations working in conflict locations now include a standard acknowledgement in their reports that, just like their female counterparts, men can also be victims of sexual violence in such situations' (Sivakumaran, 2007: 275), is a great breakthrough in itself.

BIBLIOGRAPHY

Abrahamsen, David, *The Psychology of Crime*, New York: Columbia University Press, 1960.

Agamben, Giorgio, *Homo Sacer: Sovereign Power and Bare Life*, Stanford, CA: Stanford University Press, 1998.

———, *Remnants of Auschwitz: The Witness and the Archive*, New York: Zone Books, 1999.

———, *State of Exception*, trans. Kevin Attell, Chicago, IL: University of Chicago Press, 2005.

Agger, Inger, 'Sexual torture of political prisoners: an overview', *Journal of Traumatic Stress*, 2, (4) (1989), pp. 305–18.

Agger, Inger and Søren Buus Jensen, 'The psychosexual trauma of torture', in Wilson, John P. and Beverley Raphael eds, *International Handbook of Traumatic Stress*, New York: Plenum Press, 1993, pp. 685–701.

———, 'Sexuality as a tool of political repression', in Riquelme, H. (ed.), *Era in Twilight: Psychocultural Situation Under State Terrorism in Latin America*, Bilbao: Instituto Horizonte, 1994.

Aldrich, Richard, *Colonialism and Homosexuality*, London: Routledge, 2003.

Alighieri, Durante degli, *The Divine Comedy, 1: Hell*, Harmondsworth: Penguin, 1983.

Alison, Miranda, 'Wartime sexual violence: women's human rights and questions of masculinity', *Review of International Studies*, 33, 1 (2007), pp. 75–90.

Allen, Beverley, *Rape Warfare: The Hidden Genocide in Bosnia-Herzegovina and Croatia*, Minneapolis, MN: University of Minnesota Press, 1996.

Allen, Kate, 'Rape in Iran's prisons: the cruelest torture', *The Telegraph*, 1 November 2010.

Altman, Dennis, *Homosexual Oppression and Liberation*, New York: New York University Press, 1993.

Amir, M., *Patterns of Forcible Rape*, Chicago, IL: University of Chicago Press, 1971.

Amnesty International, *Democratic Republic of Congo: Mass Rape—Time for Remedies*, AI Index: AFR 62/018, New York: Amnesty International, 2008.

BIBLIOGRAPHY

———, *Democratic Republic of Congo, North Kivu: No End to War on Women and Children*, 2008, http://www.amnesty.org/en/library/info/AFR62/005/2008/en

Anderlini, S., *Women Building Peace: What They Do, Why It Matters*, Boulder, CO: Lynne Rienner, 2007.

Anderson, Benedict, *Imagined Communities: Reflections on the Origin and Spread of Nationalism*, London: Verso 1991.

Anderson Janice, et al., *War Crimes and Atrocities*, London: Futura, 2007.

Arendt, Hannah, *Eichmann in Jerusalem: A Report on the Banality of Evil*, New York: Penguin, 1985.

———, *The Origins of Totalitarianism*, New York: Harvest, 1966.

———, *On Violence*, New York: Harcourt Inc., 1970.

Arendt, Hannah, *The Human Condition*, (2nd edn), Chicago, IL: University of Chicago Press, 1998.

Aristotle, *Nicomachean Ethics*, in *The Complete Works of Aristotle*, vol. 2, Barnes Jonathan, (ed.), 2 vols, Princeton, NJ: Princeton University Press, 1984.

Armitage, John, 'Militarized bodies', *Body & Society*, 9, 4 (2003), pp. 1–12.

Armstrong, K.G., 'The retributivist hits back', in Acton, H. B. (ed.), *The Philosophy of Punishment*, New York: Macmillan, 1969.

Arrian, *The Campaigns of Alexander*, Harmondsworth: Penguin, 2004.

Askin, Kelly Dawn, *War Crimes Against Women: Persecution in International War Crimes Tribunals*, The Hague: Martinus Nijhoff, 1997.

———, 'Sexual violence in decisions and indictments of the Yugoslav and Rwandan Tribunals: current status', *American Journal of International Law*, 93, 1 (1999), pp. 97–123.

———, 'The quest for post-conflict gender justice', *Columbia Journal of Transitional Law*, 41, 3, (2003), pp. 509–21.

Bandura, Albert, 'Mechanisms of moral disengagement', in Reich, Walter (ed.), *Origins of Terrorism: Psychologies, Ideologies, Theologies, States of Mind*, Washington, D.C.: Woodrow Wilson Centre Press, 1990.

Barkawi, Tarak *et. al*, 'Rights and Fights: Sexual Orientation and Military Effectiveness', *International Security*, 24, 1(1999), pp. 181–201.

Barkawi, Tarak, 'From War to Security: Security Studies, the Wider Agenda and the Fate of the Study of War', *Millennium: Journal of International Studies*, 39, 3 (2011), pp. 701–716.

Barkawi, Tarak and Shane Brighton (2011) 'Powers of War: Fighting, Knowledge, and Critique', *International Political Sociology*, 5, 2 (2011), pp. 126–143.

Bastick, Megan, Karin Grimm and Rahel Kunz, *Sexual Violence in Armed Conflict: Global Overview and Implications for Security Sector*, Geneva: Geneva Centre for the Democratic Control of Armed Forces, 2007.

Bataille, Georges, *Visions of Excess: Selected Writings, 1927–1939*, trans by Stoekl, A., Minneapolis: University of Minnesota Press, 1985.

———, *Story of the Eye*, trans by Neugroschal, Joachim, Harmondsworth: Penguin, 1982.

———, *Oeuvres Complètes*, I–XII, Paris: Henri Ronse and J. M. Rey, 1990.

———, *The Tears of Eros*, San Francisco: City Light Books, 1992.

Benjamin, Walter, *Reflections*, New York: Schocken, 1986.

Bilton, Michael and Kevin Sim, *Four Hours in My Lai*, New York: Penguin, 1992.

Bourdieu, Pierre, *Outline of a Theory of Practice*, Cambridge: Cambridge University Press, 1977.

———, *Masculine Domination*, Cambridge: Polity, 2001.

Bourke, A., *Beyond Security, Ethics and Violence: War against the Other*, London: Routledge, 2007.

Bourke, Joanna, 'Torture as pornography', 2004, http://www.guardian.co.uk/world/2004/may/07/gender.uk, last accessed 4 Mar. 2011.

———, *Rape: a History from 1860s to the Present*, London: Virago and Emeryville, CA: Shoemaker and Hoard, 2007.

———, 'Sexual violence, bodily pain and trauma: a history', *Theory, Culture & Society*, 29, 3 (2012), pp. 25–51.

Bracewell, W., 'Rape in Kosovo: masculinity and Serbian nationalism', *Nations and Nationalism*, 6, 4 (2000), pp. 563–90.

Breuilly, John, *Nationalism and the State*, Manchester: Manchester University Press, 1982.

Brighton, Shane (2011) 'Three Propositions on the Phenomenology of War', *International Political Sociology*, 5, 1 (2011), pp. 101–5.

Brinkley, Joel, 'Afghanistan/sexual violence against boys', *San Francisco Chronicle*, 29 August 2010.

Brochman, Sue, 'Silent victims: bring male rape out of the closet', *The Advocate*, 582, (1991), pp. 38–43.

Brownmiller, Susan, *Against Our Will: Men, Women, Rape*, Harmondsworth: Penguin, 1975.

Butler, Christopher K., Tali Gluch and Neil J. Mitchell, 'Security forces and sexual violence: a cross-national analysis of a principal-agent argument', *Journal of Peace Research*, 44, 6 (2007), pp. 669–87.

Butler, Judith, *Bodies that Matter: On the Discursive Limits of Sex*, London: Routledge, 1993.

———, *Precarious Life: The Powers of Mourning and Violence*, London: Verso, 2004.

———, *Frames of War: When Is Life Grievable?* London: Verso, 2009.

Camus, Albert, *Neither Victims Nor Executioners*, Philadelphia, PA: New Society, 1986.

Canetti, Elias, *The Conscience of Words and Earwitness*, London: Picador, 1979.

Carlson, Eric Stener, 'The hidden prevalence of male sexual assault during war: observations on blunt trauma to the male genitals', *British Journal of Criminology*, 46, 1 (2006), pp. 16–25.

Carpenter, R. Charli, 'Recognizing gender-based violence against civilian men and boys in conflict situations', *Security Dialogue*, 37, 1 (2006), pp. 83–103.

Casey, John, *Pagan Virtue: An Essay in Ethics*, Oxford: Clarendon Press, 1990.

Caton, Steven C. and Bernardo Zacka, 'Abu Ghraib, the security apparatus and the performativity of power', *American Ethnologist*, 37, 2 (2010), pp. 203–11.

Cavarero, Adriana, *Horrorism: Naming Contemporary Violence*, New York, NY: Columbia University Press, 2010.

Clatterbaugh, Kenneth C., *Contemporary Perspectives on Masculinity: Men, Women and Politics in Modern Society*, Boulder, CO: Westview Press, 1997.

Chan, Stephen, *Robert Mugabe: A Life of Power and Violence*, Michigan, MI: University of Michigan Press, 2003.

Chang, Irish, *The Rape of Nanking*, Harmondsworth: Penguin, 1997.

Chong, Denise, *The Girl in the Picture—the Kim Phúc Story*, Toronto: Viking, 1999.

Chorley, Matt and Leon Watson, 'Mau Mau fighters, raped, castrated and beaten in Kenya's uprising against Britain get £14million compensation but no apology', *Mail Online*, 06 June 2013.

Clayton, Lucy, 'MSF confronts sexual violence in Sierra Leone', *MSF*, 9 September 2003.

Cohn, Norman, *Warrant for Genocide*, New York: Harper & Row, 1967.

Cohen, Dara Kay, 'Female Combatants and the Perpetration of Violence: Wartime Rape in the Sierra Leone Civil War', *World Politics*, 65, 3 (2013), pp. 383–415.

Cohen, Dara Kay, Amelia Hoover Green and Elisabeth Jean Wood, 'Wartime sexual violence: misconceptions, implications, and ways forward' (Special Report), Washington, D.C.: United States Institute of Peace, 2013, pp. 1–16.

Cohen, Ed, 'A body worth having? Or, a system of natural governance', *Theory, Culture & Society*, 25, 3 (2008), pp. 103–29.

Couzens Hoy, David, *The Time of Our Lives: A Critical History of Temporality*, Cambridge, MA: The MIT Press, 2012.

Cover, Rob, 'The naked subject: nudity, context and sexualization in contemporary culture', *Body and Society*, 9, 3 (2003), pp. 53–72.

Dallaire, Roméo and B. Beardsley, *Shake Hands with the Devil: The Failure of Humanity in Rwanda*, Toronto: Vintage, 2004.

Danner, Mark, *Torture and Truth: America, Abu Ghraib and the War on Terror*, New York, NY: New York Review of Books, 2004.

Das, Veena, *Life and Words: Violence and the Descent into the Ordinary*, Berkeley, CA: University of California Press.

Daymon, Christine and Immy Holloway, *Qualitative Research Methods in Public Relations and Marketing Communications*, London: Routledge, 2002.

Debrix, François and Alexander D. Barder, *Beyond Biopolitics—Theory, Violence and Horror in World Politics*, New York: Routledge, 2012.

Dehghan, Saeed Kamall, 'Iran giving out condoms for criminals to rape us, say jailed activists', *The Guardian*, 24 June 2011, http://www.guardian.co.uk/world/2011/jun/24/jailed-iran-opposition-activists-rape, last accessed 6 Jul. 2011.

Deleuze, Gilles, *Essays Critical and Clinical*, London: Verso, 1998.

Deleuze, Gilles and Félix Guattari, *Anti-Oedipus*, trans by Hurley, Robert, Mark Seem, and Helen R. Lane, London: Athlone Press, 1984.

———, *A Thousand Plateaus: Capitalism and Schizophrenia*, trans by Massumi, Brian, Minneapolis, MN: University of Minnesota Press, 1987.

De Pablo, Ofelia, Javier Zurita and Giles Tremlett, 'Guatemalan war rape survivors: "We have no voice"', *The Guardian*, 28 July 2011.

Del Zotto, Augusta and Adam Jones, 'Male-on-male sexual violence in wartime: human rights' last taboo', paper presented to the annual convention of the International Studies Association, (ISA), New Orleans, 23–27 March 2002.

Dhattiwala, Raheel & Michael Biggs, 'The Political Logic of Ethnic Violence: The Anti-Muslim Pogrom in Gujarat, 2002', *Politics & Society*, 40, 4 (2012), pp. 483–516.

Dollimore, Jonathan, *Sexual Dissidence—Augustine to Wilde*, Freud to Foucault, Oxford: Oxford University Press, 1992.

Dorais, Michel, *Don't Tell: The Sexual Abuse of Boys*, Montreal: McGill-Queen's University Press, 2002.

Drumbl, Mark A., *Atrocity, Punishment and International Law*, Cambridge: Cambridge University Press, 2007.

Durant, Will, *Caesar and Christ: A History of Roman Civilization and of Christianity from their Beginnings to A.D. 325*, New York: Simon and Schuster, 1944.

Einolf, Christopher J., 'Explaining Abu Ghraib: a review essay', *Journal of Human Rights*, 8, 1 (2009), pp. 110–20.

Elias, Norbert, *The Civilizing Process, Vol. I, The History of Manners*, Oxford: Blackwell, 1969.

———, *The Civilising Process: The Sociogenetic and Psychogenetic Investigations*, Oxford: Blackwell, 2000.

Ellis, L., *Theories of Rape: Inquiries Into the Cause of Sexual Aggression*, London: Routledge, 1989.

Ellis, Stephen, *This Mask of Anarchy: the Destruction of Liberia and the Religious Dimension of an African Civil War*, New York, NY: New York University Press, 2007.

Enloe, Cynthia, *Does Khaki Become You?: The Militarization of Women's Lives*, London: Pluto Press, 1983.

———, *The Morning After*, Berkeley, CA: University of California Pres, 1993.

Epps, Brad, 'Proper conduct: Reinaldo Arenas, Fidel Castro, and the politics of homosexuality', *Journal of History of Sexuality*, 6, 2 (1995), pp. 231–83.

Ewing, A. C., *The Morality of Punishment*, London: Kegan Paul, Trench, Trubner & Co., Ltd, 1929.

Eysenck, Hans J., *Crime and Personality*, London: Houghton Mifflin, 1964.

Fanon, Frantz, *The Wretched of the Earth*, New York: Grove Press, 1963.

———, *Black Skin, White Masks*, trans by Markmann, Charles Lam, New York: Grove Press, 1967.

Fetherston, A.B, 'UN Peacekeeprs and Cultures of Violence', *Cultural Survival Quarterly*, 10, 1 (1995), pp. 19–23.

Featherstone, Mike, 'Body image/body without image', *Theory, Culture & Society*, 32, 2–3 (2006), pp. 233–6.

Fernandes, Edna, *Holy Warriors—A Journey into the Heart of Indian Fundamentalism*, New Delhi: Penguin, 2006.

Finley, Moses I., *Aspects of Antiquity—Discoveries and Controversies*, Harmondsworth: Pelican, 1977.

Fonseca, Isabel, *Bury Me Standing: The Gypsies and their Journey*, London: Vintage, 1996.

Foucault, Michel, *Archaeology of Knowledge*, London: Tavistock, 1972.

———, *The History of Sexuality: Volume I, An Introduction*, New York: Random House, 1978.

———, trans by Sheridan, Alan, *Discipline and Punish: Birth of the Prison*, Harmondsworth: Penguin, 1991.

———, 'Governability', (pp. 87–104) in Burchell G., C. Gordon and P. Miller (eds), *The Foucault Effect: Studies in Governmentality*, London: Harvester, 1991.

———, 'The subject and power', in Rabinow P. (ed.). *Essential Works of Foucault: Power, Vol. III*, New York: The New Press, 2000.

———, *Security, Territory, Population: Lectures at the Collège de France, 1977–1978*, Senellart, Michel (ed.), trans by Burchell, Traham, New York: Palgrave Macmillan, 2007.

———, *The Birth of Biopolitics*, (Michel Foucault: Lectures at College De France), Basingstoke: Palgrave, 2008.

Fox, Michael Allen, *Understanding Peace—A Comprehensive Introduction*, New York: Routledge, 2014.

Franks, Mary Anne, 'How to feel like a Woman, or Why Punishment is a Drag', *University of California Los Angeles Law Review*, 566 (2014), pp. 566–605.

Freud, Sigmund, *Three Essays on the Theory of Sexuality*, in 1953–74, vol. 7, London: Hogarth Press, 1905.

———, *Civilisation and Its Discontents*, New York: W.W. Norton, 1930.

Fromm, Erich, *The Sane Society*, London: Routledge 2002.

Garland, David and Peter Young, *The Power to Punish: Contemporary Penality and Social Analysis*, London: Heinemann, 1983.

Gatens, Moira, *Imaginary Bodies: Ethics, Power and Corporeality*, New York: Routledge, 1995.

Gear, Sasha, 'Behind the bars of masculinity: male rape and homophobia in South African men's prisons', *Sexualities*, 10, 2 (2007), pp. 17–39.

BIBLIOGRAPHY

Genet, Jean, *A Thief's Journal*, trans from the French by Frechtman, Bernard, New York: Grove Press, 1949.

———, *Our Lady of the Flowers*, trans from the French by Frechtman, Bernard, New York: Grove Press, 1963.

———, *Miracle of the Rose*, trans from the French by Frechtman, Bernard, London: Anthony Blond, 1965.

Gettleman, Jeffrey, 'Symbols of Unhealed Congo: Male Rape Victims', *The New York Times*, 4 August, 2009, p. 9.

Ghiglieri, M. P., *The Dark Side of Man: Tracing the Origins of Male Violence*, Cambridge: Perseus Books, 2000.

Giddens, Anthony, *The Consequences of Modernity*, Cambridge: Polity, 1990.

———, *Modernity and Self Identity*, Cambridge: Polity, 1991.

Gill, Rosalind, Karen Henwood and Carl McLean, 'Body projects and the regulation of normative masculinity', *Body & Society*, 11, 1 (2005), pp. 37–62.

Ginsberg, Morris, *On Justice in Society*, Harmondsworth: Pelican, 1965.

Girard, René, *Violence and the Sacred*, Baltimore, MA: The Johns Hopkins University Press, 1977.

Glover, Jonathan, *Humanity—A Moral History of the Twentieth Century*, London: Jonathan Cape, 1999.

Goffman, Erving, *The Presentation of Self in Everyday Life*, New York: Anchor Books 1959.

Goldstein, Joshua, *War and Gender: How Gender Shapes the War System and Vice Versa*, Cambridge: Cambridge University Press, 2001.

Goldstein, J. S., *War and Gender: How Gender Shapes the War System and Vice Versa*, Cambridge: Cambridge University Press, 2001.

Gopinath, Gayatri, *Impossible Desires: Queer Diasporas and South Asian Public Cultures*, North Carolina, NC: Duke University Press, 2006.

Gettleman, Jeffrey, 'Symbols of Unhealed Congo: Male Rape Victims', *The New York Times*, 4 August, 2009, p. 9.

Graham, Ruth, 'Male rape and the careful construction of the male victim', *Social and Legal Studies*, 15, 2 (2006), pp. 187–208.

Green, Russell G., *Human Aggression*, Milton Keynes: Open University Press, 1990.

Grey, John Glenn, *The Warriors*, New York: Harper & Row, 1970.

Hancock, Eleanor, *Ernst Röhm: Hitler's SA Chief of Staff*, Basingstoke: Palgrave Macmillan, 2008.

Handrahan, Lori, 'Sudan: war and rape in Darfur', *International Herald Tribune*, 24 November 2004, p. 23.

Hansen, Thomas Blom, *Wages of Violence: Naming and Identity Postcolonial Bombay*, Princeton, NJ: Princeton University Press, 2001.

Hargreaves, Sally, 'Rape as a war crime: putting policy into practice', *The Lancet*, vol. 357, 10 March 2001, p. 737.

Hatzfeld, Jean, *A Time for Machetes*, London: Serpent's Tail, 2005.

Henry, Nicola, *War and Rape: Law Memory and Justice*, New York: Routledge, 2011.

Herr, Michael, *Dispatches*, London: Picador, 2004.

Hersh, Seymour M., 'Annals of national security: the General's Report: how Antonio Taguba, who investigated the Abu Ghraib scandal, became one of its casualties', *The New Yorker*, 25 June 2007.

Hesse, Herman, *If the War Goes On... Reflections on War and Politics*, London: Paladin, 1990.

Higate, Paul (2007) 'Peacekeepers, Masculinities, and Sexual Exploitation', *Man and Masculinities*, 10, 1 (2007), pp. 99–107.

Hill, Geoff, 'Male rape, the latest weapon for Mugabe's men', *News Statesman*, 9 June 2003.

———, *The Battle for Zimbabwe*, Johannesburg: New Holland Publishers, 2007.

Hoad, Neville, *African Intimacies: Race, Homosexuality and Globalization*, Minnesota, MN: University of Minnesota Press, 2007.

Hobbes, Thomas, *Leviathan*, Molesworth, William (ed.), *The English Works of Thomas Hobbes*, vol. III, London: Bohn, 1839, p. 300.

Honderich, Ted, *Punishment—The Supposed Justifications*, Harmondsworth: Pelican, 1984.

Horgan, John, *The End of War*, San Francisco, CA: McSweeney's Books, 2012.

Howard, Michael, *The Lessons of History*, Oxford: Oxford University Press, 1991.

Howard, Michael, *Captain Professor*, London: Continuum, 2006.

Human Rights Watch, *The War Within the War—Sexual Violence Against Women and Girls in Eastern Congo*, New York: Human Rights Watch, 2002.

———, *"We Have No Orders to Save You": State Participation and Complicity in Communal Violence in Gujarat*, 14, 3 (C), (2002), pp. 1–67. http://www.hrw.org/reports/2002/india/gujarat.pdf

———, 'We'll kill you if you cry', *Sexual Violence in the Sierra Leone Conflict*, 15, 1 (January 2003), New York: Human Rights Watch.

Hume, David, *A Treatise of Human Nature*, Norton, David Fate and Mary J. Norton (eds), Oxford: Oxford University Press, 2001.

Hyam, Ronald, *Empire and Sexuality: The British Experience*, Manchester: Manchester University Press, 1990.

ICRC, *Report of the International Committee of the Red Cross (ICRC) on the Treatment by the Coalition Forces of Prisoners of War and Other Protected Persons by the Geneva Convention in Iraq During Arrest, Internment and Interrogation*, Geneva: ICRC, 2004.

Ignatieff, Michael, *Blood and Belonging—Journeys into the New Nationalism*, London: Vintage, 1994.

———, *The Warrior's Honour: Ethnic War and the Modern Conscience*, London: Vintage, 1997.

IPDISVC, *International Protocol on the Documentation and Investigation of Sexual*

Violence in Conflict, https://www.gov.uk/government/uploads/system/uploads/attachment_data/file/319054/PSVI_protocol_web.pdf, 2014.

Izard, Michael and Pierre Smith, *Between Belief and Transgression*, Chicago, IL: The University of Chicago Press, 1982.

Jackson, Stevi and Sue Scott, 'Faking like a woman? Towards an interpretive theorization of sexual pleasure', *Body and Society*, 32, 2 (2007), pp. 95–116.

Jacoby, Tim, *Understanding Conflict and Violence: Theoretical and Interdisciplinary Approaches*, London: Routledge, 2008.

Jarman, Derek, (Dir.), *Sebastiane*, Berlin: Cinegate, 1976.

Johnson, Kirsten et. al., 'Association of combatant status and sexual violence with health and mental health outcomes in postconflict Liberia', *Journal of the American Medical Association*, 300, 6 (2008), pp. 676–90.

———, 'Association of sexual violence and human rights violations with physical and mental health in territories of the eastern Democratic Republic of the Congo', *Journal of American Medical Association*, 304, 4 (2010), pp. 553–62.

Jones, Adam, 'Gender and ethnic conflict in ex-Yugoslavia', *Ethnic and Racial Studies*, 17, 1 (1994), pp. 114–34.

———, *Gender Inclusive: Essays on Violence, Men and Feminist International Relations*, New York: Routledge, 2009.

Jones, I. H., 'Cultural and historical aspects of male sexual assault', in G. C. Mezey and King, M. B. (eds), *Male Victims of Sexual Assault*, Oxford: Oxford University Press, 2000.

Jong, Erica, 'Botero sees the world's true heavies at Abu Ghraib', *The Washington Post*, Sunday 4 November 2007.

Judah, Tim, *The Serbs: History, Myth & the Destruction of Yugoslavia*, New Haven, CT: Yale University Press.

Kafka, Franz, *The Metamorphosis and Other Stories*, Harmondsowrth: Penguin, 1984.

Kalyvas, Stathis N., *The Logic of Violence*, Cambridge: Cambridge University Press, 2008.

Kantorowicz, Ernst H., *The King's Two Bodies*, Princeton, NJ: Princeton University Press, 1957.

Karpman, Benjamin, *The Sexual Offender and His Offenses: Etiology, pathology, Psychodynamics, and Treatment*, New York: Julian Press, 1964.

Kaufman, Stuart J., *Modern Hatreds: The Symbolic Politics of Ethnic War*, Ithaca, NY: Cornell University Press, 2001.

Kazi, Seema, *Between Democracy & Nation: Gender & Militarisation in Kashmir*, New Delhi: Women Unlimited, 2009.

Kekes, John, *The Roots of Evil*, Ithaca, NY: Cornell University Press, 2005.

Kelman, Herbert C. and V. Lee Hamilton, *Crimes of Obedience: Toward a Social Psychology of Authority and Responsibility*, New Haven, CT Yale University Press, 1989.

Kelly, Liz, *Surviving Sexual Violence*, Cambridge: Polity Press, 1989.

Kelly, L., 'War against women: sexual violence, sexual politics and the militarized state', in S. Jacobs, R. Jacobson, and J. Marchbank (eds.) *States of Conflict: Gender, Violence and Resistance*, London: Zed Books, 2000.

Kennedy, Rory, (Dir.), Sergeant Javal Davis, 372nd Military Police interviewed in *Ghosts of Abu Ghraib*, HBO, 2007.

Khan, Helena, *Birangana*, Dhaka: Subarna 2013.

Kiefer, Otto, *Sexual Life in Ancient Rome*, London: Abbey Library, 1976.

King, Kimi and Megan Greening, 'Gender justice or just gender? Sexual assault decisions at the ICTY', Paper presented to the 46th annual International Studies Association (ISA) Conference, Honolulu, HI: ISA, March 2005.

King, Wayne, 'Fact vs. fiction in Mississippi', *New York Times*, 4 December 1988.

Kogon, Eugen, *The Theory and Practice of Hell—The German Concentration Camps and the System Behind Them*, New York: Berkley Publishing Group, 1950.

Koenig, K. Alexa, Ryan Lincoln and Groth Lauren, *The Jurisprudence of Sexual Violence*, Sexual Violence & Accountability Project—Working Paper Series, Berkeley, CA: University of California, 2011.

Kressel, Neil J., *Mass Hate: The Global Rise of Genocide and Terror*, Boulder, CO: Westview Press, 2002.

Krieger, Nancy, 'Gender, sexes, and health: what are the connections—and why does it matter?' *International Journal of Epidemiology*, 32, 4 (2003), pp. 652–7.

Kristeva, Julia, *Powers of Horror: An Essay on Abjection*, New York: Plenum Press, 1982.

Lawrence, Thomas Eedward, *Seven Pillars of Wisdom*, Harmondsworth: Penguin, 1962.

Lazreg, Marina, *Torture and the Twilight of Empire: From Algiers to Baghdad*, Princeton, NJ: Princeton University Press, 2007.

Lean, David, (Dir.), *Lawrence of Arabia*, Hollywood: Horizon Pictures, 1962.

Leaning, Jennifer and Tara Gingrich, 'The use of rape as a weapon of war in the conflict in Darfur', paper prepared for *US AID*, October 2004.

Leiby, Michele, 'Digging in the archives: the promise and perils of primary documents', *Politics & Society*, 37, 1 (2009), pp. 75–99.

Lerner, Gerda, *The Origins of Patriarchy*, Oxford: Oxford University Press, 1986.

LeShan, Lawrence, 'The world of patients in severe pain of long duration', *Journal of Chronic Diseases*, 17, 2, (1964), pp. 119–26.

Levi, Primo, *The Drowned and the Saved*, London: Vintage, 1989.

Levi Strauss, Claude, *The Savage Mind*, London: Weidenfeld & Nicolson, 1966.

Lévinas, Emmanuel, *Totality and Infinity*, trans Alphonso Lingis, Pittsburgh, PA: Duquesne University Press, 1969.

Lewis, Dustin A., 'Unrecognized victims: sexual violence against men in conflict settings under international law', *Wisconsin International Law Journal*, 27, 1 (2009), pp. 1–49.

Lim, L. E., K. P. Gwee, M. Woo and G. Parker, 'Men who commit rape in Singapore', *Annals of Academy of Medicine, Singapore*, 30, 6 (2001), pp. 620–4.

Lind, Nick, *The Thirst for Annihilation—Georges Bataille and Virulent Nihilism*, London: Routledge, 1992.

Linos, Natalia, 'Rethinking gender-based violence during war: is violence against civilian men a problem worth addressing?', *Social Science & Medicine*, 68, 8 (2009), pp. 1548–51.

Locke, John, *An Essay Concerning Human Understanding*, 2nd edn., London: Thomas Dring & Samuel Manship, 1694.

Loncar, Mladen, Neven Henigsberg and Pero Hrabac, 'Mental health consequences in men exposed to sexual abuse during the war in Croatia and Bosnia', *Journal of Interpersonal Violence*, 25, 2 (2010), pp. 191–203.

Love, Brenda, *The Encyclopedia of Unusual Sex Practices*, London: Abacus, 2007.

Lynch, Colum, 'UN sexual abused alleged in Congo: peacekeepers accused in Draft Report', *Washington Post*, 16 December 2004.

Mack, John E., 'The Psychodynamics of Victimization Among National Groups in Conflict', in *The Psychodynamics of International Relationships*, vol. I, V. Volkan, D. Julius, and J. Montville (es.) Lexington, MA; Heath, 1990.

MacKinnon, Catherine A., *Are Women Human? And Other International Dialogues*, Cambridge, MA: Harvard University/Belknap Press, 2006a.

————, 'Women's September 11th: rethinking the international law of conflict', *Harvard International Law Journal*, 47, 1 (2006b), pp. 1–31.

Malinowski, Bronislaw, *Sex, Culture and Myth*, London: Rupert Hart-Davis, 1963.

Marcuse, Herbert, *Eros and Civilization—A Philosophical Inquiry into Freud*, New York: Beacon Press, 1974.

Maugham, W. Somerset, *A Writer's Notebook*, Harmondsworth: Penguin, 1967.

Mbembe, Achille, 'Necropolitics' trans by Meintjes, Libby, *Public Culture*, 15, 1 (2003), pp. 11–40.

McKay, Susan, 'Gender, justice and reconciliation', *Women's Studies International Forum*, 23, 5 (2000), pp. 561–70.

McGuire, Danielle L. '"It Was Like All of Us Had Been Raped": Sexual Violence, Community Mobilization, and the African American Freedom Struggle, *The Journal of American History*, 91, 3 (2004) pp. 906–31.

McSorley, Kevin, 'The reality of war? Politics written on the body', *New Statesman*, 07 June (2010), pp. 7–10.

————, 'Helmetcams, militarized sensation and 'Somatic War", *Journal of War and Culture Studies*, 5, 1 (2012), pp. 47–58.

Médécins Sans Frontiéres (MSF), *Medical, Psychological, and Socio-Economic Consequences of Sexual Violence in Eastern DRC*, Paris: Médécins Sans Frontiéres, 2004.

Medical Centre for Human Rights (MCHR), *Report on Characteristics of Sexual*

Abuse of Men During the War in the Republics of Croatia and Bosnia-Herzegovina, 1995a.

————, *Report of Male Sexual Torturing as a Specific Way of War (Torturing of Males on the Territory of Republic of Croatia and Bosnia-Herzegovina)*, 1995b.

Meger, Sara, 'Rape in Syria: a weapon of war or instrument of terror?', *The Conversation*, 17 September 2012.

Mehta, Suketu, *Maximum City: Bombay Lost and Found*, London: Headline Books, 2005.

Menon, Ritu and Kamala Bhasin (eds.) *Borders and Boundaries: Women and India's Partition*, New Delhi: Kali for Women, 1998.

Mestrovic, Stejpan, *The Trials of Abu Ghraib: An Expert Witness Account of Shame and Honor*, Boulder, CO: Paradigm, 2007.

Mezey, Gillian and Michael King, *Male Victims of Sexual Assault*, Oxford: Oxford University Press, 2000.

Millett, Kate, *The Politics of Cruelty: An Essay on the Literature on Political Imprisonment*, London: Viking, 1994.

Mishima, Yukio, *Confessions of a Mask*, trans by Weatherby, Meredith, New York: New Directions, 1958.

Misra, Amalendu, *Afghanistan: The Labyrinth of Violence*, Cambridge: Polity, 2004.

————, *Identity and Religion: Foundations of anti-Islamism in India*, Thousand Oaks, CA: Sage, 2004a.

————, *Politics of Civil Wars*, New York: Routledge, 2008.

Mondloch, Chris, 'Bacha Bazi: An Afghan Tragedy', *Foreign Policy*, 28 October 2013.

Morris, David B., *The Culture of Pain*, Berkeley, CA: University of California Press, 1993.

Morrow, Lance, 'Unspeakable: is rape an inevitable-and marginal-part of war?' *Time*, 22 February 1993, pp. 48–50.

Morton, Adam, *On Evil*, London: Routledge, 2004.

Mosse, George L., *The Image of Man: The Creation of Modern Masculinity*, Oxford: Oxford University Press, 1996.

————, *Nationalism and Sexuality: Respectability and Abnormal Sexuality in Modern Europe*, London: Howard Fertig, 1997.

Mouthaan, Solange, *International Law and Sexual Violence Against Men*, Warwick: University of Warwick/School of Law, Legal Studies Research Paper No. 2011–02, 2011.

Murphey, Dwight D., 'Feminism and rape', *Journal of Social, Political and Economic Studies*, 17, 2 (1992), pp. 13–27.

Mudrovcic, Zeljka, 'Sexual and gender-based violence in post-conflict regions: the Bosnia and Herzegovina case', in *The Impact of Armed Conflict on Women and Girls: A Consultative Meeting on Mainstreaming Gender in Areas of Conflict and Reconstruction*, Geneva: UNFPA, 2001, pp. 60–76.

Naimark, Norman M., *The Russians in Germany—A History of the Soviet Zone of*

Occupation, 1945–1949, Boston, MA: Bellknap/Harvard University Press, 1995.

Neill, James, *The Origins and Role of Same Sex Relations in Human Societies*, New York: McFarland, 2009.

Netz, Reviel, *Barbed Wire—An Ecology of Modernity*, Middletown, CT: Wesleyan University Press, 2004.

Nobles, Melissa, *The Politics of Official Apologies*, Cambridge: Cambridge University Press, 2008.

Nowrojee, Binaifer, *Shattered Lives: Sexual Violence During the Rwandan Genocide and Its Aftermath*, New York: Human Rights Watch, 1996.

Nussbaum, Martha C., *The Clash Within—Democracy, Religious Violence, and India's Future*, Cambridge, MA: Belknap/Harvard University Press, 2007.

OCHA, Discussion Paper 2, 'The nature, scope and motivation for sexual violence against men and boys in armed conflict', 2008, pp. 1–6.

Olujic, M. B., 'Embodiment of terror: gendered violence in peacetime and wartime Croatia and Bosnia-Herzegovina', *Medical Anthropology Quarterly*, 12, 1 (1998), pp. 31–50.

Opotow, Susan, 'Reconciliation in Times of Impunity: Challenges for Social Justice', *Social Justice Research*, 14, 2 (2001), pp. 149–170.

Oosterhuis, Harry, 'Male bonding and homosexuality in German nationalism', in Oosterhuis, Harry and Huberty Kennedy (eds), *Homosexuality and Male Bonding in Pre-Nazi Germany*, New York: Harrington Park Press, 1991.

Oosterhoff, P., P. Zwanikken and E. Keating, Sexual torture of men in Croatia and other conflict situations: an open secret', *Reproductive Health Matters*, 12, 1 (2004), pp. 68–77.

Oshima, Nagisa, (Dir.), *Merry Christmas Mr. Lawrence*, Hollywood, CA: Universal Pictures, 1983.

Oosterhoff, Pauline, et al., 'Sexual torture of men in Croatia and other conflict situations: an open secret', *Reproductive Health Matters*, 12, 2–3 (2004), pp. 68–77.

Pankhurst, Donna (ed.), *Gendered Peace: Women's Struggles for Reconciliation and Justice*, London: Routledge, 2012.

Paolucci, E. O. et. Al., 'A meta-analysis of the published research on the effects of child sexual abuse', *Journal of Psychology*, 17, 30 (2001), pp. 17–36.

Parker, Andrew et Al., (eds.) *Nationalisms & Sexualities*, London: Routledge, 1992.

Parker, Alan, (Dir.), *Mississippi Burning*, Hollywood, CA: Orion Pictures, 1988.

Pearsall, Ronald, *The Worm in the Bud: The World of Victorian Sexuality*, Harmondsworth: Penguin, 1969.

Peel, Michael, 'Men as perpetrators and victims', in Peel, Michael (ed.), *Rape as a Method of Torture*, London: Medical Foundation for the Care of Victims of Torture, 2004.

BIBLIOGRAPHY

Peer, Basharat, *Curfewed Nights: One Kashmiri Journalist's Frontline Account of Life, Love and War in His Homeland*, New York: Scribner, 2010.

Peninston-Bird, Corinna, 'Classifying the body in the Second World War: British men in and out of uniform', *Body & Society*, 9, 4 (2003), pp. 31–48.

Pile, Steve, 'Spatialities of skin: the chafing of skin, ego and second skins in T. E. Lawrence's "Seven Pillars of Wisdom"', *Body and Society*, 17, 4 (2011), pp. 57–81.

Pinker, Steven, *How the Mind Works*, London: Penguin, 1998.

———, *The Better Angels of Our Nature*, London: Penguin, 2011.

Plutarch, *The Life of Alexander the Great*, New York: Modern Library, 2004.

Poorgiv, Esfandiar, 'Arrested, beaten and raped: an Iran protester's tale', *The Guardian*, 1 July 2009.

Potts, Malcolm and Thomas Hayden, *Sex and War: How Biology Explains Warfare and Terrorism and Offers a Path to a Safer World*, New York: BenBella Books, 2010.

Puig, Manuel, *Kiss of the Spider Woman*, London: Arena, 1984.

Quraishi, Najibullah, 'The dancing boys of Afghanistan', 20 April 2010, 9:00 pm. *PBS*.

Rabinow, Paul and Nikolas Rose, 'Biopower Today', *BioSocieties*, 1, 2 (2006), pp. 195–217.

Rauhala, Emily, 'Rape as a weapon of war: men suffer, too', *Time*, 3 August 2011, pp. 7–8.

Razack, Sherene H., *Dark Threats and White Knights: The Somalia Affair, peacekeeping and new imperialism*, Toronto: University of Toronto Press, 2004.

Reilly, Niamh, 'Seeking gender justice in post-conflict transitions: towards a transformative women's human rights approach', *International Journal of Law in Context*, 3, 2 (2007), pp. 155–72.

Rejali, Darius, *Torture and Democracy*, Princeton, NJ: Princeton University Press, 2007.

Reuben, David R., *Everything You Always Wanted to Know about Sex but were Afraid to Ask*, New York: David McKay Company Inc., 1969.

Ricks, Thomas E., 'Tales of the Afghan military: Honestly, which officer here hasn't raped a tea boy?" *Foreign Policy*, 11 April 2013

Rieff, David, *Slaughterhouse: Bosnia and the Failure of the West*, London: Vintage, 1995.

Rodley, Nigel S., with Matt Pollard, *Treatment of Prisoners Under International Law*, Oxford: Oxford University Press, 2009.

Rodriguez, George, 'War turns neighbor against neighbor', *Dallas Morning News*, 9 May, 1993.

Rosenblatt, Roger, 'The male response to rape', *Time*, 18 April 1983, pp. 64–6.

Rousseau, G.S. and Roy Porter, *Sexual Underworlds of the Enlightenment*, Manchester: Manchester University Press, 1987.

Rummel, R. J., *Death by Government*, London: Transaction Publishers, 1997.

Russell, Wynne, 'Sexual violence against men and boys', *Forced Migration Review*, 27, 2 (2007), pp. 22–3.

Sadeghi, Shirin, 'The Rape of Taraneh: Prison Abuse of Iran's Protesters, *The Huffington Post*, 15 July 2009.

Salzman, T. A., 'Rape camps as a means of ethnic cleansing: religious, cultural, and ethical response to rape victims in former Yugoslavia', *Human Rights Quarterly*, 20, 2 (1998), pp. 348–78.

Sanday, Peggy Reeves, *Fraternity Gang Rape*, New York, NY: New York University Press, 1990.

Sartre, Jean-Paul, *Saint Genet*, trans from the French by Frechtman, Bernard, New York: Braziller, 1963.

———, *Being and Nothingness: An Essay on Phenomenological Ontology*, London: Routledge, 2003.

Scary, Elaine, *The Body in Pain: The Making and Unmaking of the World*, New York: Oxford University Press, 1985.

Schram, S. F. and B. Caterina, (eds), *Making Political Science Matter: Debating Knowledge, Research, and Methods*, New York, NY: New York University Press, 2006.

Scruton, Roger, *The Aesthetic Understanding*, London: Carcanet, 1983.

Schmidt-Harzbach, Ingrid, 'Eine woche im April', in Helke Sander and Barbara Johr (eds.) *Befreier un BeFreite: Krieg, Vergewaltigung, Kinder*, Munich: Knutsmann, 1992.

Schmitt, Carl, *The Concept of the Political*, Chicago, IL: University of Chicago Press, 1966.

Seifert, Ruth, 'War and rape: a preliminary analysis', in Stigelmayer, A. (ed.), *Mass Rape: The War Against Women in Bosnia-Herzegovina*, Lincoln, NE: University of Nebraska Press, 1994, pp. 54–72.

———, 'The Second Front: The Logic of Sexual Violence in Wars', *Women's Studies International Forum*, 19, 2 (1996), pp. 35–43.

Seltzer, Mark, *Serial Killers: Death and Life in America's Wound Culture*, New York: Routledge, 1998.

Sells, Michael A., *The Bridge Betrayed: Religion and Genocide in Bosnia*, Berkeley: University of California Press, 1996.

———, 'Crosses of blood: sacred space, religion, and violence in Bosnia-Hercegovina', *Sociology of Religion*, 64, 3 (2003), pp. 309–31.

Shanker, Thom, 'Inquiry faults commanders in assaults on cadets', *New York Times*, 8 December 2004.

Shepherd, Laura J. 'Gendering Security', in J.Peter Burgess (ed.) *Routledge Handbook of New Security Studies*, London: Routledge 2010.

Shirer, William L., *The Rise and Fall of the Third Reich*, New York: Simon & Schuster, 1960.

Silwa, Maria, 'The rape of slave boys in Sudan', *Contemporary Review*, 3, 2 (2004), pp. 1–5.

BIBLIOGRAPHY

Singh, Jarnail, *I Accuse... The Anti-Sikh Violence of 1984*, New Delhi: Penguin, 2009.

Sivakumaran, Sandesh, 'Male/male rape and "Taint" of homosexuality', *Human Rights Quarterly*, 27, 4 (2005), pp. 1274–1306.

———, 'Sexual violence against men in armed conflict', *European Journal of International Law*, 18, 2 (2007), pp. 253–76.

———, 'Lost in translation: UN responses to sexual violence against men and boys in situations of armed conflict', *International Review of the Red Cross*, 92, 877 (2010), pp. 259–77.

Skejlsbæk, Inger, 'Sexual violence and war: mapping out a complex relationship', *European Journal of International Relations*, 7, 2 (2001), pp. 211–37.

Sokolowska-Paryz, Marzena, 'The naked body in the war film', *Journal of War and Culture Studies*, 5, 1 (2012), pp. 21–32.

Sontag, Susan, 'The pornographic imagination', in Sontag, Susan, *Styles of Radical Will*, London: Vintage, 1994.

Snow, N. E., 'Self-blame and blame of rape victims', *Public Affairs Quarterly*, 8, 4 (1994), pp. 377–93.

Snyder, J., W. Gabbard, D. May and N. Zudic, 'On the battleground of women's bodies: mass rape in Bosnia-Herzegovina' *Affilia: Journal of Women and Social Work*, 21, 2 (2006), pp. 184–95.

Stemple, Lara, 'Male rape and human rights', *Hastings Law Journal*, 60, 3 (2009), pp. 605–46.

———, 'The hidden victims of wartime rape', *The New York Times*, 1 March 2011.

Stigelmayer, A., 'The rapes in Bosnia Herzegovina', in Stigelmayer, A., (ed.), *Mass Rape: The War Against Women in Bosnia-Herzegovina*, Lincoln: University of Nebraska Press, 1994, pp. 88–169.

Straub, Ervin, *The Psychology of Evil: Why Children, Adults, and Groups Help and Harm Others*, Cambridge: Cambridge University Press, 2003.

Tannahill, Reay, *Sex in History*, London: Hamish Hamilton, 1980.

Taylor, Jerome, 'Government admits Kenyans were tortured and sexually abused by colonial forces during Mau Mau uprising', *The Independent*, 17 July (2012).

Taylor, John, *Body Horror—Photojournalism, Catastrophe, & War*, Manchester: Manchester University Press, 1998.

Taylor, Christopher C., 'The Cultural Face of Terror in the Rwandan Genocide of 1994', in Alexander Laban Hinton (ed.) *Annihilating Difference: The Anthropology of Genocide*, Berkley, CA: University of California Press, 2002.

Taguba, Major General Antonio M., Article 15–6 Investigation of the 800th Military Police Brigade (The Taguba Report), 2004, http://www.npr.org/iraq/2004/prison_abuse_ report.pdf

Todd, Cain, 'Imagination, fantasy, and sexual desire', in Maes, Hans and Jerrold Levinson (eds), *Art and Pornography—Philosophical Essays*, Oxford: Oxford University Press, 2012.

Todorov, Tzvetan, *The Morals of History*, Minneapolis, MN: University of Minnesota Press, 1995.

———, *Facing the Extreme—Moral Life in the Concentration Camps*, New York, Henry Holt, 1996.

Toften, Samuel and Eric Markusen, *Genocide in Darfur: Investigating the Atrocities in the Sudan*, London: Routledge, 2006.

Tompkins, Tamara L., 'Prosecuting rape as a war crime: speaking the unspeakable', *Notre Dame Law Review*, 70, 4 (1995), pp. 845–90.

The Economist, 'Peacekeeping and sex abuse: who will watch the watchmen?', 31 May 2008, pp. 74–5.

———, 'Georgian politics—a stunning victory', 6 October 2012, p. 42.

Turner, Bryan S., 'Body', *Theory, Culture & Society*, 32, 2–3 (2006), pp. 223–9.

———, *Regulating Bodies: Essays in Medical Sociology*, London: Routledge, 1992.

United Nations, *Report of the Secretary-General on Prevention of Armed Conflict*, 7 June 2001, A/55/985-S/2001/574.

———, *Contemporary Forms of Slavery: Systematic Rape, Sexual Slavery and Slavery-like Practices During Armed Conflict*, New York, NY: United Nations, 1998:7–8. Final Report submitted by Gay J. McDougall, Special Rapporteur. E./CN.4/Sub.2/1998/13.

———, Security Council, *Resolution S/RES/1820 (2008)*, New York: UN Security Council, 2008.

———, UN Security Council, *Security Council Resolution 1820 (On acts of sexual violence against civilians in armed conflicts)*. S/RES/1820. New York, NY: United Nations. 2008, http://www.unhcr.org/refworld/docid/485bbca72.html, last accessed 10 Mar. 2011.

———, UN Security Council, *Text Mandating Peacekeeping Missions to Protect Women, Girls from Sexual Violence in Armed Conflict*. S/RES/1988. New York, NY: United Nations, 2009, http://www.un.org/News/Press/docs/2009/sc9753.doc.htm, last accessed 10 Mar. 2011.

Unwin, Joseph Daniel, *Sex and Culture*, Oxford: Oxford University Press, 1934.

van Creveld, Martin, *Men, Women and War: Do Women Belong in Front Line?*, London: Cassell, 2001.

van den Berghe, Pierre, 'Race and ethnicity: a sociobiological perspective', *Ethnic and Racial Studies*, 1, 4 (1978), pp. 402–11.

van der Veer, Peter, 'Writing Violence', in David Ludden (ed.) *Contesting the Nation*, Philadelphia, PA: University of Pennsylvania Press 1996.

van Tienhoven, Harry, 'Sexual torture of male victims', *Torture*, 3, 4 (1993), pp. 133–5.

Virilio, Paul, *War and Cinema: The Logics of Perception*, London: Verso, 1989.

Vezina, Renee A., 'Combating impunity in Haiti: why the ICC should prosecute sexual abuse by UN peacekeepers', *Ave Maria International Law Journal*, 1, 2 (2012), pp. 431–60.

Visvanathan, Shiv, 'Nation', *Theory, Culture & Society*, 23, 2–3 (2006), pp. 533–8.

Wagner, Peter, 'The discourse on sex—or sex as discourse: eighteenth-century medical and paramedical erotica', in Rousseau, G.S. and Roy Porter (eds.) *Sexual Underworlds of the Enlightenment*, Manchester: Manchester University Press, 1987.

Wakelin, Anna and Karen M. Long, 'Effects of victim gender and sexuality on attributions of blame to rape victims', *Sex Roles*, 49, 9–10 (2003), pp. 477–87.

Walker, Jayne, John Archer and Michelle Davies, 'Effects of rape on men: a descriptive analysis', *Archives of Sexual Behaviour*, 34, 1 (2005), pp. 69–80.

Walker, Kenneth, *The Physiology of Sex*, Harmondsworth: Pelican, 1952.

Walter, E. V., *Terror and Resistance: A Study in Political Violence*, Oxford: Oxford University Press, 1989.

Ward, Jeanne, *If Not Now, When: Addressing Gender-Based Violence in Refugee, Internally Displaced, and Post Conflict Settings*, New York, NY: Reproductive Health for Refugees Consortium, 2002.

Watson, Burton, *Ssu-ma Ch'ien: Grand Historian of China*, New York: Columbia University Press, 1958.

Weeks, Jeffrey, *Sexuality*, 2nd edn, London: Routledge, 2003.

Weinstein, Jeremy, *Inside Rebellion: The Politics of Insurgent Violence*, Cambridge: Cambridge University Press, 2006.

Weierstall, Roland, 'The desecration of bodies in war', 13 May 2013, http://www.bbc.co.uk/news/magazine-22528846

Wexler, Lesley, 'No more impunity: a roadmap to stopping rape in conflict', *The Guardian*, 19 June 2014.

Wood, Elisabeth Jean, 'Variation in sexual violence during war', *Politics & Society*, 34, 3 (2006), pp. 307–41.

Woollacott, Angela, *Gender and Empire*, Basingstoke: Palgrave Macmillan, 2006.

Wright, Derek, *The Psychology of Moral Behaviour*, Harmondsworth: Penguin, 1981.

Zarkov, Dubravka, 'The body of the other man: sexual violence and the construction of masculinity, sexuality, and ethnicity in Croatian media', in Jacobs, Susie, Ruth Jacobson and Jennifer Marchbank (eds), *States of Conflict: Gender, Violence, and Resistance*, London: Zed, 2001, pp. 69–82.

Zawati, H. M., 'Impunity or immunity: wartime male rape and sexual torture as a crime against humanity', *Torture*, 17, 1 (2007), pp. 27–47.

Zimbardo, Philip, *The Lucifer Effect*, New York: Random House, 2007.

Žižek, Slavoj, *Violence—Six Sideways Reflections*, London: Profile Books, 2008.

INDEX

INDEX